Theory and History
Series Editor: Donald MacRaild

Theory and History offers lively, comprehensive introductions to the principal theories students encounter while studying history.

Although some historians have been researching and writing history from a transnational perspective for more than a century, it is only recently that this approach has gained momentum. But what is transnational history? How can a transnational approach be applied to historical study?

Pierre-Yves Saunier's dynamic introductory volume conveys the diversity of the developing field of transnational history, and the excitement of doing research in that direction. Saunier surveys the key concepts, methods and theories used by historians, helping students to find their own way in this vibrant area.

Pierre-Yves Saunier is Professor of History at Université Laval, in Québec City (Canada). He has published widely in the field of transnational history.

Theory And History
Series Editor: Donald MacRaild

Published

Biography and History	*Barbara Caine*
Empiricism and History	*Stephen Davies*
Cultural History	*Anna Green*
Gender and History	*Susan Kingsley Kent*
Social Theory and Social History	*Donald M. MacRaild and Avram Taylor*
Narrative and History	*Alun Munslow*
Marxism and History	*Matt Perry*
Transnational History	*Pierre-Yves Saunier*
Postmodernism and History	*Willie Thompson*

Theory and History
Series Standing Order
ISBN 978–1–4039–8526–X hardback
ISBN 978–0–333–91921–1 paperback
(*outside North America only*)

You can receive future titles in this series as they are published by placing a standing order. Please contact your bookseller or, in case of difficulty, write to us at the address below with your name and address, the title of the series and the ISBN quoted above.

Customer Services Department, Macmillan Distribution Ltd, Houndmills, Basingstoke, Hampshire RG21 6XS, England

Transnational History

Pierre-Yves Saunier

palgrave
macmillan

First published 2013 by
PALGRAVE MACMILLAN

Palgrave Macmillan in the UK is an imprint of Macmillan Publishers Limited,
registered in England, company number 785998, of Houndmills, Basingstoke,
Hampshire RG21 6XS.

Palgrave Macmillan in the US is a division of St Martin's Press LLC,
175 Fifth Avenue, New York, NY 10010.

Palgrave Macmillan is the global academic imprint of the above companies
and has companies and representatives throughout the world.

Palgrave® and Macmillan® are registered trademarks in the United States,
the United Kingdom, Europe and other countries.

ISBN 978–0–230–27184–5 hardback
ISBN 978-0-230-27185-2 paperback

This book is printed on paper suitable for recycling and made from fully
managed and sustained forest sources. Logging, pulping and manufacturing
processes are expected to conform to the environmental regulations of the
country of origin.

A catalogue record for this book is available from the British Library.

A catalog record for this book is available from the Library of Congress.

Contents

Preface

Paradoxically, it is not easy to write an introduction to a field of scholarship when it has only recently been defined as a particular branch of study. There are no canonical theoretical strands, no agreed list of seminal books, roll-call of consecrated key authors, or compendia of seasoned methods accumulated by decades of scholarship to be quietly rehashed. This is the first dilemma for the author who does not want to set in stone an 'authorised' version of this field while it is still in the making. I have addressed this difficulty by showing the diversity of transnational history, although I have been confined by my own ignorance on many topics, regions or moments.

A second dilemma also derives from the relatively recent crystallisation of transnational history. On the one hand, this makes it necessary to cover the widest possible range of concerns and situations that have been explored; on the other, one needs to find or construct a framework to live up to the introductory mission of this book. The most obvious of these frameworks seemed impractical at best, or counterproductive at worst. An organisation of contents by historical subdisciplines (economic, cultural, international relations history...), regions (South Asia, Americas...), topics (migrations, technologies, commodities...), categories (class, gender, race...), historiographical stages or major concepts was considered and rejected. Instead, the core of the volume has been composed within a 'notional' framework, based on key concerns that can help historians to research and write history in a transnational perspective.

The result is not a book which limits the definition of what transnational history should or should not be. It is merely a guide, the validity of which is conditional on the rapid change of the landscape it purports to describe, analyse and domesticate.

Acknowledgements

A large number of colleagues have provided invaluable help in assembling the body of literature I needed to consult in the writing of this book, and the long list of their names is mentioned in the expanded online bibliographical companion that provides a further reading list of books and articles that could not be included here. This companion can be obtained by writing to pys.th.2013@gmail.com

I am extremely thankful for the feedback provided by Kiran Patel, Ian Tyrrell, Donna Gabaccia and Sunil Amrith on the complete typescript of this book, at a stage where it was written in what only I call English. Christophe Verbruggen kindly accepted to chase out the most blatant blunders in the section dealing with social network analysis. Sonya Barker and Don MacRaild have been supportive and demanding editors, just as expected, and I commend them for that. Besides, they hand-picked anonymous reviewers whose comments were useful to think with and against: thanks to them. It has been a pleasure as well to work with Philip Tye and Alec McAulay, the two copy editors whose task it was to reform my personal take on the English language without humiliating me. Mission accomplished.

Students in several classes contributed to the formulation of the elements in this book: at the University of Chicago, the Université de Montréal, the École des Hautes Études en Sciences Sociales in Paris, the Université de Genève and the Institut des Hautes Études Internationales et du Développement in Geneva.

Different aspects that eventually coalesce here have been generated, presented, discussed and amended during and after encounters in a number of seminars and presentations: at the Norwegian University of Science and Technology in Trondheim and the University of Bergen; at the Université de Lausanne, the Université de Genève and the doctoral workshops of the Conférence Universitaire de Suisse Occidentale (*sic*); with the History of International Organisations Network in Geneva; at Carleton University and the Université de Montréal; the École Normale Supérieure de la rue d'Ulm; the Università degli Studi di Padova and the Robert Schuman Centre at the European University Institute in Fiesole; the Technological University of Eindhoven; the Harvard–Yenching Institute; the Centre for Transnational History at University College London; and the European Science Foundation research group 'Making Europe: technology and transformations 1850–2000' whose participants' company has been a constant pleasure.

It was the experience of editing *The Palgrave Dictionary of Transnational History* that provided many of the resources on which I have drawn: without my co-editor Akira Iriye, the associate editors and the contributors to that volume, my horizon and this volume would have been irremediably different.

Introduction

> But not only is it true that no country can be understood without taking account of all the past; it is also true that we cannot select a stretch of land and say we will limit our study to this land; for local history can only be understood in the light of the history of the world. There is unity as well as continuity. To know the history of contemporary Italy, we must know the history of contemporary France, of contemporary Germany. Each acts on each. Ideas, commodities even, refuse the bounds of a nation. All are inextricably connected, so that each is needed to explain the others. This is true especially of our modern world with its complex commerce and means of intellectual connection. In history, then, there is unity and continuity. Each age must be studied in the light of all the past; local history must be viewed in the light of world history.

This statement was not made in one of today's forums where the need for 'a global history for a globalised world' was preached. Neither was it uttered in a graduate seminar where enthusiastic young historians present their first historical research, nor in the ever-growing number of conferences and workshops where established scholars confront their work on ideas, commodities and other items on the move. Nor was it written in the last two decades, when more and more historians have tried to stretch the limits of their investigations and imaginations beyond the restrictions of the merely national. These words were pronounced in 1891 by the US historian Frederick Jackson Turner.[1] Only two years later, Turner would again tackle the topic of the significance of history and pronounce his famous 'frontier' hypothesis. It was to become a touchstone of the idea that the United States of America was a country on a special historical track, different from other countries' trajectories, and to be narrated as such. The tension between a relational outlook and an insular national history was thus embodied in one person, a member of the generation that made history a discipline within the framework of the research-based university.

The aforementioned tension is not specific to US historians. Other national contexts have their own Turners who advocated the study of 'inextricable connections'. Karl Lamprecht in Germany, Henri Pirenne in Belgium, the Romanian Nicolae Iorga, Cheikh Anta Diop in Senegal, or the Japanese Suzuki Shigetaka could be depicted in similar terms. In some scholarly communities, like that of the orientalists, the study of interactions between civilisations was on the official agenda of international conferences as early as the late 1880s.[2] History and its practitioners certainly have been part and parcel of the nation-building process in its different embodiments throughout the twentieth century. They have gathered material, processed data and established narratives that took the national framework as their frame and horizon. But the admittedly 'repressive connection between history and the nation',[3] that this stream of linear history established, placing the nation as the central and only subject of history, was never hegemonic.

In the midst of the most nationalist historiographies, and not always against their grain, some historians also made the case to extend their gaze beyond, across and through nations. This tension never ceased to define the methodological and narrative keyboard that we historians have used for the researching, writing and teaching of history. Most of the keys play the notes of **methodological nationalism**, whereby historians explicitly or implicitly produce a tune in which the country, aka the national state, appears as the natural form of organisation of societies and the basic unit of historiography.[4] But there is an alternative which rejects the autonomy of national histories as a fiction, and favours what lies between or through national societies and other units of historical analysis.[5] In fact, does one necessarily oust the other? In the last two decades, we have simultaneously seen signs of renationalisation of history, notably in the new countries that emerged from the breakdown of the Soviet Union and its western belt, and a major overhaul of German and American history that went in the other direction. Here, a substantial effort was made to understand how these national histories were shaped by outside forces, and how they had been a factor in historical developments beyond their borders. This is not to suggest the superiority of the transnational perspective: conceiving, researching and writing history of and in one country is still worthy of the historian's attention. In regard to national historiography, what this book argues is that the transnational perspective enhances its capacity by adding the history of entanglements between countries to the checklist of national history writing.

This can happen because transnational history is an approach that emphasises what works between and through the units that humans have set up to organise their collective life. This contrasts with an emphasis on what has been happening within these units taken as **monads**. It is an approach that focuses on relations and formations, circulations and connections, between, across and through these units, and how they have been made, not made and unmade. To appraise its tentative nature, it needs to be remembered that the phrase 'transnational history' is still young, and its definition remains fluid. Chapter 1 will reposition this idea in the wider context of the social sciences, demonstrate this diversity, and connect it to the trajectory of the term since its appearance in 1842. Just as 'transnational' as an adjective is often indiscriminately used to specify a certain class of phenomena, or a spatial level, or the identity of certain individuals and the characteristics of some organisations, the recent invasion of 'transnational history' in dissertation, book and article titles covers many different meanings. Some use the phrase abundantly and under several of these understandings, others are comfortable with other generic or specialised qualifications like universal, oceanic, world, comparative, connected, entangled, shared, cosmopolitan, symmetrical, translocal, international or cross-national history. The differences between these approaches are, in my view, less important than their common emphasis on relations. Let us start with the why, when and where of transnational history, in order to see what specific concerns and angles, if any, distinguish it from some of these other relational approaches.

▶ Transnational history: what are the stakes?

If we consider what historians do when researching and writing history with a transnational perspective, three things catch the eye. They are the 'big issues' transnational history attempts to address. First is the **historicisation** of contacts between communities, polities and societies. Here, the goal is to study how exchanges and interactions waxed and waned, to appraise the changing levels of exchange, integration and disintegration between the territorialised basic units of historical understanding (countries, regions, continents): an empirical answer to questions of what is, and when was, **'globalisation'**. Secondly, the transnational perspective acknowledges and assesses foreign contributions to the design, discussion and implementation of domestic features within communities, polities and societies; and, vice versa, the projection of domestic features into the foreign. The purpose is to thicken our understanding of self-contained entities like nations, regions, civilisations, cities, professional groups and religious communities by shedding light on their composite material. Thirdly, transnational history deals with trends, patterns, organisations and individuals that have been living between and through these self-contained entities that we use as units of historical research. Here we have an opportunity to recover the history of projects, individuals, groups, concepts, activities, processes and institutions that often have been invisible or at best peripheral to historians because they thrived in between, across and through polities and societies. These three issues mark a difference between transnational history and **global history**. Global history, according to one official description of the eponymous journal, deals with 'the main problems of global change over time, together with the diverse histories of globalization'.[6] Planetary change is certainly part of, but not the whole of the above programme.

This problem-oriented agenda underpins Chapters 2–5 of this book. They build on a substantial body of scholarship, regardless of the badge it wears in book titles or keyword description, and not limited to the by-product of most recent scholarship. If the expression 'transnational history' is recent, its three fronts aroused the interest of a number of historians before the 1990s. And, the phrase 'transnational history' is hyperbolic, suggesting a specialised subdisciplinary field in ways that do not match the spirit of much of what is being written and researched under that title. Rather, the mindset is oriented towards openness and experimentation regarding the range of topics and methodologies.[7] Consider the table of contents of the special issue of *The Journal of American History* in 1999.[8] The contributors broached the environment, identities, migrations, the history of the discipline of history, the historiography of black Americans' emancipation, the labour movement, social sciences, human rights, social and development policies, race and empire, and showed how changes and patterns in US history were entangled with developments abroad, from Mexico to Italy via the Philippines. That is hardly a thematic domain, even less a subdisciplinary brief.

It may be appropriate here to think of what William Cunningham once wrote about economic history: '[it] is not so much the study of a special class of facts, as the study of all the facts of a nation's history from a special point of view'.[9] Minus the reference to 'a nation's history', this book starts from here. 'All facts': transnational history can be applied to any topic, which does not mean it will be useful and relevant to each and every one. 'Point of view': this is what transnational history claims to provide, with the idea that this special point of view will complete other points of view and not replace them. This is why I will often use the phrase 'history in a transnational perspective' to lessen the risk of the subdisciplinary hubris suggested by 'transnational history', although the latter will be frequently used for its amenity to syntax. Likewise, my use of 'transnational historians' does not mean that we need yet another brand of historians: it is just shorter than 'historians who adopt a transnational perspective'.

The list of topics included in the *Journal of American History* is familiar to any social historian. Similar topics have been covered under many other labels, especially **comparative history** – or rather, the application of comparison between different national societies (cross-national comparative history, as it were). A major reference for historians who compare national histories is an article written in 1928 by the French historian Marc Bloch.[10] Bloch's piece clearly included instances of 'filiation' and 'influence' between national societies and polities in the purview of comparative history. Yet he did not single out the study of such actual connections and circulations between countries as the 'most interesting' direction for comparing societies. Bloch expressed a preference for the comparison of countries that had no actual ties to one another, a choice vetted by most of his explicit followers.[11] Thus, it is the way comparison between national histories has developed, not the way it was conceived, that has created some distinction between the comparison of the historical fate of countries without actual ties to one another, and the study of the processes and elements that were the substance of such actual ties. This early divergence would return with a vengeance in European historiography, during the skirmishes between comparative history and *Transfergeschichte* in the 1990s. Comparative history, it was argued, had paid an excessive tribute to national histories.[12] It had accepted countries as the basic unit for researching and writing history, at the expense of regional or other units, and had no interest in actual historical relations between and through countries. *Transfergeschichte*, it was rejoined, cared for the small stuff of history with its focus on cultural products such as ideas or books: it had nothing to say on major social and political changes in European history.[13]

This debate subsided, and most now share the argument that both approaches can be combined with profit because they help to answer different questions.[14] This provided the basis for empirical attempts to combine the two approaches,[15] and historians who compare nations and historians who study connections and circulations between nations have been able to confront their respective angles more productively.[16] This helped to sharpen the distinctions as to the role of comparison in comparative history and in the history of cultural and other transfers. In comparative history, comparison is the tool historians use to evaluate different historical courses – mostly national – in search of structural causes for broad processes and patterns that will explain discrete national historical trajectories, their differences, their similarities. For those who work in between and through national histories, comparison is the tool used in the past by historical actors themselves, when they engineered similarities and differences in order to create particular historical trajectories for their polities and communities. In her study of reciprocal observations between French views of American style and American views of French fashion, Nancy Green called this 'interactive comparative history', the study of 'reciprocal visions'.[17] In fact, transnational historians do not shirk comparison between different locations, if only because they have to understand what happens to the ties and flows they follow through different polities and communities. But to them comparison is a topic of study more than a tool for the study of topics.

▶ When was transnational history?

To follow and reconstruct the operation and impact of entanglements across and through societies, polities and communities, historians can direct their attention to the 5000-year span since the establishment of literate and agricultural societies. Or to the eight million years since the date of the first known fossil of hominids: after all, it was through circulation that hominids dispersed from Africa to the whole planet. Closer to us in time are instances of exchanges, contacts, persons, patterns or conjunctures that existed between, across and through polities and societies between 200 BCE and the end of the eighteenth century CE. Historians like Jerry Bentley, Fernand Braudel, Sanjay Subrahmanyam or Victor Lieberman have thus surveyed wide chronological vistas.[18] Some historians have no qualms about placing works by these and other writers under the label of transnational history, or deploying the notion of transnational history for early modern Europe.[19] Starting from the *natio* as the group of people born within one and the same community, they stress that it is the duty of historians to trace entanglements between these nations, even if they were not the nations of more recent times, where the coalescence of state- and nation-building processes gave birth to territorially bounded units with an impulse for homogeneity. Conversely, other historians argue that, when it comes to periodisation, one should restrict application of the label 'transnational history' to the moment when national states began to crystallise. For twentieth-century historian Kiran Patel, using the term 'transnational history' for the Greek *polis*, China under the Tang dynasty or Europe under the Carolingian kings adds little value: 'who speaks about transnationalism for these times, is either using an anachronistic fashion label or introduces, by the back door, an essentialist understanding of nation that the transnational perspective wants to avoid'.[20]

This book starts from a similar position: transnational history is the chronological peninsula of a wider body of scholarship, firmly connected to it but with distinct contours. It is in continuity with the research of historians who have been anxious to investigate the entanglements between polities, societies and communities. Whether they name their quest 'global', 'world', 'connected' or 'translocal' history is secondary. A close relationship exists between all these. For instance, transnational history has especially close links with the idea of **'connected histories'** that Sanjay Subrahmanyam, drawing on previous work by Joseph Fletcher, elaborated in the 1990s in order to deal with large issues (conjunctures, empires) through the study of specific confrontations between different polities of Eurasia 'from the Tagus to the Ganges' between the fifteenth and eighteenth centuries.[21] But it is also a specific stretch of such connected histories because it deals with a moment when polities, societies and communities were increasingly defined or battered by the idea and practice of the national state as a bounded territorial unit in which authorities strove for internal homogeneity and external projection of prestige and power, and where the exclusive loyalty of citizens was required in exchange for civil rights. This 'age of territoriality', argues Charles Maier, took shape during the seventeenth century, came of age in the Age of Revolutions and crystallised in the middle of the nineteenth century.[22] Intertwined state- and nation-building processes, manifested in the control of bordered space and the ordering of the society within that space, were seen or imposed as the single best way for communities and societies to create polities endowed with sovereignty.

Since the beginning of the nineteenth century, humans have increasingly been living in a world organised by the idea and practice of the national state. True, some analysts have diagnosed a withering of nations and states in recent decades. In his text, Maier himself diagnoses a weakening congruence between identity-space and decision-space since the 1960s, and elsewhere sociologist Saskia Sassen assesses the disassembling of territory, authority and rights that characterised the 1980s.[23] Yet, as she points out, the formidable combination known as the 'nation state' is still the most widely spread and meaningful kind of polity on the planet. One may add that part of the grip of the national state resulted from the resistance or accommodation it triggered during its uneven and resistible ascension. Other kinds of communities, territorial (city states) or not (class or religious affiliation), also had their thinkers and supporters: in the name of the *umma*, the community of Muslim believers, the very idea of the nation was contested by a range of scholars, activists and intellectuals, resulting in conflicting waves of absorption into nationalism and commitment to the unity of Islam.[24] Even where the national state was not endemic, peoples, authorities and intellectuals took up a stance towards it, if only because European expansion 'hawked the nation state in the world as one of its prized export communities'.[25] It does not mean that those who aspired to create a new independent national state always abided with its most rabid territorial aspects, as witnessed by the changing geographies of the Latin American independence struggle under Bolivar, or by 'deterritorialised' Indian patriotism.[26] Neither should we conclude that the national state monopolised the imagination of those who strived to create or maintain a community: the transatlantic religious community of Candomblé, the Djedji/Jeje nation, 'came about before the "classical" age of nationalism and has endured well beyond it', James Lorand Matory reminds us.[27] The non-territorial Djedji nation was coeval with empires and national states, and in a large part these different kinds of community 'subsidised' one another as they provided economic, linguistic or personnel resources for their mutual installation or maintenance. This coevality is a crucial point for transnational historians.

The uneven and resistible success of the territorial and homogenising national state charts the chronological scope of transnational history: the last 200 years cut large, biting into the late eighteenth century and with a sharper mark from the middle of the nineteenth. By confronting the national state at its high point, we can study how interdependencies and interconnections unfolded within, against or beyond the roadblocks and incentives that derived from nationally produced orders. We can also assess the composite nature of the nation and the state, against their self-narratives of autonomous production. The pretension of the national state to be the single best way to organise polities and societies gives us a chance to research and write about how this came or failed to be, through the definition of antagonistic economic or cultural national styles, appropriations of political thought, mutual support between nationalist movements or public policy transfers.

The impulse for homogeneity of the national state led to attempts to control, rebut or eradicate flows, ties and formations across borders, while its capacity to project power entailed projects to nurture and orient them, if only to increase or protect what was defined as 'national'. The result is a bonanza of documentary evidence about the life between and through countries, with the bias that it has been gathered by authorities, agencies or individuals who 'saw like a state'.[28] But it is this material which, in the last instance, allows us to observe what stretched between locations and across polities.

This chronological scope showcases differences with related approaches that participate in a relational approach to history. Especially since its consolidation in the 1960s, **world history** has had the most ambitious goal of writing the history of humankind.[29] Some of its practitioners, like David Christian, have ratcheted it up, and his '**Big History**' starts with the inanimate universe and the possible Big Bang.[30] Nonetheless, what is generally accepted as world history usually deals with the last 5000 years, and most activity focuses on smaller but still considerable fractions of this. **Global history**, as an attempt to establish the different and changing forms of integration and convergence at the planetary level, ploughs the last 500 years, charting the course of globalisation since the world was circumnavigated.[31] The transnational perspective has a much shorter range, even if it ought to acknowledge previous historical trends and patterns. Obviously, the circulation of goods, ideas, capital and people did not start in the age of national states, and many developments in this late period happened within and against existing patterns. If we want to appraise what the development of national states and their ideals of external projection and territorial homogeneity introduced as constraints and possibilities for the direction, content and orientation of these flows, we need to consider the previous deployment and structure of the latter. Historians of science have shown the importance of straddling the eighteenth and nineteenth centuries, for instance.[32] The periodisation of transnational history, as a result, is not fixed.

The focus on the moment of growing ubiquity of nation- and state-building processes does not amount to a new ontological certification of nations as indivisible monads. However, rattling the weight of the national casing should not cause the denying of nations as **realised categories**, which have contributed so importantly to the framing of our individual and collective lives. We would lose our capacity to understand the presence of the past in the present if we systematically write without or versus the nation. Transnational historians need to think 'with and through' the nation, in order to do justice to this 'inadequate and indispensable category', as argued by Antoinette Burton, the historian of British imperialism.[33] Transnational history, then, is a perspective available to all historians of the last 200-250 years, whose research project entails researching and writing a history with nations that is not a history of nations.

▶ Where is transnational history?

Does this chronological scope bind the analytical capacity of transnational history to certain places and spaces? Chapter 6, which opens the methodological toolkit of transnational history, will delve into the issue of spatiality, but three preliminary issues need to be confronted first. Does transnational history only study large-scale processes? Is it only preoccupied with enmeshments where nations are the basic unit? Is transnational history only applicable to places where the coalescence of nation- and state-building produced bounded and ordered sovereign territories?

A positive answer to the last question would seem to limit the reach of transnational history: during the late eighteenth century and even in the first half of the nineteenth century, polities organised and conceived as national states were chiefly taking shape in Europe and the Americas. Yet the impact of the national project was strongly felt beyond this Atlantic core, well before the national state became the political best-seller of the modern age through the waves of nation- and state-building that electrified Africa and Asia following the Second World War.[34] On the one hand, the colonial projection of European nations foisted the nation state upon distant lands by means of the establishment of settlements where indigenous populations were kept out of the national community of settlers, with a consequent deep impact on the way in which the idea of national citizenship developed as a Manichean project in both colonial and metropolitan settings.[35] On the other hand, the idea of the national state set the destination for emancipation and independence movements in areas where polities were not yet organised on national lines, beginning with Haiti in the late eighteenth century. European nationalist and republican figures like the Italian Mazzini generated a storm well beyond their native land and region.[36] Early in the nineteenth century, Caribbean and American black Christian missionaries played a central role in the establishment of national definitions in Liberia and Sierra Leone, and in the prospect of an African nation.[37] How much this formed the background for the attempts to create a free state on the Gold Coast in the 1860s (the Fante Federation) is still hypothetical, but the national state was a political project in Cameroon after the First World War, well before the African independence struggles, and pan-Africanism as a national project for Africa flourished under Claude McKay and Marcus Garvey in the 1920s.[38] Similarly, nationalist ideas, anti-imperialist activists and anti-colonial propaganda material criss-crossed the Indian Ocean between territories ruled by the British.[39] Even in regions where nations were absent in their territorial manifestation, the *idea* of the national state was present in political, social, religious and cultural life. Moreover, without being conceived as national states, different polities moved towards greater internal homogeneity within a neatly defined territory in the early nineteenth century. In the Ottoman Empire, in Mirza Taghi Khan Amir Nezam's Iran or Muhammad Ali's Egypt, governments established programmes for political reform in the domains of taxation, education and the military, and pushed towards a stronger cultural uniformity within the country.[40] This created new constraints and opportunities for circulations and connections. It is not only where national states crystallised earlier, in the Atlantic world, that a history 'with and through' the nation is relevant, needed and possible.

Now we move to the kind of spaces transnational history works with and about. We started from the premise that the national state came to organise polities and societies in the last 200-250 years. But, because it leads historians to follow flows, watch ties, and reconstruct formations and relations between, across and through nations, the transnational perspective puts great strain on the nation as the basic unit for researching and writing history, from below and from above. The transnational perspective not only reveals nations as embedded in webs of interactions with other nations, but it also 'brings to the surface subnational histories of various kinds'.[41] When one maps the movement of migrants, they do not 'start' from a country, but from a specific place like a city, a village, a region, a kin group.[42] Similarly, public policies that are observed, emulated and labelled in national terms by their supporters or opponents have often been experimented with by local authorities, not by national ones.[43] The same applies to know-how, ideas and capital: detailed study of flows, ties and formations leads historians to question national tags and to reaffiliate circulations and connections to specific spatial or social segments, groups and institutions under the national umbrella. In order to deal with these subnational or non-national elements, some historians have proposed the notion of **translocality** for the capacity to identify entanglements that do not involve countries, especially in regions where the national state was a latecomer.[44] That is also my understanding of transnational history. On the other hand, researching flows, ties and formations across national units gives access to larger formations. In that guise, the transnational perspective draws from **borderland studies** and the thriving research on oceanic basins as areas of dense interactions.[45] But it also contributes to recovering forgotten zones like the Sahara, to reformulate our knowledge of 'Europe', or to reveal unexpected formations that do not match the identified regions of **area studies**, such as the mutual interest of Japanese and Ottoman intellectuals and governments.[46] Thus, paradoxically, the growing salience of nations in the last 200 years or so is a wedge to open up access to circulations and connections between other types of polities, societies and communities. Empires, city-states, subnational regions, villages, ethnic groups, regional basins of exchange and markets still contributed to organising human activity. But they all were framed by the national state and its homogenising by-products such as citizens' rights and duties, social policies, currencies, language, lifestyles, allegiances, legislations, cultural foreign policy or colonial expansion. Accordingly, when we examine interactions, circulations, constellations and interactions between and through nations with our historical camera set on transnational mode, we also put ourselves in position to capture the flows, ties and formations that have worked across, between and through other kinds of units, beginning with infranational and supranational territorial units.

The third spatial point that needs clarification is the scope of investigations bequeathed by a transnational perspective. There are indeed some connections and circulations that unfurl over a longer distance. Benedict Anderson follows the revolutionary connections that started from the improbable link between Filipino nationalists and the anarchist movement in Paris, Brussels and Barcelona.[47] His journey with José Rizal, Isabelo de Los Reyes and Mariano Ponce also leads him to faraway nodes of activism, exile and intrigue in Havana, Singapore, Tokyo and Yokohama. Quite a ride. But transnational history does not necessarily boil down to long-distance moves and far-flung circuits. The complex relations of observation, emulation and rivalry between artists, officials and intellectuals of China and Japan, France and Germany, USA and Mexico, took place on relatively limited maps.[48] The history of Palestine as a crucible of the Palestinian and Jewish peoples certainly has long-distance dimensions, but it has dramatically played out on a very small tract of land.[49] The everyday life of borders across the globe has been one of smugglers or commuting workers who did not travel to distant places but moved goods, earnings and lifestyles over short distances.[50] The Gotthard Tunnel, just 15 kilometres of track opened under the Alps in 1882, became an icon of Swiss national identity and a bulwark for Swiss territorial integrity. But it was also the by-product of an internationalised capital, know-how and workforce, and became a central axis for trade and tourism between north-western Europe and northern Italy.[51] By and large, transnational historians can keep in mind Donald Wright's successful attempt to tie the 'small place' of Niumi (Gambia) within larger systems. Because of the specialisation of the Niumi region in large-scale peanut culture and exportation, a detailed account of its daily life and society since the late nineteenth century inevitably brings to the fore its location within the imperial economy of commodities and migrations.[52] This interest in combining the big-picture view with the study of short- or medium-range circulations, of small and singular places, is the third answer to the question of where is transnational history.

▶ Conclusion

Adopting a transnational perspective has a lot to do with other relational approaches to history. It is historiographically connected with them and fosters investigations that expand beyond national units. Yet there are also significant differences of a complementary nature: transnational history is not written against or without nations but simultaneously pays attention to what lives against, between and through them; it limits itself to the last 200–250 years broadly understood; it works across the board in regard to spaces, scales and topics. This book does not aim to crystallise such distinctions or tighten the definition of what transnational history should or should not be. It is rather intended as a vade mecum that tries to convey the range of what historians, and social scientists interested in history, have been doing when researching and writing a history that contributes to the answering of the 'big issues' that were outlined at the beginning of this introduction. The flag under which they march is treated as a secondary variable.

As any guide should, the first chapter maps the territory in more detail, and accounts for the itineraries of 'transnational' as a notion. The four core chapters of the book are dedicated to specific notions, the study of which helps to capture the content, operation and impact of entanglements between polities, societies and communities: connections, circulations, relations and formations. The first two have a panoramic purpose, and their framework is meant to make readers think about other topics, places and moments than the ones they are more familiar with. Chapter 2 is dedicated to connections, and offers an overview of linkages created by human individuals and organisations, and by non-human intermediaries. Chapter 3 focuses on the flows that these linkages impeded or favoured, and insists on manners to specify their content, direction, extent and intensity. In the next two chapters, the analytical view yields to a synthetic angle, with a focus on selected instances for deeper examination. Chapter 4 places the emphasis on relations that emerge from connections and circulations, and the way protagonists are changed by this participation. With Chapter 5, we turn to the different formations that generate and are generated by circulations and connections. The last chapter returns to some methodological issues lurking throughout the preceding chapters. All along the way, I will try to draw from a range of moments, topics and regions, but with no intention or illusion of covering the field comprehensively or without bias. After all, a guide is meant to arouse curiosity about a different country, not to mirror the latter.

1 Meanings and Usages

In 2005, the American social scientist Gustavo Cano presented a substantial report on the meanings and usages of the terms 'transnationalism' and 'transnational' among US scholars.[1] He identified a start in the late 1990s, with premises as early as 1979. Building on the *Social Science Abstract Database*, Cano captured a sharp and durable rise after 1993, and illustrated the situation across the arc of the social sciences and humanities by looking for subject keywords such as 'transnational communities', 'transnational links', 'transnational migration/migrant issues' and 'transnational spaces' in publications in anthropology, economics, history, law, political science, migration studies and sociology. Cano's account locates the term only in the US, and only in the last 30 years or so. It would be tempting to conclude that transnational history is a recent fad, with history trailing behind the social science disciplines, and the community of historians throughout the world adopting another passing fashion picked up from US campuses. This chapter will complicate this view. Starting with an account of the recent success of the transnational approach in the social sciences, it explores 170 years of lay and scholarly usage of 'transnational' and its derivatives. Subsequently, it focuses on the discipline of history, with special attention paid to the way in which some historians had adopted a transnational perspective well before the phrase 'transnational history' was minted. This will lead us to finally consider why and how modern historians have increasingly adopted a transnational perspective in the last 20 years, and to assess the several agendas that are encapsulated in transnational history. Gustavo Cano rightly points out that 'transnationalism' was a 'generous' term: its use by social scientists and historians does not belie such a statement.

▶ *Fin de siècle* or the transnational *zeitgeist* in the social sciences

In the late twentieth century, the different disciplines in the social sciences and humanities were assailed by pressing requests to shake off their predominant concern for what was happening in territories shaped by the national state. In a present that was characterised as the age of **globalisation**, such concern was increasingly disparaged as inappropriate – unfitted to the capture of a phenomenon transcending these limits. In a volume that claimed to chart the horizons of sociology for the next century, American sociologist Saskia Sassen urged fellow social scientists to 'crack the casings', and her British counterpart Barry Wellmann indicted the sociology of 'little boxes'.[2] That mood characterised a moment when new rallying cries urged scholars to capture patterns and trends that escaped the grip of the territorially bounded social sciences. 'Networks', 'hybridity', 'diasporas', 'rhizome', 'meztisaje' and 'borders' were among the major keywords that chimed more or less harmoniously, and new empirical work emerged under their spell. It was on the wings of this global craze that the terms 'transnational' and 'transnationalism' gained ground. In fact, a brand new range of 'trans' terms emerged or re-emerged at this moment: 'transmigrants', 'transurbanism' 'translocality', 'translocal' or 'transnations' rhymed with the more ancient 'transnational', 'transnationalism' or 'transnationals'. Many authors in several disciplines did contribute to inventing or reviving this terminology and put it to work, but three fields contributed more consistently than others.

A conquering conceptualisation of the 'transnational' emerged from the field of cultural studies. The major powerhouse was the Center for Transcultural Studies at the University of Chicago and the University of Pennsylvania, in the USA. The Center began to develop a programme to study the internationalisation of culture and communication in 1986, under the direction of Arjun Appadurai and Carol Breckenridge. It launched a 'Project for Transnational Cultural Studies', and established the journal *Public Culture* in 1988. The Center and the journal would be the platform for an interdisciplinary group of US scholars, many with ties to India as a place of origin or a field of work, to investigate what they saw as a dramatic change in cultural forms and flows beginning in the 1970s. Beyond this US core, Appadurai's writings and English sociologist Paul Gilroy's *Black Atlantic* were the flagships of a prolific thread of cultural studies that carried the 'transnational' family of terms into a large section of the social sciences.[3] In this context, 'transnational' was clearly taken as a way to qualify, observe, assess or prophesy a new multipolar, multicultural and post-national world. Arjun Appadurai did not hesitate to suggest that 'the very epoch of the nation-state is near its end'.[4] His prolific lexical inventiveness of terms with the prefix 'trans' bore witness to his sense that the epoch called for new notions.

The study of migrations, with anthropologists and sociologists leading the march, was another domain where the transnational was given impetus. In the 1970s, some scholars of hemispheric American migrations had pointed out that many immigrants had 'their feet in two societies'.[5] From the early 1980s, anthropologists Nina Glick Schiller and Georges Fouron, among others, developed the idea that contemporary migrants in the US, especially Haitians and Caribbeans, endorsed multiple identities that did not fit with territorialised conceptions of identity. The diagnosis was that unprecedented flows of migrants and cultural artefacts (music, images) called for a reconceptualisation of migrants' identities. Neither these identities, nor the political and cultural practices of the migrants, were limited to their country of origin or their country of settlement. These identities, activities and migrants were 'transnational', a term reclaimed from the New York radical intellectual Randolph Bourne and his 1916 plea for a 'transnational America'.[6] From initially sporadic appearances in the literature, 'transnational', 'transmigrants' and soon 'transnationalism' became a rallying cry with the publication of two volumes in 1992 and 1994 by Linda Basch, Nina Glick Schiller and Cristina Szanton-Blanc.[7] This research was also an argument for the realisation of a multicultural US society. Later on, sociologists of migrations also endorsed this approach, with a focus on economic activities by migrants and the notion of 'globalisation from below', where migrant communities developed transnational economic strategies as a response to the reconfiguration of the relationship between capital and labour at the planetary level.[8] In the 1990s, then, transnationalism became the new concept to conceive of migration in a 'global age'. Discussions about the utility and 'correct' definition of the term 'transnationalism' began with these scholars of migration.[9]

There was a third field of research in which 'transnational' gained ground as a specific notion in the 1990s, that of international relations. In this case there was a lineage with usages and definitions dating back to the 1960s (see below). This was why the German political scientist Thomas Risse-Kappen could issue a call in the mid-1990s for 'bringing transnational relations back in', drawing attention to the policy impact of non-state organisations working across state boundaries.[10] The second half of the 1990s saw a number of publications in this vein, including the much cited volume by Margaret Keck and Kathryn Sikkink on 'transnational advocacy networks', i.e. coalitions between groups and movements that campaigned across national borders for social and political issues.[11] Two characteristics were common to these works. First, they all emphasised the contribution of non-state actors to the conception, installation and operation of issue area policies and global governance. Second, they hailed the existence, emergence, role and impact of a 'global/transnational civil society' as a moderating power in face of the prevailing economic and neo-liberal dimension of globalisation. In that domain, 'transnational' meant non-state.

Although they were not always aware of another, these major cores shared a similar creed: flows of capital, people, ideas or images were making nation states insufficient or irrelevant as units of analysis, and the social sciences had to account for this break in the history of the world. Unravelling this change erred on the side of prescription and prophecy, as many social scientists saw social and political purchase in their use of the transnational family of terms. These usages and meanings quickly snowballed in public usage and in academia. Newspapers in different languages embraced the idea of transnationalism to qualify migrants who were 'neither here nor there'. While until the 1990s the term was at best of sporadic use, it cropped up in new scholarly journals (*Diaspora: a Journal of Transnational Studies* created in 1991; *Global Networks: a Journal of Transnational Affairs* launched in 2001), in names for research projects (the Transnational Communities Programme led by Steven Vertovec at Oxford University, England, from 1997, or the Transnational Social Fields Network run by Ludger Pries at the Ruhr Universität Bochum in Germany during the early 2000s), as well as in graduate programmes in 'transnational studies'. All these initiatives had different methodologies, objects and goals, but they derived from a common statement of intentions: the forces of globalisation were transforming migration, politics, economics and religion, erasing their national characteristics. They needed to be conceived and researched as transnational facts and processes.

Gustavo Cano rightly observed that 'transnational' was the most commonly used term in the US academic world in the late 1980s and early 1990s, before 'transnationalism' took over after 1994. This would suggest that the semantic power of the transnational, which initially was a qualification to be appended to facts, processes, individuals and groups, increasingly came to be used as a paradigm or a world view, and even as a political project to transform the social sciences if not the actual world. In parallel to that change of terminology, a search for normative definitions took place. Debates began to define what 'real' transnationalism was, what was transnational and what was not. A cottage industry generating and appraising definitions quickly developed as the label became a must-wear. Consequently, it was also criticised for lack of theorisation. As early as 1994 an anthropologist specialising in Eastern Europe noted that the term dissolved 'when inspected more closely' and pointed to its inherent confusion between state and nation.[12] Later on, historians of migration also came to terms with the presentism and approximations they saw in the use of the notion of 'transnationalism' to study contemporary migrations.[13] This did not stop the snowball, though, and the different terms of the transnational family are now in common use well beyond the places and fields where they were coined or revitalised some 20 years ago.

This momentum has recently been captured by Sanjeev Khagram and Peggy Levitt in their proposal to establish 'transnational studies' as a new section of the social sciences. They make bold and stimulating proposals to establish the empirical, methodological, theoretical, philosophical and public aspects of transnationalism, with an insistence on the need to build up our capacity to work across territories and scales. The task of transnational studies, as they sum it up, is to 'uncover, analyse and conceptualise similarities, differences and interactions among trans-societal and trans-organisational realities, including the ways in which they shape bordered and bounded phenomena and dynamics across time and space'.[14] And the destiny of transnational studies is to change the social sciences as we know them. While Khagram and Levitt recognise that transnational scholarship is not entirely new, they do not rewind the tape very far, nonetheless; they cleave to the last 30 years' range of the *fin de siècle* globalisation mood. Yet the term 'transnational' has been with us for some 170 years. A study of its career before its recent fortune is necessary to contextualise the whens, wheres and whys of this usage.

▶ Looking backwards: 'transnational' at 170 years

The continuous expansion of full-text online databases will certainly make this claim obsolete very soon, as has already happened to previous assertions, but the Frenchman Constantin Pecqueur (1801–1887) can be provisionally cited as the first user of the adjective 'transnational'. In a memoir published in 1842, Pecqueur studied the means to achieve peace. He suggested that the best guarantee was interdependence between nations, to be established through free trade, income compensation schemes and the advent of a 'cosmopolitan power'. Only then would 'considérations d'intérêt transnational' ('issues/considerations of transnational interest' – my translation) such as peace have a chance to prevail.[15] Pecqueur uses 'transnational' to stress that peace is a topic of general interest for all nations, and the absence of quotation marks suggests the term may not have been coined by the author. It is not anecdotal to mention this first, because it points us to a specific political region. Pecqueur was a major French socialist writer of the mid-nineteenth century, formerly of Saint-Simonian tendency, who felt strongly about the establishment of international arbitration.[16] His publications are often quoted in Karl Marx's *Das Kapital*, although 'transnational' does not appear there. The next known step takes us to Germany and the linguist Georg Curtius (1820–95). The 20-year gap suggests that there were other uses in the meantime, waiting to be excavated. In his 1862 inaugural lecture at Leipzig University, Curtius insisted that all national languages were rooted in families of language, culture and racial features, understanding of which called for views that extended beyond the study of national literature. 'Eine jede Sprache ist ihrer Grundlage nach etwas transna-tionales und eben deshalb von dem Standpunkte des Philologen allein nicht völlig zu begreifendes', he wrote.[17] An anonymous US author used that quotation to support his own views in 1868 in the *Princeton Review*, translating it as 'every language is fundamentally something transnational and therefore not to be fully comprehended from the philologist's point of view'.[18] This is, provisionally, the first known appearance of the term in English.

These occurrences anchor the term in the nineteenth century and in several languages, and we see them questioning the relevance of national containers at the very moment of their consolidation. Further usage, which contrasted meanings suggests that there were different semantic streams, is attested in the late nineteenth and early twentieth century. The hyphenated 'trans-national' was then used in US newspapers to qualify transportation infrastructures like roads or waterways that connected distant sections within the country.[19] Its parallel presence as a synonym for 'international' does not seem to have been damaged by this opposite understanding.

However, the first famous use of the term was to lead in another direction with Randolph Bourne (1886–1918), a character of repute on New York intellectual scene. In reaction to widely shared expectations and anxieties about the possible disloyalty of diverse strands of 'hyphenated Americans' in the context of the European war, Bourne led the charge on the ideal of assimilation of immigrants in a 1916 article.[20] His suggestion was that the United States had to come to terms with the myriad of national origins that peopled the Great Republic, and that they should become the first 'international nation', a matrix of world citizenship. Bourne revelled in lexicographical invention to make his point. He used 'trans-national' as an adjective to describe an American population that defied simple national affiliation, 'trans-nationality/transnationality' to qualify the resulting situation, 'transnationalism' to characterise the sense of belonging that would go beyond existing nationalisms and amount to world citizenship, and 'trans-nationals' to designate the people with a dual sense of belonging. All along the way, Bourne marshalled his 'trans' terminology as a set of synonyms for 'international', 'internationalism' or 'cosmopolitanism'. He had no chance to elaborate further on definitions because of an unexpected encounter with an unhyphenated migrant, the Spanish influenza virus.

In the following years, the adjective was used infrequently but regularly. 'Transnational/trans-national' qualified elements that developed across national boundaries. Casual use of the word in English can be tracked in regional or national US newspapers and journals: 'transnational arrangements' described the operations of the League of Nations that cut across borders (1925), 'transnational trip' advertised a university study tour in Europe (1931), 'trans-national affairs' described the agenda of the annual session at the Institute of International Relations (1931). In French, 'trans-national' served as a synonym of 'pan-human' and 'universal' to denote aspects of Russian literature (1927), or to qualify the state of mind that should lead to Franco-German reconciliation and European construction (1929). It was mostly very loosely handled, halfway between a synonym of 'international' and a shorthand for 'stuff that crosses national boundaries'. Most of its users did not try to harness it to any conceptual aims.

Yet, a few decided users seized on 'transnational' to name things or processes of a specific nature during the inter war years. University of Heidelberg law professor Max Gutzwiller (1889–1989), who worked in the field of international law and arbitration, was one of them. With the phrase '*transnationale Privatrecht*', he named in 1931 new legal norms and situations that escaped the realm of 'international private law': the cases of arbitration taken up by the mixed arbitration tribunals created by the Versailles Treaty.[21] In *Fruits of Victory* (1921), the English-American journalist, supporter of the League of Nations and peace activist, Norman Angell (1872–1967), hitched the term to his argument about pre-war trade and industrial and financial entanglements among countries. Angell wrote about a 'trans-national' economy that bound European countries together and with other areas, caused by the world division of labour and the transactions between economic agents. This adjective he found 'more correct' than 'international', and accordingly used the term and its spin-offs ('trans-nationalism', 'trans-nationally') several times in his book. The success of his essays might have given some popularity to the use of the term in the US press during the 1920s. In contrast, Simon Kuznets' use of the term in a 1948 article does not seem to have been followed up despite the fame of the author. However, I find it significant that Kuznets used the phrase 'trans-national economic relations' to urge his fellow economists to consider the US economy in a larger context. To appreciate a domestic economy, Kuznets said, it was necessary to include non-material exchanges (population, policies, obligations, power projection) as well as emulation and competition between countries.[22]

Apart from a few jurists who picked up on Gutzwiller's neologism, all these uses remained isolated. Meanings were scarcely explored and certainly not disputed until the 1950s. Clusters of more systematic usage appeared around that time. These offered neater definitions and specific points of application. On the one hand, 'transnational' became a tag for developments in the real world political economy of the 1950s and 1960s. In the USA, it was increasingly used in the naming of firms during the 1950s, as witnessed by advertising blocks and business news in several newspapers. The 'trans-national/transnational' label seems to have appealed to firms in many different sectors, including some with a clear domestic orientation. It also gained ground in the early 1960s when the term 'transnational corporation' inched its way into lay and scholarly language, first as a synonym of 'multinational', and later to suggest a further stage of business integration where capital, research and other aspects were managed without any regard for the company's home country interests. Eventually, the United Nations Organisation adopted that terminology in 1975 for its new Centre on Transnational Corporations. This latter use might have been decisive for the capacity of the term to travel in the lay world. The adjective moved into the economic and political vocabulary beyond the USA, and was for instance used to designate actual or expected business consequences of European integration. Meanwhile, activists from the left began to indict 'transnational capital' and 'the transnationals'. There were a number of activist groups, journals or think tanks who began to carry the adjective 'transnational' in their names like *Agenor: Transnational Left Review* in 1970, or the research centres created by Chilean exiles after Pinochet's coup (Transnational Institute, 1974, Latin American Institute for Transnational

Studies, 1976). These were the premises of an enduring anti-imperialist under-standing of the term 'transnational' in South and Central America. On the other hand, 'transnational' had found purchase among those who tried to analyse and explain the post-war world. US commentators of the current and future world political order spoke of 'transnational cooperation' promoted by the UN and its agencies (Walter Lippmann, 1949), of 'transnational groups' to name the Soviet and American blocs (William McNeill, 1954), or of the establishment of 'trans-national communities' of scholars, scientists and others in the service of world peace (Robert Oppenheimer, 1958). Law professor Myres S. McDougal chose it to qualify groups whose composition or activities stretched across national frontiers, and so did political scientist Arnold Wolfers who stressed the role of corporations as 'transnational actors' in world politics (1959). As can be seen from this range, the meaning of the term was still open-ended: it could be used as equivalent to 'supranational' or 'international', appended to the names of governmental, inter-governmental, business and civil society actors, used by those who awaited the end of the age of nations and by those who merely described relations between nations.

It was at the meeting point of these two fields, economics and international rela-tions, that the first scholarly attempt to create a transnational paradigm took place. In February 1956, Philip Jessup, a professor of international law and diplomacy at Columbia University (USA), gave three lectures at the Yale University Law School. A couple of months later, they were published under the title *Transnational Law*. Though he did not acknowledge the former use of the term by German-speaking law scholars in the 1930s, Jessup was brimming with a similar frustration. An old hand at the State Department, the US foreign ministry, Jessup had played a role in the design of several institutions of the new world order during the Second World War, especially as assistant secretary general of the United Nations Relief and Rehabilitation Administration. He left government service in 1953, and sub-sequently worked with the Rockefeller Foundation and the Carnegie Endowment for International Peace. Jessup's 1956 conferences spelled the need for a corpus of 'transnational law', that would include all law which regulated actions or events that straddled national frontiers. This was long overdue, he said, to handle cases tied to the work of UN agencies, the development of the European institutions, the activities of business, investment and trade overseas, the global commons, the activities of non-governmental organisations and other manifestations of a 'com-plex interrelated world community'. For Jessup, foreign relations other than those between countries and states needed a legal corpus, as did problems that stretched across national borders and across the specialised and specialised categories of law. However, the transformation of the *Bulletin of the Columbia Society of International Law* into the *Columbia Journal of Transnational Law* in 1964 was one of the few immediate by-products of Jessup's suggestion. Only much more recently would transnational law again be placed on the map.[23] Although this first attempt at a transnational turn was not conclusive, it signalled a new moment where the term 'transnational' would increasingly be the object of proposals and discussions within different disciplines of the scholarly world, in order to grapple with the perceived world change.

These features were all present in the field of political science in the late 1960s, when a group of scholars defined their approach in terms of 'transnational relations' as opposed to 'international relations'. We have seen above that the term had begun to surface with some regularity among specialists of world politics from the late 1950s. Arnold Wolfers used it in 1959 to identify the role of non-state corporate actors in world politics; in 1962, the Frenchman Raymond Aaron spoke of a *société transnationale* to point to a system parallel to interstate relations, involving individuals from different countries and blocs who migrated, traded, exchanged ideas and joined with each other in celebration, competition or protest. The German Karl Kaiser penned a long development on the *transnationale Politik* emerging from growing interactions between actors located in different countries.[24] On the borderline between academy and activism, the Norwegian peace researcher Johan Galtung used 'transnational' to name the kind of loyalty he hoped would develop in non-governmental organisations that transcended national borders (1967). This trend was captured and systematised in 1970–71, when Robert Keohane and Joseph Nye, two US political scientists, organised a conference on 'transnational relations' and published its proceedings. It was an open challenge to the realist approach that dominated the field of international relations, and to its 'state-centric view'.[25] Picking up from work on economic interdependence and on multinational corporations, the convenors deliberately focused on 'contacts, coalitions, and interactions across state boundaries that are not controlled by the central foreign policy organs of government'.[26] They asserted that these were 'centrally important for the understanding of contemporary politics'.[27] The first 'transnationalism' was born, to describe their emphasis on non-intergovernmental relations in world politics. Contributors to the volume used this word to describe a contemporary condition of their world, marked by an abundance of cross-border ties that were not reducible to relations between states. And a few used it to describe a situation where national units were altogether irrelevant, understanding 'transnationalism' as a further stage in the history of human societies coming after the age of nationalism. This interest in 'transnational relations' and 'transnationalism' was soon eclipsed by the next big thing in international relations, a discipline where a new paradigm emerged every other year. But interest endured, especially among non-US political scientists.[28]

This emphasis on transnational relations with a focus on non-state actors left an enduring mark on the vocabulary of other social sciences as well as on the very actors of these relations. Transnationalism became 'in'. Non-governmental organisations found the term appealing, as it stressed their difference from interstate actors. In the year 1976, the phrase 'transnational associations' made a spectacular appearance in *International Associations*, the journal published by the Union of International Associations. The journal even changed name in 1977, to become *Transnational Associations*. This was also the moment when the hyphenated form 'trans-national', that had lost ground during the 1960s, definitely disappeared. By and large, the 1970s made the adjective a household name in academia and in the lay world.

Yet, for all their criticism of state-centric approaches to international relations, Keohane and Nye were for the most part very careful to stress they did not support or advocate the view that national states were withering away. This ambiguity had been part and parcel of the different uses of the terms throughout the previous decades. What was defined as transnational was certainly presented as a challenge to national politics and societies, but political scientists did not pronounce on the result of the contest. Even Johan Galtung, despite his enthusiasm for such perspectives, wrote in 1971 that the 'transnational', 'global' or 'world' phase, where international organisations would achieve their shift from their national touchstones, was still hypothetical. As we have seen, this post-national posture would definitely carry the day during the 1990s, when the qualification of 'transnational' became a statement on the present and a prophecy about the future. As for the past, it had never been a concern for all those who coined or toyed with the words of the transnational family. Whence a question: what about history and historians?

▶ Modern history before transnational history

In their indictment of **methodological nationalism**, Andreas Wimmer and Nina Glick Schiller rapped the knuckles of history for its love affair with the nation.[29] Indeed, history as a discipline did develop in close contact with the processes of state- and nation-building. In the nineteenth century, its sources, methods and narrative took shape alongside those of the national state, and in close relation to them. Archives and data were framed by a national perspective. The first major collections of sources, which laid the foundation for the expansion of empirical history, bore the stamp of national construction (Monumenta Germaniae Historica in1823, English Rolls Series in 1857). Political history, the first specialisation to come of age, told the tale of the irresistible but difficult birth of specific nations. This love affair with the nation endured through time, as witnessed by the role given to history in the new countries that emerged from decolonisation or from the break-up of the communist bloc. For the most part, and even without a nationalist tack, it has remained the mission of history and historians to tell the story of a given country, and the national unit is given prominence when we observe and assess change and continuity. More than sociology, geography, anthropology or economics and possibly on a par with literature, history as a discipline and a profession has certainly been the handmaiden of nation- and state-building processes.[30] As a sub discipline devoted to the study of the last two centuries, modern history was, more than other fields, caught in this service relation. Nonetheless, this does not imply that all of modern history and all modern historians have abided by this rule, as we can see from experiments they conducted before the 1990s.

The track records of **universal history**, **area studies** and **world history** bear witness that professional historians wrote history beyond the national scope. It must be said that this sometimes derived from clear attempts to expand the might of a given nation, as in the case of the *Südostforschung* (southeast studies) institutes and journals that were started in Vienna and Berlin before the First World War, with the brand of world history carried out in Japan in the 1940s, or with the rise of area studies at US universities in the Cold War context of the 1950s.[31] And, these concerns for writing history beyond the nation considered entanglements between polities, communities and societies as minor or instrumental aspects. In contrast, though, the German historian Karl Lamprecht, in a famous lecture he gave in the United States in 1904, called for 'the study of the history of the inter-relations of communities of men' and insisted on the transmission of culture, which he summed up as the question of 'influence' between nations.[32] The English historian Arnold Toynbee, who addressed 'encounters' among civilisations in space and time, was mostly concerned with contacts between Western civilisation and some of the others. He was eager to identify the laws of 'cultural radiation and reception', and this focus on contacts was taken up by his commentators such as José Ortega y Gasset or Christopher Dawson.[33] Marshall Hodgson, the first world historian in residence at the University of Chicago, constantly reformulated his plea for the 'hemispheric interregional approach' since his initial article on that topic in 1954.[34] The emphasis on ties and flows was also brought up during the discussions of projects like the *History of Mankind* launched by UNESCO in 1946. At that moment the French historian Lucien Febvre stated that this history should deal with 'everything that had been subject to circulation'.[35]

In fact, it is not too difficult to find other instances of famous and not so famous historians who have made similar statements. And yet, those who began to work across and between societies, communities and polities stopped short in the face of several limits. First, they shirked more often than not on the threshold of the nineteenth century, as if the coming of age of national states had thwarted the development of interactions and relations. Second, the major works in that vein, especially in **world history**, were masterful attempts at synthesis rather than the result of the identification, command and cultivation of original material. This pattern was reinforced when, as in the USA, world history became an element of the school curriculum and was defined as a teaching-oriented undertaking.[36] Lastly, world history or universal history were not problem-oriented: they were, as a distant echo of Immanuel Kant's 1784 essay, 'Ideas of universal history with cosmopolitan aims'.[37] They celebrated the unity of mankind, wanted to redress misperceptions among nations, or celebrate the prominence of one civilisation over the others. But they did not point to specific stakes and issues in terms of historical change and continuity. This is also why the mass of research- and problem-oriented academic historians ignored the study of entanglements.

Yet, some tried. British historian Eric Hobsbawm wrote synthetic interpretations of modern and contemporary European and world history that relentlessly inter-twined the history of polities and societies.[38] Regional specialists quietly weaved their stories of cultural and economic connections across centuries, without much attention from colleagues in other fields.[39] In the USA, the interest in inscribing American history in a web of connections with the world out there was made loud and clear in the late nineteenth century, waned in the 1920s, to be revived during the 1940s and was muted again later on.[40] This also happened in specific subdis-ciplinary contexts. Economic history, in its liberal or Marxist declension, relies on traditions that exhort us to study economic entanglements across nations in the last two centuries. Karl Marx himself cleared the ground with *Das Kapital*, which is largely a history of economic connections in the early nineteenth century. Marxist historians and social scientists of the late 1970s were on a similar wavelength when they investigated topics like unequal development and peripheral capitalism since the mid-nineteenth century.[41] Besides, today's historians tend to forget that, only a few decades ago, their counterparts had to be fluent in the language of economic cycles, understood as common conjunctures for the countries that were integrated in the modern capitalist economy. Even if Kitchin, Juglar, Kuznets and Kondratieff cycles are not what they used to be from the 1950s to the 1970s, they are reminders of that aspect of economic history. Still, despite these precedents, economic history as a discipline was caught in the vortex of national data, national territory and national appraisal of research topics and results. The history of economic entan-glements may well have provided a continuous thread in the pages of specialised US journals like the *Bulletin of the Business Historical Society* and later the *Business History Review*, but the articles were mostly about the entanglements of the US econ-omy with the rest of the world. An American historian like Clark Spence began his career by writing a major book on British investments in the American West, and eventually focused on US regional history.[42] The British historian Sydney Pollard, keen as he was to follow regional paths of transmission in his study of the Indus-trial Revolution, found it necessary to reintroduce economic nationalism as a *deus ex machina* even as he fiercely criticised his fellow-scholars' baleful tendency to consider 'that countries within their political boundaries are the only units within which it is worthwhile to consider the process of industrialization'.[43]

In other provinces of the historians' realm, some subjects were similarly dissatis-fied with the national container, for instance diplomatic historians who were not happy with their subdiscipline's focus on diplomatic agreements and disagreements between national governments.[44] Some free spirits did use that opportunity to sail on different seas,[45] but by and large this did not deter the subdiscipline from keeping its prime focus on the study of the politics of power, war and peace between countries. Generally, the conjunction of nationally framed data and nationally framed academic communities did induce subdisciplinary communities to define their research within the safe and secure container of national histories. Addressing national audiences and horizons was the shortest way to sources, audience, positions, research funding and intellectual legitimacy.

It was mostly mavericks who thought otherwise, collectively or individually. Thus economic history had its empirical workers, free riders, number crunchers and system builders who did consider the practical or systemic entanglements of the modern world.[46] Working between and across national units of analysis was also enticing to historians who tried to develop a new field. When new interests and subdisciplinary trends developed, like environmental history in the 1980s, they did not readily accept the bounds of national territories as their remit.[47] If only because they had to subvert the neat arrangement of established subdisciplines that were abiding by national specialisation. Likewise, a number of individual historians have worked between and across national frameworks without being too much concerned by where they did fit. A. O. Lovejoy's reflections on intellectual history, which in 1948 placed the emphasis on following the combination and recombination of 'unit-ideas', implied following ideas regardless of national or linguistic boundaries.[48] In 1959, the historian of literature Claude Digeon showcased the antagonistic symbiosis between French and German high culture between 1870 and 1914.[49] These individuals often remain isolated, but a transnational perspective was being eagerly applied on the fringes of the established specialisations of modern history.

More precisely, this often happened among historians and in domains that were peripheral to the social and intellectual mainstream of the discipline, as with the late nineteenth-century orientalists mentioned earlier. In these peripheries, one can observe a correspondence between the situation of historians and that of the groups they studied: both had to find resources beyond their national communities.[50] Consider the historiographies of women's, workers' and black American movements, for instance. Their earliest historians were often activists themselves, and they studied the history of these groups and their struggle for emancipation because they considered the writing of history as an element on this path to emancipation. Because of the fact that the history of these groups was, for a long time, not central in academic history, these historians had to rely on fellow committed historians abroad to build conversations and to put their object of study on different national agendas. Moreover, the historical protagonists of the women's, workers' and black American movements had created communities of action and belief beyond borders, and emphasised a language of sisterhood and brotherhood across borders. These were fundamental reasons for committed historians to pay significant interest to activities that spilled across national limits. The interest in resources that national women's movements had mustered through national borders in the late nineteenth and early twentieth centuries was thus present very early in women's history.[51] The concern to retrace class solidarity and contacts across borders was an enduring aspect in the historiography of the workers' movements, also because of the lasting role of 'internationalism' in the language and ideology of trade unionism and socialism since the 'Address to the Belgian Working Classes' penned by the English Working Men's Association in 1836.[52] It is significant that historians of the workers' movement conducted early explorations of topics that would, more recently, be emphasised in other fields such as the history of labour migrations.[53] As for black Americans, the trend was even more consistent in time. Late nineteenth- and early twentieth-century black intellectuals and scholars were very eager to write the history of the black diaspora and of pan-Africanism. W.E.B. Dubois, Eric Williams, C.L.R. James and their fellow black intellectuals kept an eye on past and current avatars or the colour line in the whole Atlantic world (and more widely). Not only were they much interested in contemporary evolution of the black diaspora, but they also participated in the worldwide revolutionary and emancipatory struggle. Later in time, some promoters of 'Black Studies' in the 1970s treated Africans and people of African descent as a single people. Robin Kelley sums up this situation by writing that 'many early contributors of the *Journal of Negro History* were attempting to write transnational history before such terminology came into being'.[54] This statement rings true for the history of women's and workers' movements as well. This stream of militant transnational history did not stop when transnational became hot. The current activities of the Tepoztlán Institute for the Transnational History of the Americas, in Mexico, bear witness to the emancipatory deliverables expected from the term 'transnational' in its anti-colonial and anti-imperialist historiographical vein.[55]

Although limited to specific moments or niches of historical research and writing, this brief exploration is suggestive. Being mindful of these earlier attempts to configure a transnational perspective can prevent current transnational historians from thinking they have invented the wheel. It also provides them with a pool of intellectual resources: topics, hypotheses, sources, methods and angles that should not be discredited as archaic or outdated. This is especially useful now when the mainstream of the discipline has begun to pay some attention to what was once the domain of mavericks, free riders and outsiders.

▶ Modern historians go transnational

The term 'transnational', the phrase 'transnational history', and the range of issues and concerns they encompass, have all become familiar in the discipline of history in the last 20 years. The term 'transnational' was only used randomly by histori-ans until then, sometimes as a synonym for 'multiple countries' or 'regional'.[56] But there was no attempt whatsoever to make it more than a loosely descriptive adjec-tive. Very few historians took an active part in the lexical development of the term since its appearance 170 years ago. Save James Field, historians did not contribute significantly to the different transnational factories opened by jurists, political sci-entists or anthropologists and sociologists from the 1950s to the early 1990s.[57] Despite the obvious interest of Arjun Appadurai and Carol Breckenridge in histor-ical developments, and although a historian like Dipesh Chakrabarty contributed very regularly to *Public Culture*, historians were rarely spotted among the partici-pants in the early initiatives of the Center for Transcultural Studies in the late 1980s and early 1990s.[58] Migration anthropologists do not seem to have connected with historians of migrations when they elaborated their views on transnationalism. This absence from the interdisciplinary debate has endured. The *Transnational Studies Reader* (2008), the most determined attempt to create an interdisciplinary research, educational and intellectual conversation about the transnational per-spective, includes a short 'Historical perspectives' section.[59] The texts of that section are from sociologists Janet Abu-Lughod and Howard Winant, cultural studies foun-tainhead Paul Gilroy, and world historian William McNeill. Although the section wants to bring to light 'ways in which the world has always been transnational', it does not include or hint to any contribution by historians who have done empirical work on entanglements in human history, not even historians of migra-tions, culture, trade or religion. Would it be the case that we are just redundant or irrelevant?

Yet, if we glance at library shelves, publishers' catalogues, journal tables of con-tents, bulletin boards or conference programmes, historians seem now to have adopted the transnational perspective. In the last 20 years, an increasing num-ber of modern history books and articles have flagged their interest in what lies in between national histories. They have appeared under the labels of 'global', 'international', 'world', 'transnational' "connected" or 'entangled' history, or have ignored labels altogether. They are now the first port of call for any modern historian who wants to adopt a transnational perspective. How did this happen?

Of major importance were discussions within and about specific national historiographies, which were taken to task for their fixation on the national. The very coining of the phrase 'transnational history' took place in that context. It was the Australian historian of the USA, Ian Tyrrell, who used the adjective and the phrase several times in a 1991 forum piece for the *American Historical Review*.[60] Tyrrell's purpose was to ambush the parochialism of American history and its touchstone, the idea of 'exceptionalism', i.e. the sense that US differences amounted to a uniqueness which made the history of the American nation incom-mensurable and splendidly isolated from the history of the rest of the world.

His verdict might have been too severe or selective,[61] but it was productive. This charge was subsequently endorsed by the Organisation of American Historians, through a series of meetings and seminars dedicated to 'The internationalisation of American history'. Their efforts were crowned by the 'The Nation and Beyond' special issue of the *Journal of American History* in 1999, and by a collected volume published in 2000.[62] Later volume-length essays offered the synthetic result of this attempt to relocate modern American history within a set of interactions with the world.[63] Interactions there were also with other national historiographies, despite the fact this US discussion was overwhelmingly concerned with the writing of US history. Some modern Spanish historians, for instance, built on the resources of their American colleagues to consider the possibility of carving research and narrative spaces that were not bound within the nation. In the workshop they organised in 1997 and in the resulting publication *La historia transnacional*, they referred to publications by Tyrrell and Thelen, and invited some participants from the Internationalisation of American History project.[64] Was this a hint that transnational history would be yet another product made in America that conquered the scholarly world in the twentieth century?

Not if we consider that Spanish historians' concern was not for US history or, for that matter, Spanish history. The project coordinators were keen to stress that going transnational was about making history for *todos terenos* (all terrain), in terms of topics, analytical levels (from the micro to the macro) and territories (cutting across subnational units as well as considering regional or global situations). Not if we turn to another major site for the emergence of the terminology and practice of transnational history, Germany. The grip of *Transnationale Geschichte* owed much of its success to its capacity to unsettle the master narrative of the German *Sonderweg* (special path), which had dominated the historiography of that country since the 1970s. This was one of the intellectual purposes of the experienced German historian Jürgen Kocka when he launched the discussion in a forum section of the journal *Geschichte und Gesellschaft* in 2001.[65] As in the USA, *Transnationale Geschichte* was a call to re-situate modern German history in the world, and to get rid of the national fixation that derived from the historiographical focus on the period of Nazi dictatorship and its roots. But there were many differences between the two situations.[66] They help us to understand that German historians were far from mimicking their US counterparts when they went transnational. On the one hand, *Transnationale Geschichte* capitalised on a number of previous attempts by German modern historians to escape the national framework, most notably **Transfergeschichte**. This notion had emerged from the study of cultural transfers between France and Germany that started in the late 1980s.[67] It subsequently aroused interest beyond the study of this specific relationship,[68] and generated discussions with comparative historians that were the background of *Transnationale Geschichte* (see introduction). Again in contrast with the US story,

Transnationale Geschichte blossomed on interdisciplinary encounters. Admittedly, the transnational moment of US modern history did develop some 'ex post' conversation with social scientists, but in the German case this was present at the creation. AGORA, a research programme at the Wissenschaft Kolleg in Berlin, was the hothouse of transnational history in Germany. At the invitation of the sociologist Wolf Lepennies and the historian Jürgen Kocka, a number of young scholars gathered between 1998 and 2001 and embarked on a fruitful conversation. This was when anthropologist Shalini Randeria definitively exposed Kocka and young historians like Sebastian Conrad and sociologists like the French Bénédicte Zimmermann to some of her ideas. Randeria insisted that the study of processes of interaction and intermixture in time, which she called the 'entangled histories of uneven modernities', made it possible to consider multiple modernities, to pay attention to original processes and patterns in non-Western societies and ultimately to bypass the focus of the social sciences and humanities on Western historical experience and trajectories.[69] AGORA had numerous direct by-products, beginning with the 2001 issue of *Geschichte and Gesellschaft* that has been mentioned earlier, and the further elaborations by Bénédicte Zimmermann and Michael Werner on **histoire croisée**.[70] More widely, its emphasis on the study of interactions and entanglements quickly caught on. If *Transnationale Geschichte* gelled as a proposal that had to do with German history, it quickly attracted German and other European historians who were interested in the modern history of Central Europe, China, or the Atlantic world, and more generally in patterns and objects that existed between and across countries or regions.[71]

By and large, these national crystallisations were singular actualisations of a larger mounting concern in modern history. Transnational history did not 'start' from the project to internationalise American history or to dismantle the *Sonderweg*. It belonged to the same *zeitgeist* that had captured the attention of cultural studies scholars or anthropologists of migration at the turn of the 1980s. Modern historians caught the transnational wind in a general climate where 'globalisation' was the key buzzword. In his introduction to *Globalization in World History*, Anthony Hopkins was right to say that 'with few exceptions (...), historians have still to participate or even to recognize the subject'.[72] Indeed, sociologists, anthropologists, economists and political scientists had been debating definitions and interpretations since the early 1990s, when globalisation began to make front page news.[73] Historians entered the fray quite belatedly, modern historians especially, and initially as the supporting cast in discussions about the chronological depth of the integrated world economy.[74] Transnational history, together with **global history, connected history** and the revival of world history, has been one of their attempts to recast these discussions in historical fashion. As often, the present worked as a heuristic device: it pushed historians to question the past in order to study interrelations and interconnections that globalisation literature said were new and unprecedented. That move not only accounted for the revival of world history as a meta-narrative of a global past composed of encompassing planetary processes, but it also created opportunities for a strand of scholarship that originated from around the world, a history of 'mobility and mobilization, of trade and merchants, of migrants and diasporas, of travellers and communication'.[75]

This atmosphere also favoured the convergence of long-term waves, leading to the emergence of new research agendas that contributed to the success of transnational history in the 1990s. An instance of that convergence was the meeting between historians of migrations and diplomatic historians in the United States. While migration history had developed in the wake of social history, diplomatic history had somehow been the intellectual foil of the latter in the 1950s and 1960s. In the last 20 years, however, they have come to share some interests because of the common adoption of a transnational perspective, something that would have been unlikely 20 years ago.[76] This intersection concluded a longer trend within each field. Since the 1970s, some historians of migrations have strived to extricate the history of migrations from the specific history of one nation (that of emigration or immigration), and to explain how migrants travelled and built their identities and lives through different locations. They stressed trajectories instead of focusing on departure and arrival points.[77] Migration history became resolutely multidisciplinary.[78] Historians of international relations, on their own track, turned towards issues of gender, race and cultural relations as Akira Iriye, Frank Ninkovich and others pushed their colleagues to include new protagonists and new approaches in their horizons.[79] This coalesced during the 1990s into a flurry of books and articles, and the prominent journal in the field soon stated that 'transnational forces and their human elements are the stuff of a new international history and should not escape our attention'.[80] The attention to the migration element of these forces eventually brought together historians of international relations and migrations, under the aegis of transnational history. The historical study of empires and colonisation has been another region whose renewal spurred the success of the transnational perspective in the last 20 years. In the late 1980s, some historians of colonial empires breathed new life into colonial history by collating coloniser, colonised peoples and territories into one analytical bundle, whereas the study of connections between metropolises and colonies, and between colonies, had been consigned to the margins by mainstream imperial history.[81] Because they tried to read the relation between empire and nation as a relation of mutual coproduction, and not just one of dominance, resistance and filiation, the historians who contributed to what later was called the 'new imperial history' embarked on thinking 'with and through the nation'.[82] In other instances, change occurred in interaction with researchers in other disciplines. This was the case, for instance, of historians of Muslim religion and politics who contributed to the 'Muslim transnationalism' group created by the English political scientist James

Piscatori and the anthropologist Dale Eickelman in the late 1980s.[83] In these different instances, use of the terms 'transnational' and 'transnational history' made it possible to point to new research directions, to open new conversations and to put a label on manifold historical studies that worked in-between and through national containers.

▶ Conclusion

In 2005, a US historian who specialises in the twentieth-century history of racial theory and categories wrote that 'interest in transnational approaches to history now reaches from the most radical to the most orthodox branches of the profession'.[84] Micol Seigel was, of course, speaking about modern history in its US garb to diagnose a 'transnational turn'. Though German modern historians might have ratified the statement, it would still certainly have been called irrelevant or premature by historians of other periods or who worked in other national, disciplinary contexts. In Europe, medieval or early modern historians' love affair with the national state was less passionate than the modern historian's romance, and they did not need any conversion or turn. The very idea of a 'turn' is also questionable if we remember past manifestations of modern historians' interest in what happened between and through polities and communities: a re-turn might be a more appropriate term. There are also national or subdisciplinary contexts that do not show any interest in transnational approaches. In any event, Micol Seigel's article reminds us that transnational history is just not the handmaiden of globalisation, a sort of second lethal hug after the one between history and the nation. Her genealogy of transnational history ties it to W.E.B. Du Bois, Eric Williams, C.L.R. James and Frantz Fanon. In her eyes, radical historians are the spearheads of transnational history, and it was 'the mobility and resistance occasioned by colonialism, as translated by anticolonial and postcolonial intellectuals, that have lit the hottest fires in the engines driving the transnational turn'.[85] As with Seigel's agenda of resistance and emancipation, historians often have specific references and goals in mind when they claim to be doing transnational history. And these agendas can be quite different. To some, it can contribute to 'one world' aspirations once pursued by the likes of Leften Stavros Stavrianos or Lucien Febvre. The latter, when he contributed to the design of the UNESCO *History of Mankind*, supported the study of connections on the basis that 'from this picture would emerge the idea that separations in the world are mere illusions, and that the earth never ceases to diversify, to enrich, to mutually fertilize with streams of peaceful exchanges'.[86] Much of world, global and transnational history has been and is being written to that purpose. Variations on that theme come from historians who hanker for peaceful mutual understanding if not a cosmopolitan democratic future at world scale, and from those who hope for a more multicultural society in national contexts.[87] Thomas Bender, in his recent *A Nation among Nations*, does not conceal his 'civic purpose' in writing a transnational history of the United States: to 'encourage and sustain a cosmopolitan citizenry, at once proud nationals and humble citizens of the world'.[88] Conversely, rather than a unifying narrative, Arif Dirlik sees transnational history as a way to debunk Western categories and proceed with the provincialisation of Europe, a further and subversive step on the path to intellectual decolonisation and the writing of a post-national history.[89] Many historians of international relations consider that transnational history is the study of non-state actors, in line with Nye and Keohane's 'transnational relations'.[90] This is not the position of others in the discipline who do take on board cross-observation by governments and public policy transfers.[91] Historians who adopt a transnational perspective certainly cannot espouse all these different and contradictory purposes and definitions together, but they need to be aware of their existence and situate themselves in relation to their different contents and goals. Yet, history is what historians do, not the definitions they give to explain what they should do. This author, and consequently this book, will navigate between the definitions, and between different meanings, usages and non-usages of the term 'transnational history'. The road map will be provided by the three 'big issues' that make transnational history a problem-oriented way of researching and writing history.

2 Connections

Phytophthora infestans is not often mentioned as a major protagonist of modern history even though it made a major contribution to creating linkages between distinct and distant places in the middle of the nineteenth century. It travelled to Europe in 1845, after a sojourn in the USA, and, as far as we know its pedigree, had origins in Central America. Under its spell, a common fate of want and suffering hit communities across Western Europe in 1845 and 1846. Irrespective of national affiliations, but according to the composition of people's diet, *Phytophthora infestans* put pressure on social policy institutions in several cities and regions. It created a European-wide atmosphere of social unrest and market riots, and affected international discussions about free trade. In the west and south-west of Ireland, at the peak of its activity, not only did it bring about the death of about 1 million people but it also boosted the importance of a migration that had started a century before, and sent about 2 million Irish men and women to England, Wales, Scotland, the United States, Canada and Australia.[1] Being the fungus responsible for potato blight, *Phytophthora infestans* is more familiar to environmental historians, who retrace the mutual impact of humans and the biosphere, than to historians of migrations and of public policies. Yet, as it literally flew with the wind from Flanders, its European bridgehead, it singled itself out for the future attention of transnational historians, to whom it gives a clue that connections are not only created by human beings but also by other living organisms. Humans matter, but so do animals, germs, things and technologies. Consequently, our journey in this chapter will take on board both human and non-human intermediaries.

There are a few preliminary caveats to be made. The first seems counter-intuitive: although our first inclination is to think about mobile actors, connectors are not always mobile. Imagination transports people who read books, watch images or listen to stories without their moving. Agreements and treaties do not move, yet they create entanglements of many sorts. The free trade treaties of the nineteenth century, or the 'open door' agreements about China in 1899, propelled foreign goods and commodities into domestic markets; the civil rights section of the Helsinki Accords in 1975 created a legal basis for monitoring committees to look at human rights issues on the eastern side of the Iron Curtain; and, from 1974, the Multi-Fibre Arrangement and its quotas have provided the impetus for the Hong Kong textile industry to invest in Thailand, Malaya, Philippines, China, Indonesia and

Mauritius (whose competitive advantage came from its access to European markets thanks to another agreement, the Lomé Convention). The non-human sphere also includes a number of immobile connectors such as hygrometric or light conditions. And it is not merely because they are mobile, but because they are scarce, that whales and other migrating species have provoked the construction of alliances and counter-alliances across borders to protect or exploit them.[2] One should keep in mind that mobility depends on immobile connectors: emigration guides that enticed or advised candidates to migrate did not move, neither do computers nor the algorithms which propel today's internet search engines, nor do pipelines. In fact, the number and footprint of these immobile connectors has increased considerably as mobility has demanded an ever larger quantity and quality of infrastructure. Everything considered, immobility is not the antonym of connection. Just as much as the migrants who return more or less regularly, the kin and friends who stay are linkages that bring the foreign into the heart of domesticity when they receive material and cultural remittances in the form of goods, ways of life or ideas that permeate the everyday life of the community.[3]

The second caveat is a prerequisite: the capacity of connectors to make, twist, maintain and terminate connections has to be considered piecemeal according to the type of connectors. Since the beginning of the twentieth century, the reproductive migration of Pacific salmon has created a landscape of negotiation and competition among local authorities, salmon canning firms and fishing societies across the US–Canadian,[4] but the salmon's agency is not as flexible as that of human emissaries who travelled the word to spread the word for a profane or a sacred cause. Resilience is also variable: it is easier to break a system of pipes and cables than to control the print medium or the radio wave. Similarly, different kinds of transport system like the horse, steamship, plane or automobile do not have identical connecting power in terms of speed, load and predictability. The propagation patterns of a germ are less subject to change than the programme of an organisation which works to coordinate internationally the political action of the working class. The sturdiness and impact of connections have to be appreciated afresh in each case.

The third caveat also has to do with fine-grained contextualisation: connectors do not work in a vacuum. On the one hand, they are often part of a more or less organised system, be it a loose set of informal relations or a structured organisation. Their connective contribution draws from the resources of other connectors, to whom they are themselves connected. On the other hand, their activity derives possibilities, as well as constraints, from past connections. In the middle of the nineteenth century, each time another escaped slave arrived in England and started a lecture tour to muster funding and support for the anti-slavery movement in the United States, he or she benefited from the success of all the others who had come before and tied the cause of English or Irish working men to that of black slaves across the Atlantic.[5] Even when linkages were actually created anew during the last 200–250 years, they were enmeshed within former connections and the landscape of possibilities they had created. Early twentieth-century Islamic reformers, in their attempts to spread the word throughout the Muslim world, could rely on students who came to study in Cairo and returned to their homeland, on hajjis who returned from the Mecca pilgrimage, on sailors and merchants who were ready to smuggle printed material into South East Asia on their way back from the Middle East, and on thousands of madrasas (religious schools).[6] All these pre-existed by several centuries the decided attempt by Muhammad Rashid Rida to reinvigorate Islam throughout Muslim communities, and were staple resources to his endeavour.[7]

With these concerns in mind, we can now turn to research that has been done on how, when, where and why connections were made and unmade. We begin with human-made connections.

▶ Human-made connections

The role of individuals and groups is probably the most studied aspect of connection work. Traders and raiders, sailors and warriors, migrants and vagrants, artists and scientists immediately come to mind for their capacity to link between the different polities and societies they included in their travels, operations and horizons. Early modern historians call the tune here, with an abundance of studies on these issues.[8] *The Brokered World*, a recent collection of essays by early modern historians that focuses on go-betweens in the production and circulation of knowledge, offers useful tips and leads for organising the study of human connectors.[9] Its contributors insist on the confrontational aspect of connection work as much as on its exchanging aspects: connecting is far from being a peaceful and well-meaning activity, a fact that modern historians tend to forget because of our view of connections as positive, as we have seen in the previous chapter. Also, *The Brokered World* covers the North and South Atlantic, Pacific, British Empire and Luso-Brazilian regions. Generally, exponents of modern history are a long way away from that situation where scholars of a domain such as religious studies gather to construct a common framework to analyse the role of intermediaries in Islam, Protestant churches and the Catholic world, in the production and dissemination of religious knowledge between and through polities and societies over the last 200 years or so. *Religious internationals*, a collection that was published in 2012, is very much a first of its kind.[10] A large part of modern history scholarship on connections and intermediaries has been produced within relatively narrow, specialised geographical or topical fields, and is unknown to historians of a different region or theme. Early modern historians also spur us to fill some of the yawning gaps in historical research over the last 200 years. We modern historians have given most of our attention to cutting out profiles of intermediaries, whether they belonged to the ruling elites as authors, businessmen or politicians, or to elites of rebellion as revolutionaries, pirates and activists. Cecil Rhodes and Jean Monnet vs Marcus Garvey and Mohandas Karamchand Gandhi, so to speak. Sanjay Subrahmanyam, in his wide-ranging work on South Asia between the sixteenth and eighteenth centuries, has instead reconstructed the work of small bureaucrats, drifting merce-naries and unlucky renegades.[11] Linda Colley, whose study of ordinary imprisoned Britons stretches across early modern and modern history, also provides incentives to expand our range as she assesses the power of their autobiographies to shape the perception of the other and the conception of Britishness.[12]

For all this, connectors are difficult prey for historians. Intermediaries, go-betweens and brokers lived and operated in-between large social and political constructions. As a result, their traces are often peripheral to the large bodies of pub-lished and unpublished primary sources we (modern) historians have been trained to work with. Film entrepreneur William James Dixon, if we believe national histo-ries of the film industry, is a secondary figure. The importance of his innovations in commercial practices only comes out when you reconstruct his trajectory and oper-ation in Canada, Great Britain, Australia and the United States of America.[13] The task is even more complicated when intermediaries are involved in cross-border activities that have to do with smuggling, trade in counterfeit goods or transporta-tion of subversive political items. Then they have to be pursued with even more tenacious and cunning research strategies.[14] Another difficulty has to do with the fact that many of these brokers operated not only between polities, societies and communities, but also across fields and domains. In his portrait of the intellec-tual Cedric Dover's 'colored cosmopolitanism', Nico Slate demonstrates that Dover not only banded together the energies of 'coloured and subject people' against colonialism and racial oppression between the 1920s and the 1950s.[15] He also interweaved science, arts and literature with his politics of 'counter racist racialism'.

In face of this capacity to elude classification in terms of place, profession and domain, historians have nonetheless found ways to frame such characters and account for what they do. Historians and social scientists who study migration, trade and social movements have recently expanded our awareness of modest intermediaries in the modern age, be they resettled refugees, ordinary migrants, border commuters, missionaries, mercenaries, activists or traders. On the latter, we can now learn from both studies of the formal ventures of Shikarpur and Hyderabad merchants in the nineteenth century, and of the activities of the 'globalisation ants' from Afghanistan and the Mediterranean, those indispensable intermediaries of licit and not-so-licit trade in late twentieth- and early twenty-first-century Eurasia.[16]

This section draws on these studies to develop its forays into connectors' life and lore, on three exemplary sites of observation: situations, roles and **circuits**.

Situations

Travel, trade and transplantation are the three situations we will use to appraise the limits and possibilities of making and unmaking connections. They are far from being the only situations that create conditions for individuals to act as connectors, of course, but they are sufficiently different to give us clues about what the study of connections can contribute to the 'big issues' of transnational history.

Speaking of travel today brings tourism to mind, especially in the mass forms that have emerged or generalised since the 1860s and Thomas Cook's early attempts to sell collective excursions for the British middle class to discover first Britain, and then, soon after, Switzerland, the Holy Land, Egypt or Jerusalem. The latter destinations indicate how much tourism was sold to individuals as an aesthetic and spiritual voyage to the springs of civilisation, or to those of religion, not unlike today's shows of 'authenticity' that attempt to convince us that attending some ritual dances connects us to the 'genuine' Africa, Bali, or Italy.[17] The industry of tourism has been dedicated to the selling of such situations of connection to other places and other epochs. But tourism was also a matter of public policies, and in this case, transnational historians are interested in the capacity of tourism to create a cultural, political or economic linkage between a place and the rest of the world. This created tension within autarchic political regimes of the twentieth century,[18] although hopes of breaking diplomatic isolation, generating prestige and attracting hard currency often overcame political prejudice. Spain under General Franco opened up to mass tourism in the late 1950s despite his desire to isolate Spanish society from outside influences and the Falange leadership's scorn for 'foreigners coming in and showing off their hairy legs'.[19]

But tourism is just one version of travel. Scientists, activists, workers, to name but a few, have also moved across borders in the last 200 years or so. Travel is a complex act where travellers (and their supporting cast, from family to transportation companies) act as intermediaries at all stages, from preparation to the travelogue in its private or public form. In each of these stages, travellers create or join a discussion about the relative characteristics, positions and roles of the places they visit for fun, work, profit, or spiritual and secular enlightenment: the linkage is also about comparing 'home' and 'abroad'. This makes travel a propitious site for transnational historians, as a topic per se or as an element in a larger narrative. In the latter case it provides a thread through which the history of connections comes alive, unveiling the actors' agency. The travels of women missionaries, whether they stay put or criss-cross the globe, thus unveil their capacity to mediate between

America and the places they tried to place under its 'moral empire'.[20] A set of cases drawn from the study of the Indian Ocean region by Sugata Bose demonstrates the gains to be made by studying travel and travellers.[21] The study of Indian travellers (soldiers, capitalists, pilgrims, labourers, poets) hammers home the message that the Indian Ocean did not stop being an interregional arena during the nineteenth and early twentieth centuries, for all the constraining power of British rule and large-scale capitalism. Boses's emphasis on the hajj – the pilgrimage to Islamic holy places in Mecca and Medina – highlights specific individuals like the *muallim/mutawwif* (service provider and guide), a central character of the hajj who acted as intermediary between a group of pilgrims of similar origins and the places they visited. The travel situation was also crucial for the articulation of thoughts and notions, as with Rabindranath Tagore's (1861–1941) travels in the years 1916–30 that contributed to his ideas about the nation and his conception of India's universal role.

Trade and its different human agents comprise another situation where connections can be read through. In the large form of corporate or family trade companies and their well- arranged organisation, that of the bazaar economy which characterised the Indian Ocean trade, or under the many versions of community-based peddling (French peddlers from the Alps region in Mexico from the early nineteenth century, Muslim and Christian Lebanese in the Americas since the early twentieth century, Mouride peddlers in Europe today), and across the many functions entailed by trade (from ship chandling to payment), traders created or maintained ties between distant locales by ordering, carrying, pricing, marketing and selling products which originated in different material cultures. Studies of nineteenth- and twentieth-century trade have recently done much to expand our views far beyond the Atlantic or the Mediterranean, possibly the most studied trade basins in the history of humankind. Ghislaine Lydon's study of trans-Saharan trade in West Africa is illuminating from that point of view because it not only presents caravanners in their role of traders, but also Islamic men of law (*qadis* and *muftis*) who provided the legal mediation that made transactions possible.[22] The 'paper economy of faith' disclosed by Lydon is a reminder that connections rely on conventions and rules, especially in a space disputed between different authorities (Spain, France, Morocco). Indian Ocean trade and traders comprise another topic that has received much attention recently, shedding light on a number of intermediaries, including individuals, families and urban and regional communities. These studies underline that it is essential to address the fine grain of trading situations to document how far traders can contribute to entangling distant locales. Following the Vaniya merchants, a group of Hindu and Jain merchants from Gujarat, we see that their success was connected to their capacity to tune the supply from Jambusar weavers in Gujarat to an estimate of demand in east-central and south-east African markets – what is now Mozambique.[23] There ensued a domination in that market until the 1830s, based on centuries of trade experience in the region, flexible mechanisms of procurement and sustained contact with the trade hubs of the coast and the Zambezi valley. Being in-between was key. Thousands of traders from different communities of the Indian peninsula bet on that same card in East Africa. From the middle of the nineteenth century, they used the 'Mare Nostrum' status of the Indian Ocean under British rule to expand their ancient trading presence in East Africa. As the presence of their small shops extended far beyond the coastal region, they became the indispensable intermediaries for trade within, and in the direction of, this region, and tied it to Indian products to the point that the rupee was a familiar currency in many coastal and interior places.[24] British officials schemed to build on this intermediation to strengthen the Empire, seeing the Indians as middlemen liaising between Europeans and Africans in the racial construction of the region. This was one of the rationales behind the attempt to attract Indian migration to rural British East Africa, which for a time captured the imagination of some imperial British civil servants. This idea was a token of the mediating capacity attributed to transplantation, the last of our three situations.

Transplantation played a role in the very definition of some national communities: *Krios* and *Sàro*, as the slave returnees from Brazil were called, standardised the Yoruba language in Lagos during the nineteenth century, notably when they translated the Bible from English.[25] Subsequently, these Afro-Brazilian groups made large contributions to cultural nationalism and to the first national elites of Dahomey, Togo and Nigeria after independence. Historians of migration, when they shifted their attention to the way migrants lived in-between different receiving and sending locales, showed the full breadth of the connecting work done by transplanted populations. Through the multiple affective, economic and political links that they maintained with China, Chinese Americans were thus able to launch or support political and economic undertakings in both countries, creating a space in-between that generated 'diasporic moments' such as the 1905 boycott of American products in China in reaction to US legislation against Chinese migration, or the wave of investments by Chinese Americans after Deng Xiaoping's economic reforms in the 1980s.[26] The situation of these migrants transplanted into a new place generated multiple ties with the homeland, from the trade in Chinese products in one direction and the flows of remittances in the other, to exceptional investments like the railroad which the returning Taishanese Chen Yixi built in the Pearl Delta region from 1904.[27] Other situations of transplantation, more limited in time, scope or space, similarly drew on the creation and maintenance of ties with home. Exiled political communities relentlessly tried to embody the 'genuine' spirit of their existing or possible nation for foreign audiences, in order to create channels of mobilisation for their cause. This was a crucial aspect of the activity of the Free French in the United States during the Second World War, the Cameroonian nationalists in their Ghanaian operation base in the mid-1950s, or the different waves of exiles that punctuated the political history of nation-building in the nineteenth and twentieth centuries.[28] More generally, connections born out of migration shaped political ideas through the channels of 'long-distance nationalism'.[29] The experience of Indian soldiers, policemen, traders, railway workers, bureaucrats and indentured workers in British-controlled regions of the Near East, South Asia and East Africa was thus used as an incentive for action by a number of anti-imperial Indian activists. They commented about their situation in the travelogue, the booklet and the press: transplantation generated the conditions to contest the condition of being transplanted.[30]

Travel, trade and transplantation are 'sites' in the metaphorical sense, but connections did take place in specific locales. 'Middle grounds', in Richard White's expression, were places of conflict and encounters, the locus where connections were refused, made and unmade between polities and societies.[31] Such places need not be a large region like White's American Great Lakes. A restaurant in Manchester can also provide a rewarding observation post for the historian.[32] Such sites increasingly attracted attention in the 1990s, which Charles Bright and Michael Geyer characterised as a 'sorting out' moment.[33] It was also when some historians took inspiration from notions developed in other disciplines, such as literature scholar Mary Louise Pratt's 'contact zones' and anthropologist Homi Bhabha's 'interstitial spaces'.[34] The result was a strong emphasis on diasporas and borderlands as sites where friction defined and redefined national identities, but also on hybridity and *mestizaje* as outputs of these frictions.[35] One of the issues under discussion in this growing body of studies has been whether the coming of age of national states, with their apparatus of norms and controls, has destroyed these middle grounds and diminished the number of situations where middlemen could flourish.

The fact that goods and people were increasingly identified, traced, scrutinised, controlled and labelled according to national origins and concerns also created new incentives for connections and new opportunities for connectors. Borders are one of the spatial, political and social places where these incentives and opportunities materialised. Eric Tagliacozzo has shown that the development of a 3000 km border between the English and the Dutch empires in nineteenth-century South East Asia, established the perfect conditions for smugglers to thrive because they offered the cheapest through-linkages.[36] The 'undertrade' (illicit commerce) thus profited from all the attempts by the colonial nation states to tighten their capacities of political control, trade monopoly and taxation. State authorities themselves established new connections to control undertrade protagonists, as well as the revolutionary forces that contested national borders: the linkages that republicans, anarchists, Irish nationalists or communists installed through the borders of national states created common landscapes of anxiety and repression that translated into police cooperation among German European states in the nineteenth century and evolved into attempts at planetary organisation.[37] Thus, the establishment of national states did not ruin the business of connections across polities and societies: it rather gave it a new impetus, if we think of the trafficking in arms, ammunition, supplies or narcotics that nationalist movements have favoured since the beginning of the nineteenth century. In the direst of situations, human connectors found ways to shun the plans for enclosure. Even the erection of the Iron Curtain in post-Second World War Europe generated its own intermediaries who liaised between the Soviet and Western blocs. Artists, scientists and ordinary people moved ideas, images and goods.[38] Most of them were double agents of sorts, as for example Bulgarian truck drivers. On the one hand, they were unofficial emissaries of communist societies and their achievements while travelling abroad, but on the other they brought back narratives, images (the catalogue from a German retail firm, Neckermann, was a must-bring) and products from the other side, and thus underwrote the Cockaigne image of the West in Bulgaria.[39] If we historians can develop a growing appreciation of this complementary relationship between the crystallisation of well-demarcated polities and societies on the one hand and the development of connections between and through these units on the other, we gather the elements that allow us to appraise the timing, intensity, rise and demise of interconnections between polities and societies: a central issue for **historicising** what has been called **globalisation**.

Roles

Such situations, and others, offered opportunities and constraints for individuals or institutions to adopt specific roles and develop specific mediations between communities, societies and polities. The capacity to juggle different roles seems to have been important in becoming a recognised and successful intermediary, although specialisation also occurred. Diplomats, who seem to be highly specialised, were not mere official go-betweens for negotiation and adjustments of the world order. Some of them, while they were stationed abroad, used their talents to convey the atmosphere of a foreign country into domestic literature, as Stendhal did in France for Italy, or to partake in the international republic of letters – think of Pablo Neruda, Carlos Fuentes or Miguel Ángel Asturias. More modest diplomats still played many different roles, especially in times or places where diplomacy was far from being the exclusive province of national specialists. The consular service, in general, was a mixed domain where private interests mingled with the imperatives of governmental representation. Native merchants provided much of the consular personnel the British needed to represent their empire in Arabia and Persia in the nineteenth century,[40] and a similar situation prevailed for other countries in that region or elsewhere well into the twentieth century – and even today. As a result, diplomatic and trading interests were insolubly mixed, and intermediaries skilfully adjusted their allegiances, *dragomans* in the nineteenth-century Mediterranean being experts at this game.[41]

In general terms, the high visibility of one of their roles should not divert our attention from the multiplicity of roles that individuals or groups can play. Indian artists from the Tagore clan who received visits from Japanese artists in the early twentieth century did not merely 'import' the brush and ink style, but appropriated the technical features and symbolic power of Japanese design to illustrate the possibility of an Asian artistic sphere.[42] Their chief figure, Nandalal Bose (1882–1966), also gained inspiration from his own trip to Japan, which he documented through sketches, photographs and a collection of prints, postcards and life stories of Japanese painters. The visited was also a visitor, the artist also a collector, the importer also a creator. This multiplicity stands out when historians delve into the lives of individual intermediaries with a determination to follow them through all their facets and many different sources, as illustrated in a recent book by Roger Levine.[43] Jan Tzatzoe (1792–1868), the son of a Xhosa king educated by London Missionary Society missionaries, served as interpreter to the first missionary who ventured out of the Cape Colony in 1816. Tzatzoe did more than translate during diplomatic negotiations and religious conversations. He shaped the very terms of the religious encounter between the Xhosa and Christianity by preaching the Gospel himself, a role where he was in charge of choosing the terms of equivalence for evangelical notions. He also conducted negotiations on behalf of the missionaries in his unique capacity of the only man able to evaluate the expectations and interests of the different parties (the chiefs, the mission, the colonial government). Tzatzoe added other roles to his repertoire: he worked for other British and German missionaries, translated biblical texts, travelled to Great Britain to testify before the Parliamentary Select Committee on Aborigines and to lecture the British public, and his role in the Xhosa Wars is too complex to be put in a nutshell. From this example, as with diplomats, emerges an arc of roles with blurred boundaries between them, and intermediaries successively or simultaneously occupying several of the positions on this arc.

Using an analogy from the world of business and trade, one of the strongest temptations of historians who study individual and collective intermediaries is indeed to classify them as 'importers' and/or 'exporters'. Fine-grained studies warn us against a rigid adherence to these two categories. From the second half of the nineteenth century, the Hong Kong-based *jinshanzuang* (Gold Mountain firms) supplied Chinese food and goods to the overseas communities in South East Asia and the Americas, but they also took charge of transporting letters, money and information to the family back in China.[44] Moreover, they offered credit and saving accounts, as well as a set of services for legal and illegal emigrants, from the 1880s to the 1940s. If we place them in separate boxes tagged 'importers' or 'exporters', we are kept at a distance from what fosters their unique capacity to connect and liaise between societies and polities. This only prevents us seeing which societies and polities they mediate between and understanding the content and importance of their mediation work.

Daniel Rodgers's book on progressive American visitors to Europe from the 1870s to 1945 teaches a similar lesson.[45] Because they selected and sifted European social policies into the domestic US public sphere, the pilgrims of progressivism seem to operate as 'importers', striving to appropriate social policies in order to change the status quo at home. Yet, because comparison with the USA was their major concern during their observation travels abroad, in their publications and in their subsequent work as policy advisors, politicians or administrators, they also presented American situations and solutions to European partners or adversaries. The Europeans used these references in their own struggles, and these two patterns sometimes caused North Atlantic controversies where American progressives and other intermediaries (often their informers) were carrying ideas, concepts and proposals back and forth. This was the case notably with the discussion about municipal ownership of water, electricity, gas and transportation infrastructures in the late 1900s.[46] And, when events turned the tables, as happened with the First World War and the mobilisation of the progressive elites for relief work in Europe, importers turned into exporters. Roles such as importer and exporter are not categories, but positions adopted by intermediaries in order to achieve their goals. This is a warning against attempting to establish typologies based on a strict distinction of roles, and against forcing intermediaries into any single one.

Circuits

'Only connect'. E. M. Forster's *Howards End* would have provided a fitting motto for those who strived to establish linkages across polities and communities in the last 200 years. One needs to add, though, that in parallel with connections come disconnections, and that singular connections can be part of organised sets of linkages. To stay with progressive American proselytes of social policies, their US opponents were not alone in wishing to disconnect the American scene from European social policy references: progressives themselves got cold feet when the wind changed. Faced with their failure in selling German-style health insurance, and in view of the low 'purchasing power' of European references on the US public scene in the 1930s, the American Association for Labor Legislation abandoned its 'borrowing from Old Europe' argument. The shocks of the Second World War further contributed to the revival of the phoenix of American exceptionalism, argues Daniel Rodgers, and unplugged progressive America from its Atlantic viewpoint. Yet, the tie was redefined rather than entirely broken: for decades to come, policies and public debates in Europe and different regions of the globe were actively shaped by American references in the course of the great Cold War contest.[47] A different **circuit** took shape. The study of this and other circuits unveils the work of the actors involved in creating or operating them (or in fighting to destroy circuits established by others), and forces historians to acknowledge that intermediaries are part of systems of intermediation.

These systems can be large. During the Cold War, the government of the Soviet Union installed its own circuits throughout the then 'Third World', based on military assistance, political advice, trade and technical assistance. Although they are likely to be biased, Central Intelligence Agency (CIA) figures are impressive. In 1978, they noted about 70,000 Soviet economic technicians working in the Third World (plus 12,000 Cuban advisors), and some 50,000 Third World students and technicians trained in the Soviet Union and Eastern bloc countries.[48] The latter were meant to be intermediaries in charge of moving economic, political and technical frames between different polities and societies. A recent publication helps us to understand the content of such circuits, through the case of the relationship between communists in China and the Soviet Union.[49] From 1921, and with changing intensities, content and direction, this circuit was a huge government-sponsored affair which involved an intense traffic in deeds, texts, money, people, ideas and technologies as well as a continuous cross-observation between the two giants. The stakes were high: achieving the success of communism in both countries and defining the shape of universal communism. This circuit is highly relevant for us because it includes a major disconnection: the Sino-Soviet split of 1960, which derived from a growing number of political divergences, ended the flows of trainees and advisors. Yet the linkage persisted in terms of mutual interest, with authorities and specialists in both countries still very curious about one another. Even the disappearance of one partner did not stop this cross-observation: the fall of the USSR has been a subject of study for several official research programmes in China during the last two decades. The Sino-Soviet case demonstrates that circuits need to be studied in the long term, to appraise their interruptions as well as their capacity to revamp and endure.

The sturdiness of these massive bureaucratic circuits should not elude us, though. Nor are circuits always complex and confusing systems like those which have been erected to hide fiscal evasion or perform money laundering, through a cascade of bank accounts and societies in offshore financial centres and tax havens.[50] Intermediaries also operate on shoestring infrastructures based on inventiveness. Contemporary French-Moroccan women who live in France and visit their kin in Morocco during the summer holidays do not need to establish sophisticated logistics to increase their symbolic and financial resources. As they travel, they carry goods in both directions, to be used as presents for relatives or to be sold to neighbours and acquaintances: the existing systems of transport infrastructure and of kinship are mobilised to create the circuit they need.[51] Part of the work of transnational history is to disclose such unobtrusive use of existing circuits, and to unravel the dedicated and original circuits assembled by individuals in order to make connections work. Women of the 'first wave' of feminism, who were active between the 1830s and the 1860s, thus established a complete circuit across North America, Great Britain and continental Europe: they corresponded with one another, published their respective manifestos, translated one another, circulated their respective publications in their different countries, read others' addresses before assemblies, crossed oceans to attend conventions, visited their sisters or, occasionally, took part in revolutions together.[52] One of them, the Quaker Anna Knight (1786–1862), developed a comprehensive paraphernalia of leaflets, 'stickers', handbills and placards that she sent her correspondents to multiply linkages. It was no small feat to create this travel and paper circuit, even if these were also the years when the penny post made international post cheaper and easier, and when steam compressed transportation times.

The tenuous nature of circuits created by individual commitment did not mean that they were less durable than those generated by governmental bureaucracies. Retracing the life of the Chang family, whose members moved back and forth between Guangdong province and California from 1915 to 1950, Haiming Liu shows that these circuits could last for decades.[53] The Chang migration, suggests Liu, 'was not an individual adventure but a rational choice based on aspirations for social advancement': the circuit of letters, newspapers, remittances and personal sojourns allowed the Changs to fulfil this project and actually live between two worlds for decades, defying the controlling projects and bureaucracies of national states. Moreover, small circuits could evolve into large formal structures. The Communist Correspondence Committee created by Marx and Engels in Brussels in early 1846 aimed at systematising linkages between a handful of German, French and English socialists, and turned out to be one of the platforms from which emerged the international socialist movement. On the other side of the class divide, the British engineer Charles Le Maistre (1874–1953) evangelised for technical standardisation and for voluntary consensus standard-setting in Britain, Europe and the world from 1906 to 1953, helping to create national standard bodies, building up the International Federation of Standard Associations and acting as one of its first secretaries.[54] Those whom sociologists John Braithwaite and Peter Drahos call 'model mongers' in the field of business regulation at the end of the twentieth century precisely draw on their ubiquity in multiple forums, organisations and publications.[55] This is exactly what the study of circuits helps us to understand: how do intermediaries float ideas or goods in different milieus and places? We are right where the historian Frederick Cooper suggested historians should go to historicise globalisation: it is the dissection of circuits that makes it possible to restore the agency of those who lived in-between and through polities, to circumvent loose arguments about 'influence' of the foreign in the domestic, and to dissect the actual operation of integration and disintegration processes.[56] Taking account of non-human intermediaries will help to complete our exploration of the insights offered by the study of connections.

▶ Non-human connections

In 1869, the American W. C. Gardenhire toured the Fiji Islands, in the South Pacific. On his return, he exhibited (and sold) native people and artefacts in San Francisco, under the title of 'Fiji Cannibal exhibition'.[57] Knives and forks allegedly used for eating human flesh, and a large number of weapons, were central in this attempt to impress a specific vision of Fiji on to the visitors. In 1875, Anatole von Hügel arrived in the same islands and decided to begin an 'ethnological collection' to scientific ends. At international exhibitions in Sydney and Melbourne in 1879 and 1880, a 'Resources and progress of Fiji' section included cloth, mats and pottery to demonstrate the positive effect of the idea of empire on a savage population of natives. The vision that was articulated on these occasions was different, but in each instance it was objects that were given the role of mediating between their place of origin and the audience abroad. Of course, it was individuals who selected, collected, sold and gaped at these objects, but it was *things* that were endorsed with the capacity to bridge and distinguish the worlds of colonised and colonisers.

Historians have not neglected the study of material culture in the past, but when it comes to objects that create ties between polities and societies, there is much to be gained by walking in the anthropologists' footprints. Nicholas Thomas provides inspiration, as do path-breaking scholars like Margaret Mead and Bronislaw Malinowski, who interrogated respectively the potlatch system among northern Pacific American tribes and the Kula ring in New Guinea, or the anthropologists who placed the emphasis on the 'biography of things'.[58] Yet, it would not be enough only to take on board the connecting capacity of things, artefacts or machines in this section. Other non-human intermediaries have contributed to making and unmaking ties between human polities and societies in the last 200 years or so: animals, plants, germs, natural elements of the biosphere and atmosphere shaped situations, issues and solutions across and between polities.

Climate change and the way that it has been assessed, disputed and addressed by activist groups and governments as a planetary constraint; the print media (books, journals, newspapers) and their capacity to mobilise minds and energies across borders; the intertwined system of satellites and computers which has become the dependable basis of daily life in many parts of the world when people surf the World Wide Web, draw banknotes from a cash machine, drive with the help of a global positioning system (GPS) or send short messages from their cellphones with the global system of mobile communications (GSM): all these immediately come to mind when one tries to think about non-human intermediaries that currently current work through and across polities, blur the distinction between the foreign and the domestic, and contribute to integrating different places in a discontinuous spatial fashion. This chapter will draw on a sample of non-human intermediaries whose role may be less visible, in order to press readers to think about the range of things and natural elements that create linkages.

Objects

At the beginning of *Dominance by Design*, US historian Michael Adas recounts how, when forcing Japan to open up to American trade in 1854, Commodore Matthew Perry (1794–1858) brought and displayed an armada of objects, including a miniature train, clocks and farm machines.[59] Perry relied on them to convey an impression of US might. Technologically sophisticated objects certainly can create connections. It was the combination of computers, design digitisation and high-speed data transmission that reorganised industrial supply chains through the adoption of the **modular production system** in the clothing and electronics sector in the late 1990s. 3D-printers (aka 'additive manufacturing') may take this reorganisation a step further in the future. The talking machine and musical records of the early twentieth century also vouch for machines' connecting capacity,[60] together with television and radio sets that followed. But relatively simple objects also contribute to connect distinct and distant places: in 1929, an Indian pilgrim to Mecca was dismayed that even the prayer mats and beads were imported from non-Muslim countries. These objects embodied a linkage between the European and the Muslim worlds that he felt was humiliating for all Muslims.[61] Important political statements such as boycott campaigns against foreign goods resulted from the repulsion entailed by similar linkages around common commodities, starting with the 1830s boycotts of sugar and cotton produced by slave labour. Likewise, other non-technological objects represent distinct and distant places through the effects and senses of their users. One upscale version is the African and American native art that European surrealists collected from the 1930s – and with increased intensity during their American exile –, for their capacity to connect them with a land of myths that was germane to their conceptions of poetry.[62] From that breadth of possibilities, I have chosen a few objects whose invocation invites us to consider different kinds of linkages.

Our first object has the material capacity to make connections possible, and as such it stands for the whole family that includes the map and the maritime chronometer. It is the small L-shaped piece of metal that you can find in the pocket of many train attendants throughout Europe. The creation of this 'Berne key', as it is named, was one of the results of the 1886 railways conference in Berne

(Switzerland). On the agenda of the conference was the harmonisation of rolling stock and gauges in continental Europe, as well as conditions of access to railway carriages. The Berne key was an answer to that last problem. With one of its extremities, you could open the locks on the carriages of most Hungarian, German, Austrian, Italian and Swiss railway companies. At the other end, you could unlock doors of rolling stock of the major French companies, and some Italian ones too. The key, albeit a plain and unsophisticated thing, made it possible to establish a smoother connection at borders for freight transportation.[63] Connecting objects also contributed to transport more than goods or people. The ballast water tank, which began to be used in the 1880s, has been and still is a tie that binds together different ecosystems. Together with the water that bigger and bigger ships have been uploading and downloading came marine organisms (fish, shellfish, crustaceans, alga) or plain water with different salinities, all causing disturbance to many ecological systems.[64]

The second type of object has a capacity to create connections beyond the mere moment and place of its own presence, and to install a protracted interdependence. This is especially the case of high-tech objects. They require maintenance, and often need to be supplemented with a whole range of other objects (spare parts) and non-material resources (knowledge, techniques, standards). Weaponry is a good instance of this snowball effect. When a navy buys a battleship, new or used (the Brazilian and Argentine navies did buy a number of US and British ships after the Second World War), it also needs a host of big and small objects to provision and maintain it, like the floating dock Brazil bought from Britain to repair the second-hand dreadnought *Minais Gerais* in the early twentieth century.[65] When Kuwait acquired US jets in the late 1980s, it also had to buy US Navy certified dimensional, electric, space or time standards without which the planes would have been 'as useless as without an air strip'.[66] Buying new weaponry is also, for a military, the start of enduring linkages that not only include ammunition, but likely military advisors to train soldiers to use it and to reorganise the army in order to get the best return. Objects create linkages beyond just their materiality.

Our third item deals with objects that are declined and appropriated into several variations, leading to both integration and differentiation. Thus the *bàta* drums that were used in the *Sàngó* cult of the Oyo Empire, the Yoruba-speaking polity of western central Africa that disintegrated between the 1810s and the 1830s. The drums (and many other objects) tied together communities of enslaved people in Brazil, Trinidad and Cuba with the homeland of West Africa.[67] But their appearance as well as their musical and religious uses were customised to these different locales. The history of consumption is replete with similar objects. They are available in many places, and thus have a sort of universal stain attached to them, but have been the chosen vectors of appropriation when users tried to demarcate domestic styles or join foreign manners. This latter point is demonstrated by the ruling and trading elites of Mutsamudu town on Nzwani Island, in the Mozambique Channel, during the nineteenth century. They proved to be 'masters in similitude', by using British ways and goods to assert their (unsolicited) loyalty to the crown and improve their situation as traders, rulers and adventurers, edging their way into the cracks and prejudices of British imperial pride. 'Mutsamuduans', their historian concludes, 'were largely successful at using things that signified Englishness to direct imperial means for local ends'.[68]

Our last group consists of objects whose use create a shared and contested landscape of identity, imagination and practices. Some of these objects work in combination. From the 1920s, the match-up of the Singer sewing machine and paper dress-making patterns allowed millions of women to 'tinker with Paris'.[69] The Singer company, an American corporation that had turned the Frenchman Thimmonier's industrial invention into a domestic product, sold hundreds of thousands of sewing machines throughout the world from the mid-1870s. On the other hand, the paper pattern developed considerably in the late nineteenth century, as a product on its own or associated with a flowering fashion press. When feminine fashion turned to more direct and functional lines in the 1920s, the possession of a sewing machine combined with paper patterns and their users' manuals – acquired by correspondence – made it possible for women to replicate, adapt or subvert Parisian fashion. The sewing machine–paper patterns duet was the material arrangement which expanded the clout of Parisian fashion well beyond aristocratic circles and upper-middle-class women who could use the service of haute couture houses or a dressmaker. Similar combinations can be observed with, for instance, recorded music and the musical partition from the late nineteenth century. Or with the VCR and its VHS tape that were the vector for Nigerian-based film piracy and production, which plugged sub-Saharan African spectators into films and plots of Bollywood, the powerhouse of Indian cinema, in the last decades of the twentieth century. Both created far-flung linkages in trade, but also in the imagination and affect of the individuals involved.

Transportation and communication infrastructures

Powerful as these combinations have proved, more formidable systems of objects have created connections and disconnections. In the last 200–250 years, transportation and communication infrastructures have been hailed for their capacity to integrate different polities and societies, a celebration George Orwell was one of the few to shun.[70] In the winter of 2011, many commentators on popular protest in North Africa and the Middle East credited communication infrastructures as they pointed to the role of cellphones, websites and social utilities like YouTube and Facebook in organising and disseminating rebellion against dictators, both within and across borders. This belief in the capacity of communication infrastructures to annihilate geographical and political distance has been commonplace since the days of the telegraph. Successive instantiations of electric communication (telephone, radio, television, the internet) generated similar claims that the world had been ushered into yet another new era. This outlook was supported by promoters, builders and operators of transport and energy systems, and by those who substantiated projects for political integration by the existence or prospect of these infrastructures. The French engineers who adopted the Count of Saint-Simon's (1760–1825) theories on industrial democracy, and his emphasis on organisation, were the first to contribute. As early as 1832, Michel Chevalier (1806–79) took up the hymn to the civilising and integrating power of waterways, shipping lines, and most of all railways in his *Système de la Méditerranée*. Saint-Simonians worshipped the 'redeeming network'.[71] Well before the satirical English journal *Punch* lampooned Cecil Rhodes as a colossus holding up a telegraph line between Cairo and Cape Town (1892), mid-nineteenth-century British imperialists stated that the construction of more lines between Britain and India was a condition for the success of the imperial civilising mission.[72] Builders of what historians of technology call **large technological systems** have never stopped humming variations on that tune. Thanks to a recent massive research effort on the history of infrastructure in Europe, we can go beyond the mantra, and consider both the connective and disconnective cross-border capacity of material infrastructures.[73]

Networked infrastructures of transportation, energy and communication indeed generated European systems that straddled political borders. Thus, the plans for a European electricity system that gained acceptance between 1929 and the late 1930s, have given way to a vast increase of material interconnections after 1950 or so, which now literally plug countries into one another.[74] The blackouts of 2003 and 2008 have made this very clear to Italian citizens or to inhabitants of regions of Austria, Belgium, France, Germany and Spain. The same goes for other energy networks. When the Russian company Gazprom interrupted its deliveries to Ukraine in 2006, it deeply affected places further down the pipeline in other Eastern European countries.[75] From the mid-nineteenth century for railways, and from the 1920s for roads, political, business and technical actors with explicit projects for creating integrated markets across Europe bet on transportation infrastructures to achieve their goals. These infrastructures contributed to increased interdependence in terms of agricultural and industrial trade, production and distribution, and were important wedges for the penetration of foreign technique, capital and workforces in many European places.[76] Historians of technology have thus built a strong argument for the role of infrastructures in the 'hidden integration' of Europe.[77] But they have also insisted that there was a hidden fragmentation at work in the very process of building infrastructures.

Connecting some places implies that others are not connected. Electricity infrastructures demonstrate an organisation in several regional blocks, while the history of oil infrastructures underlines the differentiation between Eastern and Western Europe.[78] Last but not least, this body of work also makes it clear that 'linking, while sometimes creating structures of long duration, can be followed by de-linking'.[79] Recent electric or gas cuts are not isolated events: the strengthening of existing borders or the creation of new ones has broken existing infrastructures and impeded new linkages. West Berlin was cut off from the electric grid by the Soviet authorities in 1948, and there are still few train links between the Baltic countries and Russia. Communication infrastructures, whose connecting role has been relentlessly celebrated since the advent of the electric transmission of words, sounds and images, have also been subject to interruptions on purpose. A war of waves raged in the ether during the Second World War and the Cold War, when Soviet authorities resorted to different jamming technologies to prevent entire regions from listening to Radio Free Europe, Voice of America or Radio Liberty.[80] Jamming has been regularly employed in specific crises like the covert operations of the CIA in South America, or in situations when governments wanted to prevent a population from accessing news from unwanted sources (Iran, China, the Koreas).[81] Last but not least, the robustness of infrastructures vaunted by system builders must not veil that they were and are still sources and sites of vulnerabilities of all kinds.[82] These European-based examples underline that studying connections is a matter of more than celebrating their role in bringing people closer together. Disconnections also come to the fore, as well as the range of technical, political and social issues involved in establishing infrastructural linkages across and through different polities.

Natural elements

Many infrastructures have come of age in order to monitor, exploit, control or resist natural forces. Systems of measurement, data transmission and diffusion of information have been established across nations and regions in order to monitor major risks such as earthquakes (International Federation of Digital Seismographic Networks, 1986), tsunamis (Pacific Tsunami Warning System, 1965), storms (with coordinated observation of meteorological data on land and on seas beginning in the late eighteenth century and crystallising from the mid-nineteenth) or epidemics (Global Influenza Virological Surveillance, 1952). These systems were crucial for the definition and recognition of natural elements as forces and resources, and often resulted from decades of scientific collaboration and controversies across national and disciplinary limits, as in seismology.[83] Just as the fledgling cooperation between continental European observatories was given new impetus by the storm that wrought havoc on the French fleet in the Crimea in 1856, many monitoring systems were created out of common experiences and fears of the desolation and death wrought by events in the lithosphere, hydrosphere and biosphere, to use John R. McNeill's terms.[84] The perception of common risks created connections among polities before the late twentieth century, the moment when sociologist Ulrich Beck saw these risks as a central factor in the creation of 'cosmopolitan society'.[85]

Historians have told the story of these systems in different areas. They became more familiar with the formal organisations and agreements that were imagined to chart and map pathogens and vector-borne diseases, from networks of national labs and their imperial projections to multilateral intergovernmental agreements and institutions: the Office International des Épizooties (International Epizootic Office, 1924), the international sanitary convention signed in Venice (1892) whereby the European powers set up their control of the Mecca pilgrimage, or the work of the Health Organisation of the League of Nations from 1921.[86] Norms and rules that pervaded several national sovereignties resulted from the process, together with new international organisations in charge of maintaining and expanding them. Similar institutional and official linkages are highly visible when one looks at agreements between national or regional governments on topics like air pollution, acid rain, climate change or dwindling animal and vegetal species. Some of these domains also generated scientific and social mobilisation across borders. 'Desiccation theory' was a household topic in the nineteenth century among foresters working in different countries and regions, and provided a common rhetoric to supporters of reforestation. Its topicality was promoted by the Indian Forest Service, which operated as an experimental platform for forestry and an expert body for the creation of new forest authorities throughout the English-speaking world in the late nineteenth and early twentieth centuries.[87] The unobtrusive lobbying by social elites who participated in the first International Congress for the Protection of Nature in 1909, or who supported the protection of migratory birds in North America is, in this respect, to be given as much attention as the spectacular public interpositionings of Greenpeace activists between the whaling boats and their prey in 1975.[88] Monitoring systems, agreements, research and mobilisations were not the only linkages generated by natural risks. Following major storms or earthquakes, or the outbreak of some cattle fever, the food supply or administrative machinery of countries have often been, partly or wholly, dependent on foreign aid or foreign markets. And although the forthcoming rise in sea level may lead to unprecedented numbers of 'environmental refugees', natural events such as the severe drought throughout the West African Sahel in the early 1900s also led millions of people to migrate, sometimes across imperial borders. It is often in the direct consequences on humans that the connecting capacity of non-human connectors resides.

Natural resources

Yet risk and its anticipated or actual impacts on humans do not suffice to define the connecting power of nature. Natural elements are also coveted and exploited as resources by human combinations that straddle borders. Above or under the ground, natural resources have been the reason for the development of a number of human activities and institutions, many of which had to work around or against the demarcation of polities and societies. Labour migrations, wars, foreign direct investment, pricing mechanisms, technology transfers and scientific controversies have played out in the exploration and subjugation of mineral, vegetal or animal resources across polities. Diamonds and gold can help us to explore this further, although guano, hardwood, oil or fisheries would also do the job. In 1908, diamonds were discovered in German South Africa, near Lüderitzbucht. Their presence was the cause of a number of entanglements between the German colony and its close and distant surroundings: migrants from the nearby Cape Colony were used as a workforce; food and water were imported across the imperial border; traders and adventurers from Europe and the rest of Africa flocked in to provide groceries or prostitutes; the colonial German administration copied the legislation of the British-controlled Transvaal to distribute the profits of diamond production and trade.[89] The number of mixed-race Cape Colony workers involved in the migration eventually challenged the racial system of German South West Africa from the in-between of empires, with Cape Colony workers using the British consular system to have their 'white' rights recognised. Still in the same region, the discovery and production of gold in South Africa triggered the massive flows of capital and work-forces that respectively came from Europe and Africa, mostly from Portuguese East Africa.[90] The abundance of South African gold provided the wherewithal to ratchet up the availability of liquidities that were guzzled by the international trade and investment boom of the late nineteenth century. The Bank of England, capstone of the international financial system based on the gold standard, became increasingly dependent on this South African gold.[91] Starting from diamonds, or gold, or from some other natural resource and the different stages of its exploitation and usage, opens up a variety of entanglements authorised or contrived by the the resource's existence and attractiveness. A set of insights which the specialised study of capitalistic arrangements, trade patterns or migration alone would not deliver.

Natural invaders

It is not only between human-occupied territories that linkages have been created: separate ecological territories have also been bound together by natural elements. Climate variations or human assistance have allowed animal and vegetal species to occupy new territories, possibly with more force than ever in the last 200-250 years.

This has been called 'acclimatisation' when the linkage was created by humans in the hope of economic or cultural returns, something that happened mostly between European countries and their colonial empires.[92] It is called 'invasion' when the new species' presence or prosperity escaped human control. The second aspect receives attention here, with its biological, economic or health impacts that were labelled 'national problems' and 'international issues'. The connectors at play have been a mix of humans, objects and living species. The opening of the Suez Canal in 1866 started the 'Lessepsian migration', from the name of the French engineer who directed the canal project. Hundreds of Red Sea species have since found a home in the Mediterranean, and have been the object of investigation for scientific conversations and consortia across nations since the 1920s. The linking of the Erie Canal (1825) and the Saint Lawrence seaway has likewise created an avenue for non-endemic aquatic organisms to set valve or fin in the hydrographic system of North America. This added another layer of entanglements in the Great Lakes system, a region that is still the theatre of many agreements and disputes between the federal and provincial governments of Canada and the United States. 'Invasive species', as they are called by biologists and public authorities, thus created ties between ecosystems and between nationalised natural domains. They entailed both disputes about their introduction and common problems linked to the eradication of native species, pest control and animal diseases. In the process, improbable in-between ecological systems were sometimes created.

Think of biological control strategies, which were thought up to resist these invasive species and have involved the search for and importation of natural predators. To fight the rabbit and its ravages after its deliberate introduction as hunting game in 1859, Australian authorities imported the myxoma virus from South America. Bugs, moths, mites and flies, although less visible, have played a similar role of go-between among ecological systems. The coffee berry borer *Hypothenemus hampei,* a Central African beetle which found a ticket to Latin America and South Asia in the first decades of the twentieth century, or the cassava green mite *Mononychellus tanajoa,* a major pest that made the reverse trip to Africa in the 1970s, eventually attracted their best enemies into their new biota. In Colombia especially, *H. hampei* has been fought by acclimatising some parasitoid wasps from Central Africa. And, in order to control the cassava mite in Africa, entomologists chose *Typhlodromalus aripo*, another mite from north-east Brazil. *T. aripo* was moved to the cassava front line in Benin in 1993. It is now present in a dozen African countries, thus strengthening the presence of a sample from the Brazilian tropical ecosystem in Africa, the cassava itself having come to Africa from South America in the sixteenth century. Between 1996 and 2011, biological control research, methods, information and policy resources for the control of invasive species were pooled in the Global Invasive Species Programme, thus adding an organisational layer to ecological entanglements. Many other stories of biological invasion and control invite historians to work through the limits of regional or continental biota and ecological systems. Until now, such studies have been done by biologists, and it is timely to blend biology and history to work out the establishment and operation of these peculiar linkages. The recent call by historians Jane Carruthers and Libby Robin to 'narrow the gap between the historically ecological and the ecologically historical literature' should be of interest to transnational historians in the future.[93]

Nature across borders

The variations of El Niño and La Niña connect climate conditions and the fate of humanity over large areas of Latin America and South East and South Asia, through storms, droughts, floods and the variation of fisheries. Quite tellingly, it was the hypothesis that climatic conditions in such distinct and distant regions of the world were correlated through atmospheric pressure fluctuations that caused his fellow-scientists to chide Gilbert Walker, the British head of the Indian Meteorological Service, who suggested such a connection in 1924. This long-distance linkage through natural elements was deemed a fantasy or an overall simplification at the time. That Walker's hypothesis was mathematically and empirically verified only some 50 years later should be an incentive for historians to insist on studying connections in general, and natural connectors in particular.

Some situations are of special interest for transnational historians, when natural elements are located, or operate precisely, at or across the limits that polities try to consolidate. Natural limits like mountains or rivers were used to draw borders when countries began to consolidate these sites of entanglement, and they were the staple of nineteenth-century treaty negotiators and nationalist pundits.[94] Yet natural elements and resources mostly create linkages because of their role as sites of interaction. Their subterranean extension through distinct polities has generated conundrums between different protagonists contending for their control and use. This is one aspect of the history of natural resources that still plays out under our very eyes, as the drawing of the border between Sudan and South Sudan is conditioned by the location of oilfields and natural pastures. Consider also some 20 years of civil and international wars in the African Great Lakes region, where so many parties have coveted the resources of tantalum and cassiterite, precious ingredients for the electronics and military industries. But resources are not the only natural elements to create linkages because of their situation between and through countries. The recent rise of sea and ocean history is based on their redefinition as connecting areas. The 'new thalassology' has chiefly dealt with whole oceanic and sea basins.[95] But there are also more limited and specific stretches of water that geographers have identified as **interfaces**: straits, channels and rivers. The latter will be our chosen instrument here. Rivers with two or more riparian countries have worked as interfaces on multiple planes: irrigation, navigation, hydroelectricity, flood control or drinking water. Historians, geographers and political scientists have given us fine-grained accounts of one or the other, and they have isolated complex entanglements between countries and communities that so far have not given way to 'water wars'.[96] The study of rivers shows that it makes sense to place a natural element at the centre of historical investigation precisely because of its capacity to create linkages between polities and societies. This was how Mark Cioc studied the River Rhine.[97] This river, which was turned into a 'seamless conduit of internationalism' after the Conference of Vienna in 1815,[98] has brought the economic interests of riparian regions, countries and firms into an integrated system centred on the transportation of raw material and commodities, despite the fact that the Rhine never ceased to be the major line of geopolitical conflict between France and Germany from1870 to 1945. Cioc's eco-biography of that river does not merely unveil rivalry and cooperation between riparian actors; it sets the river as an actor through its capacity to connect economic interests, engineering capacities, ecological concerns, administrative methods and public policies in different countries, regions and municipalities.

Water bodies are not the only natural elements to invite us to pay attention to natural connectors. Nomadic pastoral communities and their herds, because of seasonal cycles and droughts, have been and are still moving across political borders, despite attempts by national states to prevent these seasonal migrations. In the Horn of Africa, and sub-Saharan Africa in general, migrating livestock have been relentlessly challenging the demarcation lines established by imperial powers and sanctioned by the Organisation of African States in 1964.[99] Animals, domesticated or wild, create linkages between spaces that are not supposed to be easily connected.[100] Still in Africa, the massive migration of millions of wildebeest, zebra and gazelle has been the reason for conservationists to push for the creation of cross-border conservation areas. The Serengeti National Park and Masai Mara Reserve were established in the 1950s and 1960s across Tanzanian and Kenyan territory, in order to cover most of their migration area. The capacity of animals to create linkages is enhanced by the fact that what seems to be a porous border for wildebeest has mostly been closed to tourists since 1977, the closure being maintained in order to increase the respective countries' share in the revenues from tourism. It is useful here to insist that the natural movement of wildebeest not only creates ties of information, negotiation, dispute and organisation between two national territories, but also between a range of actors, including different types of public and private wildlife reserves, farming and pastoral communities and international non-governmental organisations. This underlines that it would be a serious mistake to focus only on the ties between countries, or to see wildebeest as facilitators. They are not a force to annihilate the capacity of polities to demarcate and enforce their sovereignty, any more than are the wild salmon that enter US rivers in south-east Alaska and Yukon in order to spawn upstream in Canadian territory, and which have been a bone of contention among governments, fishermen and the canned food industry since the early twentieth century. The linkages they created are as much about cooperation as about antagonism.

▶ Conclusion

This chapter has listed a number of different reasons and ways to study human and non-human intermediaries that help us to write history in a transnational perspective. They can be arranged in two different concluding statements. One has to do with research results: a close look at the capacity and agency of intermediaries as connectors unveils the way connections work. Intermediaries make it happen. They enter or create situations where they can act as go-betweens, they use certain mechanisms and tools to accomplish their connecting performance, they are active in one region, or one moment, and not in another, they create ties and unmake them. They are the historians' Trojan horses, penetrating formidable impressive arrangements like capitalism, science, revolution, ecology, to unravel facts, trends and patterns that contribute to answer the three 'big questions' of transnational history. The other reason why, in Daniel Rodgers's words, 'there are gains to be made by starting from connections',[101] is that it has a strong heuristic return. The study of connectors provides us with the leverage to go beyond the mere identification of the ties that bind, to shrug off very general hints at 'influence' or 'interdependence' between regions, nations and groups, to reconstruct the circuits in which they operated, and to identify the actual ways and means that characterise the encounter of their historical trajectories. It also compels us to work across the different levels we are used to considering as nested geographical scales, because following the activities of a specific human connector illuminates its capacity to mobilise resources and occupy positions that cut through these different levels. Nor is it possible to decontextualise your work when you follow what connectors do, because their actions, their words and their impact are always located. Last but not least, connectors remind us that connections are made and unmade, and that their existence (and study) are not subsumed in the expression or celebration of benign outcomes.

3 Circulations

Plants and germs, things and the knowledge of how to make them, ideas and the ways of conceiving them, people and the techniques to govern and define them, were moving across and between polities well before the last two centuries. But these last 200–250 years have been the time when borders have been increasingly adopted and installed to control movements between national states. State, nation and nationalism progressively became banal, incorporated in bodies, minds and institutions through a host of rituals and routines.[1] As a result, the very attributes and instruments of national sovereignty have been concerned with mobility. Constitutions or military organisation have been widely compared, adapted and traded. Nationalism itself has been a composite fabric. In nineteenth-century Europe, national identities were defined with a very similar nation-building kit that mobilised grammatologists, educators, artists and folklorists.[2] Bengali activists of the **Swadeshi** (self-sufficiency) movement of the early twentieth century constantly drew parallels with, and inspiration from, other national insurgencies against imperial powers.[3] And later, the liberation struggles of decolonisation in Africa were shaped by the circulation of anti-colonial leaders, notions, weapons and assistance provided by the new independent governments of Egypt, Algeria and Ghana.[4] What goes for political dimensions also applies to other domains: ideologies of free trade as well as those of protection have been promoted, moved and resisted across limits of national discourse.[5]

Even ideologies and technologies invented to limit circulation between and through countries have been shared, adapted or sold. David Edgerton illustrated this paradox of the technologies of enclosure and autarchy, citing Nazi Germany's sale to Franco's Spain of a patent for processing synthetic oil, and its use in embargoed South Africa in the 1980s.[6] The members of autarchic regimes followed similar routes: former Nazis and their European collaborators sold their political-repression skills to South American dictatorships after the Second World War, seconded by Western democracies during the 1960s and 1970s;[7] Soviet advisors nurtured the Stasi, the East German secret police, and in the 1980s North Korean military forces trained the infamous Zimbabwean Fifth Brigade, which was accused of brutality and murder in Matabeleland in the 1980s. Should it come as a surprise? Not if, once again bearing in mind the words of George Orwell,[8] we break with the fervour, hope, distraction or laziness that make us associate circulation exclusively with generous ideas and practices. European fascists and former collaborators with the Nazi occupation rallied immediately after the Second World War to advocate an ascetic, corporatist, organic and white-only Europe no less fervently than Christian democrats who were in favour of European reconstruction.[9]

Has everything been in flux over the last 200 years? What have been the changes in quantity and quality of those flows over that course of time? The humanities and social sciences have been increasingly engaged with these questions. A growing number of research programmes, conferences and workshops scrutinise the circulation of people, knowledge, capital, ideas, technologies, artistic motifs and much more. The scope of historical research now extends beyond the most obvious circulations (migrants, capital, goods, political creeds, religious faiths) to include less visible or even clandestine circulations. As they expanded their interest in circulations, historians tried to grasp the order in the space of flows. The world is not flat and has never been: circulations are created, avoided, desired, constrained, controlled, resisted and oriented. This chapter looks for ways to make sense of the regularities that underlie these processes.

The notion of 'circulatory regime' will help us to systematise the search for order that underpins this recent scholarship. In this chapter, the term 'regime' is applied in a sense similar to its usage in physical geography, rather than its political science sense.[10] When they study an alluvial river, physical geographers often begin by establishing its 'regime', understood as the combination of factors that characterise the ordinary aspect, behaviour and impact of that river. They locate its current and past riverbeds, and map its **catchment area**; they figure out discharge, width, depth, slope and their relations; they study the variation of these characteristics throughout the course of time in response to precipitation, temperature, evapotranspiration, and drainage basin characteristics. The combination of these factors provides them with the identity kit of the river. This chapter looks for the functional analogues of these factors. Circulatory regimes are the relatively stable patterns that characterise circulations in terms of content, direction, intensity, extent and a few other factors. More than merely a riverine metaphor, the reconstruction of circulatory regimes is proposed here as a checklist for historians who must try to make sense of circulations.

▶ Looking for order in the space of flows

In the 1990s and 2000s, the sociology of Ulrich Beck, Anthony Giddens and Zygmunt Bauman was epochal for its emphasis on fluidity and movement at the expense of territoriality and situation. British sociologist John Urry argued that the increasing importance of mobility in the modern world made it necessary to research and think 'sociology beyond societies': the study of societies and their territorial embodiments was a thing of the past.[11] Historians may fear that an emphasis on what lies in-between and through polities and communities will lead to some kind of offshore and footloose history that would follow restless objects, ideas and people without paying attention to the fact that these movements are impulsed, resisted and managed by specific individuals or organisations rooted in specific contexts. If so, transnational history would give up on an elementary duty of historians: the contextualisation of events, facts, people, groups, processes and institutions. But historians who held to this first impression would be misconstruing the contribution of social scientists.

Anthropologist Arjun Appadurai is not the only scholar to stress that paying attention to the 'world of flows' does not mean that 'everything is flowing and fluxing'.[12] John Urry, who emphasised global fluidity in *Sociology beyond Societies*, was considerably more nuanced in other works.[13] Most social scientists who have called for a greater attention to fluxes have usually ended up recommending the study of specific contexts, in order to identify loci of power within the space of flows.[14] In this chapter, we will focus, similarly, on attempts to reconcile an interest in mobility with the requisite of contextualisation. Our reliance on the picks and shovels of the historians' trade obliges us to abstain from a breathless chase after ideas, people, capital and objects; we must examine these fleeting items in specific contexts, moments and places, in correlation with the action of specific institutions, organisations and individuals, or within structural mechanisms. Three shavings from recent historical research will help us to get this going.

'How does a book become an international best-seller?' asks the first line of the blurb of Isabel Hofmeyr's *Portable Bunyan*.[15] The question is largely rhetorical, as the book she studies was more often given than sold: she is writing about *The Pilgrim's Progress*, a Puritan religious text originally published in England (1678 and 1684) and transported to distant places through migration paths and missionary work. What happened to the book's shape, content and usage when it was translated into some 200 languages on different continents and used as a 'second Bible' in many instances? More specifically, Hofmeyr focuses on what happened to and with the *Pilgrim* in Africa, where it was translated into some 80 languages between the 1860s and the 1960s. Retracing the routes of the multiple publications of the *Pilgrim*, its text and its images, makes it possible to identify the orders that shaped this translation process, and the orders that the translations shaped in their turn. The *Pilgrim* did not simply move from English or other European languages into African ones. It also travelled sideways between African languages. Neither did translations leap instantly from European missionaries to African converts: the context of specific missionary sites and the contribution of converts themselves were key to adapting the words, rhetoric and images of the *Pilgrim* over the long stretches of time that were necessary to translate the book into Zulu or Kele. Imperial authorities certainly promoted the *Pilgrim* as a tool for colonial domination, but its translations also gave leverage to its African readers. Last but not least, the *Pilgrim*'s progress in Africa eventually looped back on the politics of nonconformity in England and contributed to its installation into the canon of British literature. Hofmeyr, a historian of literature based at the University of Witwatersrand in South Africa, reconstructs all the thickness of flows through time and space, and clearly identifies their underlying orders.

Our second book was written by Australian historians Marilyn Lake and Henry Reynolds. The authors follow racial ideologies and corresponding responses across the English-speaking world. They attempt to

> trace the transnational circulation of emotions and ideas, people and publications, racial knowledge and the technologies that animated white men's countries and the strategies of exclusion, deportation and segregation, in particular, the deployment of the state-based instruments of surveillance, the census, the passport and the literacy test'.[16]

But the book is not only about unravelling and drawing complex **circuits**. It also exposes a racial order project involving substantial sections of white settlers' democracies and nations. The project participants shared a common concern for racial distance, the definition and implementation of which was fuelled by constant observation, emulation and borrowing between South Africa, the United States and Australia, with the last often a 'role model' of sorts in the first two. Lake and Reynolds also show the thrust of resistance and anti-colonial politics triggered by the racialisation of these societies, notably through the cluster of initiatives emanating from the Japanese government and Japanese intellectuals after the Russo-Japanese War of 1905. Lake and Reynolds teach us that flows are ordered, resisted and resistible.

A third clue to the capacity of historians to pinpoint order in flows and hierarchies in ties is provided by the US environmental historian Michael Egan, part of his wider project to follow mercury pollution across time and space in the last 50 years or so.[17] In his article, Egan starts from Iraq, where, since the early 1970s, tens of thousands of people have died or suffered neurological damage after exposure to methyl mercury. The Iraquis suffered because of their consumption of wheat and barley seeds that had been dressed in methyl mercury, still used in shipments to Iraq long after mercury-based fungicides had been banned in Scandinavia and North America. After a disastrous series of floods and droughts, the Iraqui government bought large quantities of grain in Mexico in 1971. The wheat seeds were those developed by Norman Borlaugh as part of the Green Revolution project of the Rockefeller Foundation, and the long, hot sea journey between Mexico and Basra meant that treatment of the grain with highly effective fungicides was essential. Following the massive free handout of the seeds to Iraqi peasants at a time when their stocks of grain were low, many of the pink-dyed seeds were not sown but were used to feed chickens, livestock and human beings. Neither the warning on the sacks, being written in Spanish, nor the dying of the seeds, alerted the users. Egan's work is not only about retracing that particular load of seeds. He reveals the economic and political orders that presided over its trajectory: mechanisms of supply and demand that made mercury-based fungicides the cheapest solution as their price fell following the banning of mercury derivatives in North America; protective measures that served inhabitants of the developed world but not those living in other countries; channels of a long-distance market for buying food supplies and agricultural commodities; Iraqi politics; and technical assistance projects by the Rockefeller Foundation and other international agencies to create and disseminate new plant hybrids with higher yields obtained through natural gene selection. Neither methyl mercury, nor any other item on the move, floats freely: its mobility is inscribed in specific projects carried by specific protagonists.

▶ Caveat: circulation beyond mere motion

At first sight, circulation seems to be a simple action. An item, of material or spiritual nature, living or inert, is moved from one place to another. This item is well defined, and its points of departure and arrival clearly identified. We just have to map its trajectory and appraise the causes and consequences of its movement: easy. Sadly, this neat view is quickly blurred.

First, circulation does not amount to the mere transportation of an immutable entity. People, ideas and objects often have to be changed to be moved, or they change because they move. This applies to style and substance. Migrants are transformed by the experience of migration, as suggested by frequent twists in gender roles: Russian male former aristocrats and tycoons lost much of their control over their families when they were driven into exile after the 1917 Revolution,[18] and young Indian nurses from Kerala, who have been staffing the hospitals of the Persian Gulf countries since the 1970s, are no longer seen as members of a profession without clout but respected as breadwinners for the family at home, and coveted brides.[19] Even material vectors of circulation can be transformed by their own circulation: the sampans that were introduced into Hawaii in the 1890s by Japanese migrants became customised to fishing and seafaring conditions and were gradually adopted as 'typical' Hawaiian ships, whereas the junks that had begun to populate Californian waters only slightly earlier remained unchanged, and disappeared as one of many consequences of the anti-Chinese legislation of the late nineteenth and early twentieth centuries.[20] And it should not be forgotten that though the object may remain the same, its use and signification are different according to the moment and location. The AK 47 assault rifle started out as an entry for a competition launched in 1943 to design the future basic weapon of the Soviet Army. More than 70 years later, and after having been moved in the millions to every hot-spot on the planet, it stands as the favourite weapon of rebels and mercenaries across the world, featured on the flags and coats of arms of several countries and political movements, and is increasingly used in criminal activities in continental Europe. Words also take on different meanings when circulated, even when they seem to be immutable because of their sacred importance. The *Bhagavadgita*, a section of the Sanskrit *Mahabharata* epic, was given different meanings by its readers and translators, European or American.They tweaked the text to their own political, poetic, religious (theosophical and Christian) or philosophical ends on many occasions between the late eighteenth and the mid-twentieth centuries.[21] And these meanings were rejected or contested by different Indian readers and translators of that same text. Circulation is a creative process that affects the items that circulate; as a result, historians need to follow closely the trajectory of an item to capture the different usages and appropriations. Beware, though: we can run into what art historian Erwin Panofsky named *pseudomorphosis*: identical forms in distinct and distant times and places that carry identical meanings, although no contact can be asserted between the loci or the moments.[22]

The *Gita*, anyhow, did not go 'from India' to 'the West': it has constantly been reworked and reappropriated in-between by individuals, institutions and journals who worked with it and about it. This is our second point: circulation is not a straightforward spatial phenomenon that happens between distinct place A and distinct place B, with items leaving A once and for all, reaching B in marching order to quietly wait before proceeding to points C or D. Even if it may seem appropriate to think this way about single contained items, such as an object or person, whose materiality cannot be in several places at the same time, we should note that humankind has invented means for individuals or objects to have a presence in A and B at the same moment: memory, images, the printed word and other methods of communication make it happen. Besides, groups of beings and series of objects have an uneven and non-linear movement: as a group, migrants come and go between countries and continents; a disease can be spread by germs simultaneously in several sites; a musical phrase is heard and commented on in different places at the same moment. Immaterial items like information, ideas and know-how, which are not confined to a single container, do not always move from one place to another in cascade. They are disseminated synchronously but appropriated in different places at different paces, and their origin cannot always be easily attributed to one specific place. The case of nineteenth-century ideas on social reform is quite instructive. When US reformers travelled to Germany to study housing policies in the 1880s, they knew that some 'German methods' they observed and commented on were partly the result of the German reformers' observation and appropriation of schemes initiated in London some time previously.[23] US reformers who labelled their general social policy proposals 'made in Germany' knowingly omitted to mention that they were composite products combining experiments carried out by different local or national authorities from other countries in Europe or beyond.

Many circulating items are not 'from' somewhere and going 'to' somewhere else, they live through and in-between different places. Kapil Raj cogently makes this point when he analyses several instances of scientific knowledge in South Asia and Europe (mapping, legal knowledge), and insists that they were not created in one place and then moved from this place to others, but that they emerged from circulation, and from the interaction between actors who worked in several locations.[24] Relocating these actors and these circulations is what matters, and the attribution of origin is not what historians should look for, argues Raj. The case of *tiryaq* brings that argument home: as a medicinal commodity its elaboration, consumption, prescription and legitimation defies attribution to a given 'place of belonging'.[25] The same default of attribution applies to the missionary colleges that zealous US evangelists established in Kyoto (Japan) or Beirut (Ottoman Empire): these were not copycat US colleges, nor brand-new educational institutions. Their special characteristics, including their non-denominational aspect and interest in local knowledge, emerged from the circulation of ambitions and personnel of the American Board for Commissioners for Foreign Missions.[26] Whence the need to 'relocate' the circulating objects we study, to ground them in specific contexts where they are seen, used and changed, even those that seem to be context-free or placeless. After all, even the Internet is not everywhere, it is located in different places (entry points, data servers, wireless access spots, transmission lanes) and operates on different bandwidths, protocols and backbone networks (optic fibre, telephone cables). The current effort to map the Internet is a suggestion of how historians can use maps, for their own use and for the instruction of readers, when they want to locate not only the movement of material and immaterial items, but also their usages and appropriations.[27]

Third, circulations define a space of their own, often a very specific one. The circuit is the context, so to speak. Each type of commodity that has been moved in the last 200 years has generated its own space through the different stages of production, trade and consumption. The geography of tin is not the same as that of coffee.[28] And such geographies do not amount to country-based localisation. In recent years, the differences in legislation for oocyte donation in Europe have created an incentive for French women over 43 to go to Belgium, Spain and Greece for medically assisted procreation.[29] But they do not go 'to' Belgium or Greece; they head for specific cities, attend specific medical centres that are recommended by informants, friends, acquaintances and associations. This circulation has its distinct space, precisely located, which is the theatre and agent of social relations, financial transactions and life-changing experiences that result from the intersection of biological, individual and legal horizons. Circulations define spaces of their own which do not amount to the sum of their spatial parts. These spaces are the many middle grounds and contact zones where we have seen connectors at work in Chapter 2. They are sites for the production of attitudes, roles, situations, objects and institutions.

These are clues that circulations are more complicated than they seem. Each circulating item behaves differently, frames its own kind of space, generates different consequences. And it is far from easy or necessary to see where the motion starts and when it ends. For all this complexity, can we think of ways for historians to see through it and organise their attempts to reconstruct and analyse circulations? The notion of circulatory regimes tries to capture the relatively stable extent, direction, intensity and organisation of circulations, and the following guidelines offer suggestions for analysing their durable presence and effects.

▶ Guideline 1: know your riverbed

When container shipping replaced bulk shipping for cargo between the late 1950s and the 1980s it meant more than a different way of packing goods in motion.[30] This new way to organise cargo drastically decreased the number of hours necessary to unload vessels, made shipping a capital-intensive rather than a labour-intensive industry, allowed easy connections between ship, rail and truck and cleared the ground for industrial processes based on the fragmentation of production (just in time, outsourcing, the **modular production system**). It also involved new infrastructures with dedicated harbours, multimodal hubs and a computer-based system that today manages the flow of almost 20 million standardised containers. Last but not least, it changed the relationship between employers and labourers in many harbours of the world. Following that disruption, an inert box of metal is now of vital importance to the circulation of goods in our world: it underpins the current international division of labour by its capacity to circulate things.

The inert metal box does matter. Just as one needs to specify the characteristics of riverbeds to understand where streams can go and what can be done with them, it is of vital importance to be specific about the conduits and vectors of circulation. Their characteristics create particular opportunities and constraints, and the minutiae of their operation condition their possible impact. Once technical rules for assembling and laying submarine cables were formulated by the British Joint Committee on Submarine Telegraph Cables in 1861, their reliability quickly increased: it became possible to lay cables in difficult waters, cables now filled with additional wires that made telegraphic communications faster, more numerous and bidirectional. But it is not only in technological aspects that vectors matter. If migrant remittances are made through the hands of returning fellow migrants, the clearing houses of 'Gold Mountain firms' (*Jinshanzhuang*), the elaborate inter-individual chains of compensation of *hawala* (the popular alternative remittance system in South Asia) or the corporate web of Western Union Inc., this does not amount to the same thing: the issue of trust between partners is radically changed, as is the number of intermediaries feeding on those remittances or the capacity of governmental authorities to estimate or control remittances. Similar issues appear when one compares the familial bonds that carried information and investments throughout the House of Rothschild in the nineteenth century, with the constraints of duty and contract in a late twentieth-century major corporate bank like HSBC.[31] Or, consider that if translation of religious texts is carried out by first-language converts rather than by second-language missionaries, then these translations may not be loaded with prior theological conflicts. The vectors of circulation need all our attention.

The importance of knowing your riverbed also has methodological consequences. Only when one is aware of how things travel can one know where to capture and record their movement. This may sound obvious: quarantine stations and local authorities' records are unsurprisingly the places to document movements of germs along maritime roads. But imagination also calls the tune when it comes to locating less conspicuous sites and sources, as when financial historians use exchange bulletins to reconstruct the circulation of capital between different financial centres.[32] In the same vein, because she wanted to know how French painting became a reference in the nineteenth-century German world despite general public hostility to anything French, France Nehrlich paid attention to sales catalogues in addition to her analysis of public collections, travels of individual collectors in Parisian studios, sales catalogues and the artistic press.[33]

This is an indication that, most often, studying circulation implies considering different vectors at work simultaneously or successively. Someone interested in how musical styles and fashions evolve across and through national or regional styles will have to pay attention to the movement of records, instruments, studio recording hardware, musicians and musical scores. The range of topics to be investigated will include the musical press, sales figures of instruments and records, recording policies of recording companies, travels of migrants and tourists, the machinery of festivals, peer-to-peer conversations and inspiration among musicians as well as tours by orchestras, but also the governmental propaganda machines that touted specific musical styles and performers as messengers of national or civilisational grandeur. The roles of these different conduits have of course waxed and waned over the course of the last 200-250 years, but taking these different conduits into account has made it possible to appraise the success story of Beethoven's Ninth, the popularity of the Brazilian bossa nova, the fate of jazz during the Cold War, the Caribbean musical crucible, the iconic status of Oum Kalsoum in the Arab world from the 1950s or the presence of ethnic musical recordings on the early twentieth-century US market.[34] A daunting task, certainly, to cover all these bases, or their equivalents for other objects of study. Especially when, as with music, circulation seems to be planetary. But if vectors tell us about the style and substance of circulations, they also deliver clues about the places they reach and those they do not. Paying attention to vectors of circulation helps delineate the space of circulations. In his study of regional anarchist networks in the Gulf of Mexico and the Caribbean, Kirk Shaffer identifies two different subsets of interchange based on different journals and organisations that worked as conduits for information and mobilisation.[35] It is from our knowledge of vectors that we can demarcate the catchment area of circulations.

▶ Guideline 2: demarcate a catchment area

For ten years or so, there has been a boom in the history of commodities. One can read about the history of the world told through six beverages, or follow the pineapple or curry in their tribulations. A number of successful titles, written in academic or popular fashion, are now available. The subtitle of one of these, Mark Kurlansky's *Cod: A Biography of the Fish that Changed the World*, published in 1997 and translated into 15 languages, has become an inspiration. Several trade and academic books have struck up that tune, from Larry Zuckerman's *The Potato: How the Humble Spud Rescued the Western World* (1998) to Heather Streets-Salter, *Commodities, Culture, and History: the Products that Changed the World*, a forthcoming two-volume set. Yet, which world is it that is 'changed'? Is the word to be understood as a synonym of 'planet Earth', or as a special sphere, as in 'the world of Italian theatre'? Much can be said about the ubiquity of major commodities like electricity, but there are still places on Earth where they do not come from nor go to, and this uneven geography changes over time. Chocolate is still not often consumed in Africa, or Asia outside of Japan. India became a tea-drinking country only after much effort was put into the acquisition of new consumers by Ceylon tea producers in the late nineteenth century.

'Circulation occurs in a bounded space', writes Kapil Raj, adding that this bounded space changes over time.[36] This could be printed on a handbill and pinned above the desks of historians working in a transnational perspective: 'It's the catchment area, stupid !'. The identification of this bounded space, a sort of catchment area / drainage basin of the circulation they study, is a vital task, even when the very idea of limits seems to be counterintuitive. Long-distance circulation, like acid rain, industrial smoke plumes or the Chernobyl and Fukushima atomic clouds, hovers above certain places and not others: it follows the routes of atmospheric currents. Although such currents do not stop at national borders, as infamously stated in France in the aftermath of the Chernobyl disaster, there are areas they do not reach. The financial system is now commonly described as a 7/7 and 24/24 seamless flow of information around the globe. But stock exchanges are organised in bounded clusters by capitalist and logistical infrastructures: Euronext resulted from the merger of several stock exchanges (mainly Paris, Amsterdam, Brussels, New York) that started in the 2000s, while eight stock markets around the Baltic Sea are served by a single network of fibre-optic cables and an information system managed by a single IT company. At first sight, it also seems counterintuitive to suggest different spaces of circulation for electricity, when one considers the grid of cables and the interconnected networks of the hardwired European peninsula at the beginning of the twenty-first century. Still, a major divide results from different frequency standards on high-tension lines: the Continental European Synchronized Area includes Turkey and North Africa, while the British Isles and a large part of Scandinavia live on a different beat. This is why the European blackout of 2006, which started with an incident in northern Germany, shut off the lights in Morocco and Tunisia but hardly affected nearby Scandinavia.[37] Knowledge of the catchment area of the circulation under investigation tells one where it can and cannot have an impact. It contextualises interconnections, and forces us to be specific about the spatiality of circulations, instead of tagging anything far-flung as 'global'.

This is especially worth mentioning because the transnational perspective is often associated with long-distance circulations that involve large quantities of capital, goods and people. Distance and size are certainly two important aspects in appraising the extent of circulations. Distance makes face-to-face interaction more difficult for individuals, and the transmission of information and goods requires additional infrastructure to make up for distance (e.g. intermediary compression stations for pipelines or coaling / fuelling stations for ships). For firms that began to operate out of their domestic markets from the 1850s, it required a lot of invention and energy to establish organisation frameworks and management values that would allow the manufacture and selling of objects and services across countries, continents, languages and religious areas.[38] But neither distance nor size precludes the interactions that derive from circulation. Transnational historians in fact combine the large/small number of protagonists and the long/short distance of circulation without prejudice.[39] Cemil Aydin works on the three fronts of transnational history as he pursues pan-Asian and pan-Islamic thought and activities across continents, but so does Caitlin Murdock when she focuses on the circulation of people, goods, observation and power in a small region across the once Saxon–Bohemian and now Czech–German border.[40] They are both very specific about the space of circulation they study, despite the incommensurability of their catchment areas in size and distance.

Perhaps more than size and distance, limits and duration are essential characteristics regarding the catchment area of any given circulation. The establishment of limits does not amount to drawing a line or spreading a colour on a map, in order to include this country and exclude that one. Conflating location with country is one of the consequences of **methodological nationalism**, a propensity of historians and social scientists to consider the national framework as the only valid unit of observation and understanding.[41] But, the labelling of a circulation as going from one country to another is an instance of 'ecological fallacy', that logical error by which statisticians infer the characteristics of a single unit from the aggregate statistics of the group it belongs to. This is one of the reasons why some historians coined the term **translocality**, to indicate that circulations and entanglements have been taking place between specific locales.[42] Indeed, relocating circulation implies more than a crude country localisation, and calls for painstaking research of places that were included or excluded from the catchment area of the circulation we study. The circulation space of German exports and imports in the early twentieth century, i.e. its economic ties to the world, had its nerve centre in the port of Rotterdam, in the Netherlands. The journal *Al-Manar*, which title claimed the ambition to be a 'lighthouse' for the reform of Islam between 1898 and 1935, was not a journal 'from' Egypt that was read or highly respected 'in' Russia, eastern China or the Malay–Indonesian world.[43] It was within specific communities, around some determined individuals and through the graduates of particular religious schools, that the Islamic revival project launched by its Syrian-born editor Muhammad Rashid Rida from its headquarters in Cairo was heeded and emulated. Likewise, migration chains do not tie one country to another, but rather connect a given region or even a village to another: the hinterlands of Thanjavur, Tamil Nadu, India, to the plantations around Perak and Selangor in Malaya; Valdengo, province of Biella, Italy, to a specific neighbourhood in New York City or Buenos Aires; Taishan county in south-west China to Old Chinatown in Los Angeles, California, USA. It is a very rough approximation to map the coffee trade as an arrow between producing and consuming countries: the beans are in fact moved from specialised and specific production areas to the processing mills and warehouses of roasters which have come to control this market in recent decades. Circulations are seen to happen between one country and another only if you 'see like a state': that is, if you adopt the point of view of national authorities who create and handle aggregate numbers of people or quantities of goods going out or coming into the national territory. Establishing the limits of a drainage basin is not equivalent to turning out a list of countries. One has to follow things, people and notions through the specific places, organisations and segments of social groups where they are assembled, used or stationed.

Coffee also provides clues for thinking about duration. The geography of the coffee chain has changed several times between the early nineteenth and the late twentieth centuries, in all its different stages (production, transformation, consumption).[44] These changes not only tied or disconnected different places in terms of wages, technology, price and consumer habits, they also changed the conditions for all protagonists in the chain, from the working conditions on plantations to the taste of the beverage. The first aspect of duration is thus about the very existence and stability of a drainage basin. Limits and locations can change, as with coffee, but the whole basin can also crumble and the circulation actually disappear. Most of the Peruvian guano catchment area was shattered by the advent of chemical fertilisers at the end of the nineteenth century.[45] The massive influx of free and forced labour from China and the South Pacific Islands stopped, as did the flows of guano to the USA and Europe. But duration is also an internal factor: how long does it take to travel between different places within a catchment area? Franco Moretti has studied the time it took to translate major French, Russian or German novels into English during the nineteenth century in order to understand how England 'became an island' in literary terms.[46] Early Russian classics, he says, were translated into French on average 20 years after publication; into English 43 years after. There are different temporalities at work in the catchment area of a specific item, and they create different contexts and conditions for relations between different participants: English translations and receptions of Tolstoï were different from French ones not only because of the language, but also because they did not happen at the same time. Capturing these temporalities is not easy. The French philosopher Victor Cousin presented the elements of Hegelian philosophy to the participants of his course in Paris in 1828, but the first translations of Hegel's texts into French did not take place until 1850, long before the Russian immigrant Alexandre Kojève fully reformulated the interpretation of Hegel's *Phänomenologie des Geistes* in his seminars at the Ecole Pratique des Hautes Etudes between 1933 and 1939.[47] Estimation of how long it took Hegel's work to 'reach' French philosophy – or even Parisian philosophy – is thus quite a vexing question. All the more since every new version and appropriation of his work had to deal with the presence of former ones: duration is a multi-layered dimension. Only detailed attention to these different layers of duration can allow us to observe the operation of the Franco-German catchment area defined by the circulation of Hegel's writings, the rationales for interest in his work and the different interpretations of his thought. This needs to be conducted in relation to specific places and milieux (institutions, cities) of the French intellectual scene in order not to take the part for the whole: again, relocation is key to be specific about duration. This also points to the fact that catchment areas are not homogeneous. In terms of our hydrological metaphor, there are different tributaries with different throughputs in a single catchment area.

▶ Guideline 3: identify your tributaries

Some flows have more throughput than others. An individual writes more often to some correspondents than to others, a scientist favours references to a limited number of foreign texts, migrants leave from specific regions and travel from a limited number of seaports, a factory will get more supply from and send more goods to particular areas. In cultural history, studies of transfers have focused on highly visible flows such as bilateral relations between Germany, Great Britain and France, or on twentieth-century American cultural projection defined as Americanisation or cultural imperialism. This is justifiable when one consider that high throughput can correspond to deep impact: it makes sense to place an emphasis on the circulation of US culture because it has been a major bone of contention in receiving societies, while the Franco-German antagonistic affinity has been important to the history of modern Europe, and to the way these two countries imagined themselves.[48]

However, too much attention on the most visible or thickest streams of circulation can be deceiving. Economic historians have long been aware that capital-importing countries can also export capital: this has been the case, after all, of the USA from the late 1880s to the First World War, with both massive influx of British capital, and significant direct investment in Latin America.[49] Historians of colonial empires somehow strained a similar point when they recently insisted that the state, culture and political economy of the colonies and the metropolis were part of a single analytical field.[50] Whereas the study of colonialism and the colonial state had privileged the circulation of capital, personnel and might from the metropolis to the colonies, they insisted that the study of circulations between the colonies themselves and between the colonies and the metropolis would give a more appropriate view of the colonial condition.

What is most visible and intense should not take exclusive possession of our historical curiosity. This is an observation that especially applies to specific topics like the study of circulations of people, capital, beliefs and ideas by and within migrant communities. There has been a lot of research on Italian, Chinese or Jewish migrants, but the processes that emerge from these specific segments are not per se more important or relevant to transnational historians than the study of the Armenian, Hadhrami, Lebanese or Sikh diasporas. There are a number of hidden, forgotten, denied or merely unobtrusive flows that participate in the establishment and operation of circulatory regimes, and we are prone to neglect these 'low throughput' streams. Historical protagonists are sometimes responsible for the consignment to oblivion of these low-key circulations, such as Italian socialists failing to acknowledge the experiments and principles they borrowed from their Belgian counterparts and used as frameworks for their social, ethical and economic activities at the turn of the nineteenth century.[51] Daniel Rodgers's American progressives similarly placed public emphasis on their German or British examples at the expense of what they learned from 'small' or 'archaic' European countries, or from New Zealand. But it is mostly our own biases that prevent us from looking beyond the most visible streams of circulation. Opium and cocaine have been objects of historical interest for their role in the political, social and cultural history of Europe, but reconstructing the different circulatory regimes of narcotics over the last 200 years also requires inclusion of the trade and consumption of narcotics in Africa and the Middle East.[52] For historians, going transnational has often meant looking at circulations to and from their original area of expertise: we start from a familiar town, country, continent or region and follow things from and to there. This makes sense for practical and intellectual reasons (access to sources, command of literature and language, further exploration of already familiar issues), and it also fits the organisation of our discipline according to national or regional specialisation. This approach has heavily influenced the current development of studies of entanglements between one place and the rest of the world, or between two countries or two regions. This has remained highly productive, and we have gained a better knowledge of circulations within South and South East Asia, or between Europe and Asia.[53] Yet, as a result of this bilateral tropism, we are still struggling to appraise these streams in relation to others.

This becomes apparent when streams are studied separately, between two countries, where they are in fact part of larger 'topical' catchment areas. Take film history in the Soviet bloc: US films were deemed politically dangerous, so alternatives such as the *Indianerfilm*, counter-westerns made in East Germany, were shown across the Eastern bloc.[54] Yet, by the 1950s, films from India found an audience in Russia, Bulgaria and elsewhere in the socialist world and in the Third World.[55] These two streams are hardly compared. A similar observation applies to the circulation of films in today's world. Bollywood and Hollywood productions vie for audiences in the Middle East or in South East Asia, but it is misleading to limit the study of the circulation of feature films to these two powerhouses. This leaves aside the production of 'Nollywood' and 'Nigerian video', popular feature-length films in English that are distributed in Ghana, Kenya and South Africa.[56] The relation of these different streams, an essential aspect of the circulatory regime of films as cultural products, is hardly studied as a whole even in regional settings. Likewise, the flows of university students who enrolled abroad during the nineteenth and twentieth centuries have been scrutinised by historians of Europe, often in a bilateral or transatlantic context. But the international political economy of student migrations in this epoch also incorporates students from South East Asia studying in Japan, and students from the Islamic world who experienced the madrasa circuit (madrasas are schools of Islamic theological and juridical higher education), attended Cairo Al-Azhar University for its prestige in the study of classical Islamic texts, or enrolled in Pakistani technical schools and the higher education institutions of the Gulf states in the 1970s. These different streams still have to be analysed together.

Nonetheless, it is not beyond our powers to widen the perspective to include both weak and strong streams. In his study of exiled and diasporic cinema, Hamid Naficy uses a series of topical sections and close-ups on a number of films and film-makers to cover an impressive range of situations.[57] Jeffrey Hanes, in his biography of the political economist and mayor of Osaka Seki Hajime, does not privilege US schol-arship over German social science, and fans out the range of foreign texts and colleagues on whose work Seki drew.[58] Both examples suggest that life histories can help us to recognise and take account of different streams that an individual has been part of. Yet these two examples seem to imply a choice between mul-tiplication of individual trajectories or focus on a single one. Fragmentation or concentration?

One interesting solution to the dilemma is the joint publication of comple-mentary articles or chapters by several authors who fragment a topic. Journal special issues and collected essays have long been organised this way, but for transnational historians the aggregation of distinct chapters and articles has the potential to be more than the collation of singular research pieces. Such arrange-ments, for instance, make it possible to reconstruct the different streams of power, capital, ideas and people that joined in Harbin (Manchuria) to make it a very spe-cial town in-between countries.[59] The historiography of anarchism offers another instance of the added value of this higher type of joint venture. Although histo-rians of anarchism never ignored the movement of individuals and ideas between and through countries, they focused predominantly on the European and North Atlantic region.[60] For the past 10–15 years, the history of anarchism has incor-porated many other streams by means of monographs that have documented, for instance, the strong ties between Cuban and Filipino anti-colonial fighters, the Mediterranean hubs of radicalism, or the exchange of support and methods between Bengali and Irish activists in their common fight against British power.[61] More than a simple spatial expansion of knowledge, this recasting of the history of anarchism has included a determined attempt to assemble the different streams together, to appraise each in relation to others, and to grasp the patterns that have presided over the circulation of anarchist ideas and personnel. This has been made possible by the collective work of researchers who elaborated a common language through a series of meetings and workshops, and published synthetic accounts that capitalised on recent research.[62] Such collaborative work does not amount to a geographical division of labour, or to the search for a consensus, or to the annihilation of individual research interests. It is an invitation to devise appropri-ate solutions to uncover the salient and not-so-salient tributaries that constitute circulatory regimes.

▶ Guideline 4: where there are slopes, there are flows

Isaac Friedlander was known as the Grain King of California in the 1870s. His power relied on his ability to collect information about future crops in the region, and to charter vessels to ship grain to England. Thanks to his repeated successful antici-pations, Friedlander controlled shipping and dictated the price for transportation, and, in consequence, the price of grain and the conditions for its commerce.[63] He 'cornered' the market.

The cereals business was well known for attempts to corner the market. In 1909, US film director D. W. Griffith released a short film called *A Wheat Corner* that featured a wheat speculator cornering 'the entire market of the world' from the Chicago Board of Trade.[64] Such anticipation was made increasingly easy by new trading processes such as futures (i.e the sales of crops to come). You could set up a corner on your own or with partners, for any kind of commodity that could be bought (for instance, the sacks that were used to pack the California wheat, imported from Dundee, Scotland, also came under such schemes). Corners became a synonym for an artificial creation of scarcity in order to increase price and profits. They were one of the devices that speculators created to orient, control and take advantage of circulations. The key here was to freeze circulation by way of antici-pated purchase and storing, as if to prevent the flow of goods from following the slope of demand and supply. Our hydraulic allegory is useful, again, to remind us that dams are not the only devices that control the slope of rivers: banks and levees orient water when it flows too weakly or too strongly, locks help ships to over-come steepness, spillways counterbalance the effects of slope. The manipulation of river flows even includes bidirectional flow: the Chicago River was forced to flow out of Lake Michigan, against its slope, by the Chicago Sanitary District in 1900, but researchers have recently shown that during the winter, deep below, water still runs west to east, into the lake. The conflicts between upstream and downstream users of a river, mentioned in the previous chapter, are themselves a reminder that natural slopes do generate entanglements between polities and communities.

However, the analogy has its limits: most of the circulations studied by historians have no 'natural' slope. They depend on human action and, more often than not, are multi-directional. The story of circulations is also a story of the devices and pro-cesses conceived and implemented to initiate, orient, control, monitor, block and resist these directions. These devices and processes have made and unmade cir-culatory regimes: examples include the cartels signed between firms, the passport system installed by governments, the web of branches established by news agen-cies, the monitoring stations for recording weather data, the quotas of migrants fixed by states, the concepts and barriers of economic nationalism that try to curb flows of merchandise and capital, as well as the transport fares that influence the flows of goods. For each circulation, the identification of the devices installed for its control reveals the slopes that have been created, followed or resisted.

Where is the place to observe these devices at work, and evaluate their capacity to constrict circulations? National borders are obvious sites: there, from the mid-dle of the nineteenth century, legal and material devices were installed to identify, screen, filter or reject people and goods. Checkpoints, border inspections, censors' desks and customs warehouses may now have been substituted, in a few places, by smoother processes like those operating on the USA–Canada border (NEXUS), or have altogether disappeared, as within the European Union 'Schengen space'. In the last 200–250 years, though, by and large borders and borderlands have been characterised by the presence of loose capital, an accumulation of mobile labour, an abundance of trading or manufacturing installations, a strong polic- ing or military force, a wide variety of walls and barriers and a concentration of national anxieties: they are the sites of continuing attempts to control flows on the outer limits of national territories.[65] Other obvious sites are the hubs and cores that polarise circulations: slopes start or lead there. In the early twenti- eth century, hundreds of thousands of standardised library index cards, codified by the contributing correspondents of the Répertoire Bibliographique Universel, clogged the desks and pigeonholes of the International Office of Bibliography in Brussels, where Paul Otlet and Henri La Fontaine had implemented their scheme of a universal bibliographic repertory.[66] Around the same time, information about the rubber-plantation atrocities in the infamous King of Belgium's Free State of Congo converged towards Edmund Dene Morel in his Liverpool headquarters, where he coordinated the campaigns of the Congo Reform Association.[67] Orienting flows towards one centre was seen as the optimal strategy and a condition of effi- ciency by many international movements or associations that pursued a scientific, professional or political goal through the mobilisation of energies across borders.

The polarisation of flows, though, does not always lead to a centralisation in the large metropolises now known as 'global cities', and polarities are to be identified for each circulation. In the last 20 years, the Islamic financial services sector has developed considerably. Compliance of these products with religious rules must be theologically certified to attract investors, and each Islamic financial service firm has a board of *sharia* scholars who vouch for this conformity.[68] The interlocking membership of a large number of these boards suggests that a limited elite of sharia scholars contribute certification across the Muslim world, and Manama, in Bahrain, is the place that contributes most scholars to these interlocks. Manama is not a central node of religious scholarship like Medina, but has been a major offshore financial centre of the Middle East since the 1970s. It is in Manama that regulatory bodies have developed to certify sharia compliance of financial products, and it is predominantly from that milieu of religious and financial experts that the stan- dards that shape the development of Islamic finance in the Muslim world have emerged.

Polarisation can also be about affect and allegiance more than about flows of people, things or information. Despite the metamorphosis of Kodokan judo from a moral and physical uplift body discipline into a 'sport' during its transport to Europe and the Americas by migrants and amateurs, its millions of practitioners over the world still consider that its symbolic core lies in Japan. The facilities (*dojo*) they frequent, the body techniques and spiritual ethic they learn, the rules they respect, the vocabulary they use, the iconic judokas and masters they celebrate are chiefly identified with Japan.[69]

In any case, the polarisation of material or symbolic flows results from a continuous effort by individuals or organisations to control and orient flows. Even in highly centralised and hierarchised circuits like the Catholic Church or the Communist International, this power is always at hazard. There, especially in the 1960s and 1970s, some subcommunities of belief challenged the power of the centre and tried to define, orient and control their own circulations of principles and positions under the headings of theology of liberation or Eurocommunism.[70] In that case, as within the polycentric galaxies of anarchism, Islam or Protestantism, moments of subversion are attempts to establish new slopes in the space of flows. Identification of such attempts to change circulatory regimes is the last aspect we will cover in this chapter.

▶ Guideline 5: pin the blame on regime makers

The identification of projects to establish, operate or subvert circulatory regimes is far from easy. The notion of 'forces' or 'system' is often used to qualify durable patterns that preside over historical complex circulations, as in 'international monetary system'. Yet historians can pinpoint the protagonists who imagined the vectors, drainage basins and slopes that currencies should or should not follow. Some national governments agreed to form monetary unions like the Scandinavian Monetary Union (1873) where the value of coinage was harmonised to make monies interchangeable. Central banks in the North Atlantic world devised rules and practices to stabilise the circulation of gold and currencies in the late nineteenth century, and many other devices were implemented or dismantled to control the flows of capital and the relations between currencies. They were conceived and debated by politicians, economists, businessmen and financial agents, and implemented through conferences, treaties and institutions, the best-known being the 'Bretton Woods system' that contributed to installing the US dollar as de facto international currency.[71] There is agency behind the financial world, financial historians tell us. There are also projects and designs behind the complex circulations in **large technological systems**. When US historian Thomas Hughes began to study the installation and demise of the electricity infrastructures, which defined where and how electricity could go, he emphasised the role of 'system builders', 'inventors, engineers, managers and financiers' who designed and operated electric networks.[72] Further research on large technical systems has added public authorities, institutions, pressure groups and consumers as protagonists of system building, suggesting that circulatory regimes are made and not given, and that systems emerge from competing projects and purposes.

If we consider circulatory regimes as the result of conscious attempts to sta-bilise characteristics such as slope, tributaries, riverbeds and catchment area, then we must identify regime makers: individuals and organisations who try to estab-lish patterns for these characteristics, and to maintain their balance long enough for the regime to fulfil their visions. These regime makers can be highly complex organisations, like big corporations that arrange for their supply of inputs and the transportation of their products. From the middle of the nineteenth century, the German firm BASF has created and maintained a circulatory regime centred on its Ludwigshafen site, on the River Rhine. By ship, train, road and pipeline, tons of oil, coal, pyrites, salt and other components for dyestuffs or fertilisers converged on Ludwigshafen through a fabric of transportation infrastructures, trade agree-ments and business deals minted by an army of firm engineers and managers.[73] Regime makers are not less likely to be simple individuals working though face-to-face interaction in order to create the conditions for their schemes to expand. Souleymane Kanté (1922–87) created the N'Ko alphabet in 1949, which he con-ceived as the first original script for African languages.[74] In order to popularise N'ko among the speakers of Mande languages in West Africa (from Mauritania to Nigeria), Kanté tried several times to convince the authorities of different West African countries to use N'Ko for their alphabetisation policy. But he mostly relied on his own contribution to extend the reach of N'Ko, teaching his script to foreign merchants in public squares, transcribing and translating religious Islamic texts, copying his alphabet by hand, relying on a master–disciples chain to spread the word. Kanté can be said to have been a low-intensity regime maker, as he did not establish a specific organisation for circulating his alphabet. But he grafted N'ko onto the circuit of migration, pilgrimage, trade and religious education in West Africa, as far as Libya or Saudi Arabia.

Whether conducted by individuals or large bureaucratic apparatuses, the mak-ing of circulatory regimes usually results from the cooperation or confrontation of several parties. Many protagonists had a vested interest in the circulation of people and beliefs that constituted and resulted from the pilgrimages of Muslims to Mecca. From roughly the middle of the nineteenth century, they openly vied to make these circulations conform to their interests. Shipping companies tried to attract pilgrims to their routes, English authorities anxiously monitored the presence of the germs of anti-colonial protest as much as of cholera, the Ottoman Empire matched its hajj policy to its pan-Islamic sketches, and the new Saudi dynasty attempted to shape a geography of the pilgrimage in accordance with its own version of Islam. The dif-ferent communities of pilgrims also had their own ideas about what the itineraries of journey and worship should be, according to their place of origin and the cur-rent of Islam they were part of, and the *muallim/mutawwif* (the intermediaries who provided services and guidance to religious visitors) also tried to create patterns that served the interests of their trade.[75] At the intersection of sanitary politics, colonial concerns, political contestation, trade and business interests and the contest for religious orthodoxy, different protagonists confronted each others' views, and it was this confrontation that shaped the circulatory regimes of the pilgrimage.

▶ Conclusion

With the publication of *The Information Society*, and its companion volumes, the name of Manuel Castells and the notion of 'network' became household terms in the humanities and social sciences.[76] They come up almost inevitably in works that try to reconstruct historical movements of people, goods, capital or commitments.[77] This notion of network has not been used here, despite the focus on connections and flows, chiefly because Castells emphatically contrasts the network with other forms of social structure: the state, the army, the apparatuses of religions, bureaucracies 'and their subsidies for production, trade and culture'. According to Castells, these structures are vertical, hierarchic and centralised and power in their midst is characterised by 'one-directional flows of information and resources' in their midst. For Castells, the network society is a product of the 1980s–1990s, and the flows it generates are a challenge to these 'older structures'.[78] It would have been inappropriate to graft Castell's understanding of 'networks' on to an argument that suggests that there are vertical, hierarchic and centralised aspects in the distribution of flows and that the very emergence of 'older structures' was coeval with the development and arrangement of multidirectional flows. Besides, Castells also insists that his 'space of flows', this new arrangement of space and function in our societies, was defined in opposition to an older conception he called the 'space of places', for it rattled and abolished territoriality as a basis for such an arrangement.[79] This contrasts with the idea of 'relocation' that has been placed to the fore in this chapter.

However, Castells also formulates several proposals that are 'good to think' for transnational historians when they try to establish circulatory regimes. For instance, he addresses power holders in networks, whom he characterises as either 'programmers' who align the network operation with their goals, or 'switchers' who are in a position to connect different networks together. He also puts forward another proposition that is very relevant to the conclusion of this chapter. Networks, says Castells, cooperate or compete with each other, and the outcome can be the destruction of a network, by replacement of its interconnected nodes with others, or by substitution of elements transmitted within the network. The relation between networks makes them historical creatures. In their conversation about transnational history, historians invited by the *American Historical Review* asked the question of how the transnational perspective could contribute to the study of change over time, which is no less than how we historians sell our discipline to the public.[80] One of the answers to this question might be that circulations across and through different countries, continents or areas are so important, for their content and their consequences, that the change in their patterns deserves to be studied per se. The rise, demise and adjustments of circulatory regimes would then provide a narrative of change and continuity that would be proper to the transnational perspective.

4 Relations

Connections and circulations are not just worthy of study for themselves. They also create relations between different entities and participants brought together by flows and ties. Relations are the effect or relevance these entities have on and for one another, but they are not an automatic consequence of connections and circulations. It may also happen that connections and circulations come to nothing, in the sense that no change seems to take place in the behaviour of participants. One famous example is the lack of adaptation in military strategy following the Russo-Japanese War of 1905. Despite numerous reports and recommendations by European officers who observed the conflict, there were no major responses in strategic thinking and military equipment in the British, US, French or Austro-Hungarian armies. When the First World War began, they were not ready to cope with hand grenades, trench mortars, barbed wire, field artillery and machine guns.[1] The history of 'lessons unlearned' and of rejections is still mostly waiting in the aisles for the attention of transnational historians: this chapter will instead concentrate on situations where parties involved in ties and flows across polities and societies had their behaviour affected by that participation.

How can we conceive of relations? A wide variety of factors are featured in relations across polities and societies. A relation can be appraised through its intensity, its outcome, or the number of participants and their degree of consent and constraint. According to disciplines and subdisciplines, scholars have characterised relations across polities and communities in relation to these and many other different factors, and assessed their effects under different names. Economic historians juggle with 'integration', 'convergence', 'cycles', specialists of civil society with 'movements', 'alliances', 'waves', international relations historians with 'systems', 'alliances' and 'treaties', historians of religion with 'conversion' or 'syncretism'. Scholars of culture have been especially creative from this point of view, and this chapter starts with their attempts to characterise relations across and through nations, empires or regions.

▶ Characterising relations

In their attempts to follow the impact of US cultural products on Latin American cultural forms during the last two centuries (and before), Latin American social scientists and artists have analysed such processes with the notions of cultural digestion, imperialism, domination, **transculturation**, *mestizaje* and, eventually, hybridity.[2] Each of these notions had a different content, and stressed different aspects of the relations across the hemisphere or across the First World/Third World divide. When the relation was characterised as imperialism, as in Armand Mattelart's work, it was shaped by the iron laws of domination, and its process and results were about reproduction of, or resistance to, the cultural practices and notions that the US hegemon tried to impose on Latin American societies.[3] When it was captured in the sieves of hybridity by Nestor Garcia Canclini, emphasis was on the combinations that occurred between distinct structures and practices and on resulting in-between cultural objects, structures and notions.[4] The social sciences and the humanities being sensitive to political context, these Latin American variations were tied to changes in domestic and international politics between the early 1970s and the late 1990s. But these variations also signal that, historically speaking, relations can rarely be boiled down to pure concepts. Appropriation can take place within relations marked by domination, and domination and reproduction are not absent from relations of interchange. This is why historians have tended to diverge from pure types, as in discussions about the history of the cultural encounter between European societies and the USA. From the lens of 'hegemony', a concept defined by the Italian Marxist Antonio Gramsci to point to the capacity of elites to exercise consented domination of subaltern groups through culture, the characterisation of these encounters incrementally shifted to translation and adaptation.[5]

If we move from the Americas to Europe, 'transfer' is the term that has been most used recently, particularly by modern historians who use it to qualify the relations they observe in culture, technology, public policy history and other domains. The study of *transferts culturels* (cultural transfers), which historians Michel Espagne and Michael Werner put on the map in the 1980s, started from their desire to study the actual mobility of books, authors and ideas between France and Germany from the late eighteenth to the end of the nineteenth century, especially in the disciplines of philology, literature and philosophy. The initial emphasis was on how the differences between two cultural national contexts would inform the emission and reception of authors, notions and texts, and change them according to usages of importing or exporting actors. Thanks to subsequent refinement by its promoters, and also because it spilled out of its original Franco-German test tube, the notion of cultural transfers quickly expanded to encompass processes of appropriation, rejection and translation that could imply more than two national cultural formations, as well as entities that were not subsumed in nations (regions, groups).[6]

Transfers have come to be used as a synonym for the study of what happened between cultures, although other notions were also proposed. The British historian Peter Burke thus argues that 'cultural exchange' is preferable to 'cultural transfer' because of the former's emphasis on encounter.[7] However, he is not that sanguine over distinctions. Concluding a presentation of the various terms that were used to characterise cultural entanglements, he notes that the one usually tends to obscure what the other enhances: electing one notion above the others would then bring more losses than gains.[8] If so, the search for the best characterisation seems to be vain, although each different notion that we have listed adds to the arsenal of transnational historians.

If no single characterisation will do justice to the variety of relations that are generated or created by historical circulations or connections, this chapter has to work around that roadblock. It would be vain to start from stylised notions like cultural transfers or hybridity, to list all types of relations that historians have observed or to propose a typology to classify all relations under 'pure' types. We will instead return to the history of connections and circulations to isolate 'tropes' that can help us consider what the study of relations can contribute to answering the 'big issues' of transnational history. A trope is not a singular example, nor a universal category: it is a part of a relation, of a property, an instance of them. Four tropes will be presented in this chapter. The first is 'dedication', a trope of conversation that places the emphasis on relations where protagonists join together by mutual consent for some mutual benefit or common goal. The second is 'dominance', which touches on the issue of asymmetry and reciprocity between participants in a relation. From there we will move to 'mobilisation', a trope of usage, in which the focus is on how some actors establish a relation where other partners are barely affected at all. The last trope will be 'alignment', a trope of convergence, where all participants are affected by the creation and adoption of a common set of references.

▶ Dedication

During the last decades of the nineteenth century, Victor Joseph Viviand-Morel was the chief gardener at the experimental garden created in the early 1840s by botanist Alexis Jordan in Villeurbanne (France). An important aspect of his work of conducting Jordan's experiments on plants was his active contact with dozens of other botanists in France and beyond for some 30 years. This circle increased when he became the chief editor of the journal *Lyon-Horticole* from 1879.[9] In addition to correspondence, Viviand-Morel published in British journals, taught in Geneva (Switzerland) and contributed to Ellen Willmott's *Genus Rosa*, the bible of twentieth-century rose lovers. He was one of many participants in the circulation of information, specimens and seeds among botanists and other naturalists. In order to do so, he joined scientific societies; attended conferences; subscribed, edited and contributed to specialised journals; corresponded with and visited foreign individuals who shared his passion. None of his correspondents and hosts was compelled to contribute to similar activities: they willingly engaged in the conversation with a sense that their individual participation in the collection and dissemination of horticultural knowledge was beneficial to all gardeners, nurserymen, sellers of seeds, and to themselves as well.

This horticultural snapshot is an episode in the history of circulating knowledge about the natural world. This circulation grew in scope after the world was 'looped' between the late fifteenth and the late sixteenth centuries, and the results of this Great Columbian Exchange are still with us today.[10] What is relevant for this chapter is that, during the eighteenth century, participants increasingly conceived of this relation as a conversation, a mutually consented interpersonal communication that aimed at advancing comprehension of nature: acquaintance and knowledge were then enmeshed in the practice of correspondence.[11] It is under their aegis that this section is placed, because this idea of conversation helps us to focus on relations as a process of dedication to a common goal, although this does not exclude individual objectives. In that relation, the capacity of protagonists to affect or be relevant to one another resulted from what they deliberately offered (or refused to offer) to one another in the pursuit of a common goal: information, things, funds, ideas, commitment of their own person. In order to show how these conversations affected the individuals, groups and places that were included, we will examine political and civic mobilisations before returning to the domain of knowledge.

Political and civic movements start from decisions by individuals to join with others to work for a common cause. The last 200 or so years have seen the multiplication of organisations created to facilitate such work and make it more effective: parties, associations and clubs have flourished to propagate and defend ideas about the organisation of societies and polities. The study of organisations that appeared or operated across and through national polities and societies has long been part of the historians' domain, especially in the case of social and political movements identified with workers (socialist trade unions and organisations), or for other progressive causes like the abolition of slavery or the emancipation of women. Such studies have provided one of the bases for the development of transnational history in the United States of America: Ian Tyrrell based part of his 1991 call for a 'new American international history' on observations he drew from his study of the World's Woman's Christian Temperance Union; Leila Rupp published her article on transnational women's organisations in the *American Historical Review* in 1994; and the *Journal of American History* 'Nation and beyond' special issue (1999) included an article by Kenneth Cmiel on human rights organisations. Yet, it was sociologists, political scientists and anthropologists who took the lead in the historical study of advocacy groups, which they understood as part of an emerging world/ global/ transnational civil society. A growing number of historians have now undertaken original research on international associations, movements and non-governmental associations in the last 200 years or so. One of their findings is of particular interest here because it contributes to our understanding of how much the foreign and the domestic are composite affairs. Studies of movements, organisations and events in which individuals developed a conversation to define and defend a cause across and through national borders have all insisted that these international organisations were working both with and through the national framework, institutions and loyalties. For instance, the presence of the nation could be simultaneously enhanced by the constant presence of national symbols, both in imagery and discourse, accepted as the framework for creating national branches in charge of collecting fees and organising operations, and rejected as opposing the cause and its values. Recent studies of freemasonry have made it very clear that these different takes on the national element were passionately debated by the protagonists themselves.[12] Deciding with whom the conversation was to take place was indeed a crucial matter: it shaped the expansion and operation of the cause when it came to deciding upon the opening of lodges abroad, the creation of ties with masons from other countries, or the incorporation of members from the other side of the colonial – and colour – line. A sociability that was created by and between individuals from different nations thus contributed to the very definition of national differences, and to the definition of nations themselves.

There were other cases where the gathering of energies into a common activity for the advancement of a cause had an even more decisive effect on the making of nations, or on the rise and demise of governments. Well before the age of socialist, communist or anti-colonial movements, the nineteenth century saw conversations by deed, where bodies, monies and weapons were circulated to follow or resist the shocks of the Age of Revolutions. Early in the nineteenth century, the disintegration of the Spanish Empire in Latin America was facilitated by the presence of foreign fighters. Many had solid experience from years of war in Europe, and their reasons for being committed to the Bolivarian cause swung between their revolutionary past and their search for mercenary occupations.[13] Some of these men returned to the Old World to continue the fight far away from the Gulf of Mexico, contributing to one of the earliest causes that developed across and through Europe's national borders: philhellenism. Whether they fought for freedom, the Christians' God or humankind, whether they contributed in blood, kind or cash, a community of supporters emerged throughout Europe and North America to bankroll Greek nationalists during their war of independence against the Ottoman Empire in the 1820s. For most of the century, in fact, southern Europe was a region where the fate of nations had much to do with this kind of conversation by deed. 'National struggles in the nineteenth century were above all an international affair', writes Eric Pécout about the international volunteers who participated in the Italian Risorgimento wars.[14] Events in Mediterranean Europe certainly support his assertion. During Carlist insurrections in Spain and Portugal from 1833 until 1876, or in the various phases of the Italian Risorgimento from the 1840s to the 1860s, foreign volunteers flocked on both sides, out of a sense of friendship and solidarity with like-minded liberal or conservative domestic 'brothers' and with the certitude that these specific insurrections and wars contributed to the advancement of the revolutionary or counter-revolutionary cause in the whole of Europe.

Although there were some secret organisations recruiting men, buying weapons and shipping them to theatres of operations, conversation by deed was not institutionalised in the same way as conversation by words. Many science societies had flourished under the patronage and direction of monarchs in eighteenth-century Europe, but it was in the revolutionary conflation and its aftermath that scientific activities came to be increasingly conducted within institutions that placed their national affiliations at the forefront: 'national societies of...', national museums, national congresses. The development of the research university in the late nineteenth century, and the increased presence of research agencies and centres especially after 1945, impelled the nationalisation of the production of knowledge well beyond Europe. This nationalisation of science did not preclude the continuation of inter-individual conversations across these tighter national domains: travel, correspondence or the exchange of specimens were still part of the scientists' work. When naturalists Cuvier and Valenciennes gathered material at the French Natural History Museum to write their *Natural History of Fish* published in 1830, they borrowed specimens of Japanese fish from the Berlin Natural History museum – some of which were never returned.[15] In the era of 'big science', after 1945, and although the conversation was fraught with competition, different understandings of scientific sociability and nuggets of Cold War politics, molecular biologists Melvin Cohn, Joshua Lederberg, Sol Spiegelman and Jacques Monod flew letters, bacteria strains and experimental results over the Atlantic.[16] These and other circulations resulted in publications, prizes, discoveries and feuds: they contributed to the shaping of reputations, of scientific practices and of results for the different parties involved.

Characteristic of the nineteenth century are new patterns of scientific conversations that begin to emerge as dedicated infrastructures for the circulation of knowledge, conceived to harness the combined forces of science specialisation and nationalisation. The international conference, the international association, the international expedition, the international research laboratory were meant to create appropriate moments and opportunities for scientific conversation across disciplinary, national or political divides.[17] The earliest of these dedicated infrastructures, the international scientific congress, was from its moment of origin squeezed between the discourse of 'universal science' and the rhetoric of 'national scientific schools'. The Belgian polymath Adophe Quételet (1796–1874), astronomer, mathematician, statistician and economist, was the force behind the organisation of two of the earliest international scientific congresses in 1853: a congress of statisticians and a maritime conference. Later, he would write of congresses as moments of collective intelligence where scientists would meet in a spirit of conciliation and fraternity in order to decide common investigations based on uniform methods. To him congresses constituted an attempt to keep the 'eye of science ceaselessly open' all over the planet, a prospect he had had in mind since the early 1820s.[18] But Quételet also conceived of conferences on the basis of national and governmental delegations, and he organised the conferences in Brussels to mark a place on the map for the young little kingdom of Belgium: the latter was to be the coordinator and facilitator of such international undertakings, a national state with an international vocation. International conferences, associations, expeditions and laboratories thrived because they lived on this complementary balance of science as a common endeavour and science as a field for national assertion. These dedicated infrastructures installed a new pace for the presentation of research findings, created the conditions for the institutionalisation of new disciplines, established the reputation of scholars, and validated results on new fronts of theoretical and experimental research, fuelled controversies and fostered a sense of friendship among scientists.[19]

Not that the existence of relations of conversation was a by-product of some universal essence of scientific knowledge. The different participants had an effect on one another not only through cooperation or debate, but because of the ceaseless national rivalry that characterised congresses, expeditions, research centres and associations. They were the arenas where the Olympics of international science were played out, with nations – or blocs of nations – competing for laurels of recognition or trying to catch up, while individuals embraced or resisted that competition.[20] Once again, scientific national 'styles' or schools were defined through the relation across polities and societies.

▶ Domination

The exhibition of humans was a successful commercial enterprise from the early nineteenth century until the Second World War, from the small-scale exploitation of the 'Hottentot Venus' Sawtche in London and Paris to the big touring machines that Buffalo Bill, Barnum or Hagenbeck drove around Europe and North America, with a special mention for the 'native villages' that every international fair and exhibition included until the middle of the twentieth century. Although they sometimes featured inhabitants of peripheral regions of European countries, these shows mostly exhibited peoples from other continents, from the other side of the colour line, or considered to be living beyond the reach of civilisation. These 'human zoos', argue their historians, were the stage where the massive encounter between the West and the rest took place, rather than through actual colonisation itself.[21] They brought the foreign into the domestic, only to crystallise the racial line and the division of the world into civilised and other peoples. They were central in justifying the subjugation of the non-civilised. The crude scenes of racism offered by these shows seem to epitomise a relation of domination, when some participants have total control of what the others could do (including their mobility). However, some of the exhibited people had a labour contract that established mutual obligations, others used the tour to subvert colonial domination and perform rituals that were forbidden at home, several retooled their experience into opportunities to denounce colonialism. Moreover, the exhibitions also aroused criticism in the societies where they took place. All these actions had an impact on the fate of the colonial relation. This does not lessen any of its brutality, but it is a warning that while the relation was massively asymmetrical, there was some reciprocity in the interstices.

This provides the prompt for this section. Most relations studied by transnational historians are asymmetrical. Usually, some participants get more from it than others, and develop sophisticated or brutal methods to affect the behaviour of others. Yet even the most dominant of protagonists can be affected by the relation, beginning with when their plans are deflected by forms of resistance. The indivisibility of the history of the metropolis from that of the colonies has been one of the major arguments made by historians who have, since the late 1980s, re-energised the historiography of the British Empire, and is one of the reasons for the impact of their contribution to the crystallisation of the transnational perspective (see Chapter 1).[22] While they also reconnected with the work of scholars who had insisted on the need to consider the 'colonial relation' as a whole (anthropologists like Georges Balandier or anti-colonial writers such as Frantz Fanon), the historians who convened or were aggregated under the label of 'new imperial history' have played a crucial role in deepening the study of colonial domination. Their work underlines the need for a critical view of asymmetry as the key feature of the colonial relation. For this chapter, it is a clue that our understanding of asymmetry is enhanced when the reciprocal effects of the relation are incorporated in a study.

The history of the relations that joined US governmental and private actors with other participants in the world is rich in asymmetrical situations. While trying to understand the order in circulations and connections, many historians of the twentieth century come forth with the capacity of US actors to shape these relations. US power has chiefly to do with its ability to deploy devices that affect the behaviour of governments and people in foreign countries: advice and guidance in public policies, huge public information programmes and the more or less successful engineering of *coups d'état* when thought to be necessary. Therefore, it is appropriate for this chapter to select one moment of this asymmetrical history in order to identify the elements of reciprocity it may have included. Two recent books offer an opportunity to do so. They deal with relations between the polity and society of the USA and other societies and polities abroad, between the mid-nineteenth and the mid-twentieth centuries. They partly overlap with the period that historians have characterised as 'dominance by design' and 'irresistible empire', when the relation of domination was created by and around technological and cultural products 'Made in the USA'.[23] Both Ian Tyrrell and Kristin Hoganson look for the reciprocity within such an asymmetrical relation.[24]

Tyrrell focuses on attempts by private US citizens and organisations to make the world in their own image through moral uplift campaigns from the 1880s to the 1920s. Most of these individuals and groups were propelled by the desire to spread the Gospel of Protestant Christianity, directly or through its moral and social values, and to alter the beliefs and behaviour of people to be converted and reformed. Yet, when Tyrrell explains how they operated in the field, liaising together to pressure the US authorities for support, he touches upon the effect that these reformers' worldwide network had on American society at home. The domestic organisation of these groups was set up to collect funds, food, pledges and signatures dedicated to foreign work. Missionaries on furlough, and foreign students coming from Christian missions abroad, lectured throughout the USA to inspire male and female students for foreign work or plead for non-denominational 'all around Protestant' initiatives. The narrative of moral reform that was projected abroad was also intended to revitalise a dwindling domestic religious enthusiasm, at a moment when Christian organisations diagnosed a growing secularisation of US society. In addition to this strategic use of the foreign to uplift America, Tyrrell also identifies missionary work that impacted on the domestic scene. Campaigns against alcohol and drugs at home were closely associated with campaigns abroad,[25] while fighting caste in India and lynching in the USA were seen, by a few, as two sides of the same coin. Some dissenters eventually drew on missionary work abroad to question the social and economic conditions of Asian immigrants or black Americans on US territory. Former missionaries themselves turned their eye on the domestic scene after concluding that America and Americans needed moral uplift more than those overseas, or they indicted the formal empire that was taking shape in the Philippines in the early twentieth century. Last but not least, moral reform work brought knowledge of foreign places and culture deep into the life of the average American through the newspapers, magazines, lecture tours, lantern slideshows, exhibitions and poster campaigns that circulated around church halls and religious groups.

This is where Hoganson takes up the study. The contribution of missionaries is one aspect of the travel culture whose rise she charts through touring associations, exhibitions and lecture programmes in women's clubs, because 'armchair travel' is one of her chosen instruments to study the production of US domesticity. She works her way into the homes of America and the cosy atmosphere of domesticity honed by 'native-born, white, middle class to wealthy women' who were, among other things, in charge of the transmission of US patriotic values. Hoganson looks for objects and practices that brought foreignness to interiors (decor, cooking, travel clubs), playing an important role in the assertion of social differences in Main Street America. From the sophisticated Japanese-style cosy corner arranged by a decorator to knick-knack installations drawing on curio shops and pack peddlers' items, from canned chilli and tamales to chutney recipes, Hoganson finds that goods and manners from Europe, Persia, Africa and many other regions of the world penetrated middle-class American parlours at the very time that the world was said to be becoming Americanised. In addition to being enjoyed for their look, taste or feel, these foreign goods and manners also asserted the distinctiveness of these middle-class women: a touch of cosmopolitanism was a token of class, ethnical and civilisational power. These cross-currents produced American domesticity – and thus part of the idea of American national identity – as well as a specific sense of being in the world for the women who collected these goods and enjoyed these practices: the world as a bazaar for consumers, a cosmopolitanism mediated through goods and performances. If we follow the clues laid by Tyrrell, Hoganson and others, asymmetry and reciprocity are not two opposing sides of a coin, but processes that constitute one another. One more reason for historians not to look for pure types of relations.

▶ Mobilisation

Art historians have made great use of the notion of 'influence' to point to stylistic similarities between individual artists, or between local and national ways of painting, sculpting and decorating. Yet, despite early and decided attempts by early nineteenth-century art historians to trace Byzantine artists' travels and works in early medieval Italy, for instance, 'influence' has remained a vague notion. In many exhibitions, catalogues and books of art history, it serves as a hint of formal similarities, rather than a clue for detailed investigation into the dynamic of connections between the minds and hands of creators. The art historian Michael Baxandall indicts the lazy and limited use of the term by art historians writing on individual artists. His 'excursus on influence' stresses that, for artists and groups of artists, claiming to be 'influenced' by an artist, school or work has been a way to locate themselves in a filiation, to rewrite art history and to find a specific place in it.[26] Baxandall does not broach claims of influence that spill across nations or civilisations, or between 'national schools of art'. Yet, claims of being influenced by foreign creators, or of influencing creators abroad, are clear attempts to establish filiations and to claim a specific place and role in the history of art. They are ways to situate a national art (and its practitioners) on a ladder of appraisal that ranks national artistic expression in relation to others, or to subvert national canons by reference to foreign aesthetics. Painting's avant-gardes have been especially good at such mobilisation, for instance in relation to African aesthetics, from Picasso to the surrealists.[27] This example from art history is a clue that the mobilisation of foreign elements is a dynamic process, and that its domestic protagonists expect something from it: something that can change their standing, improve their value, support an assertion they are making as to their own significance and role, or substantiate their claims to have achieved some universal dimension. This also calls our attention to relations that may not affect all the participants in connections and circulations, and to cases where the 'owners' of mobilised elements may not even be aware of the mobilisation. Historians of cultural products, mass consumption, social movements, political ideas, public policies, nation- and state-building have characterised such relations in terms like borrowing, imitation, mimicry, cross-reference, adaptation, and translation. All cases where domestic actors attempt to affect their own situation by the mobilisation of foreign elements.

Historian Vicente Rafael analyses the discursive aspects of Filipino nationalism in his book, *The Promise of the Foreign*.[28] The phrase suggests that transnational historians must attend to the expectations and strategies of those who mobilise foreign elements, to the fact that not all promises are kept, and to the creative misunderstandings that characterise the process of building on the foreign. This section will draw from two contrasting situations to explore these promises. Rafael himself, with a chorus by Benedict Anderson, covers a situation where the mobilisation of foreign elements participates in the struggle for national emancipation from colonial rule.[29] For Rafael, the early generation of Filipino nationalists who contested Spanish domination used the instruments of this domination to frame and propel their discursive offensive in the decades that preceded the revolution of 1896–98. This included translation properly speaking – Spanish plays turned into vernacular theatre – and translation in a figurative sense – Filipino authors taking the structural patterns of Spanish drama, painting or political thought and reformulating them into weapons against the Spanish presence. But it was also the case when they used the Spanish language as the lingua franca of the nationalist movement, valuing its capacity both to address Spanish power and to overcome the multiplicity of languages in the archipelago. Translation, remarks Rafael, was about replacing and appropriating what was foreign. Benedict Anderson reminds us that the promise of the foreign also had practical dimensions for Filipino revolutionary nationalists of the 1890s. They used cities like Brussels, Yokohama or Paris as shelters, and these urban literary and political milieux were used as channels to nourish and publish anti-colonial statements. The Cuban insurrections were especially important to them: they provided an example of a long-lasting unrest, as well as comradeship in the attempt to shake off Spanish domination. Even if weapons proposed by the New York Cuban Bureau of General Information do not seem to have made their way to the Philippines, other Cuban materials did: in 1897, the Cuban constitution was thoroughly plagiarised to produce the first Filipino constitution proclaimed by the insurrection. Even the gaols of Spanish cities, notably in Barcelona, where several Filipinos were kept at different times, had the unintended effect of putting Filipino nationalists in touch with anti-colonial agitators and anarchists from Spain, Italy and Cuba. Last but not least, Anderson underlines that mobilisation often takes place in cascade, and that 'inspiration' and 'model' are eminently dynamic processes. Only one consignment of weapons almost reached the hands of Filipino nationalists – the ship was lost in a typhoon. The Chinese nationalist leader Sun Yat Sen arranged the shipment from Japan in 1899, following his encounter with the exiled Filipino nationalist Mariano Ponce, at a time when the insurrection was fighting the US army. Like other members of the Chinese intelligentsia, Sun Yat Sen had followed the Filipino revolution closely and used it as a resource to conceive of the political situation of China in the world.[30] If Filipino nationalists mobilised foreign resources, they in their turn were mobilised as a resource by other nationalist or anti-colonial movements. For a model to exist, there must be attempts by actors to establish their given situation or trajectory as replicable, as well as desire by others to observe and learn from that situation. Notwithstanding the fact that the resulting 'model' is often itself the result of simultaneous or preceding mobilisations of foreign resources.

Our second case lies at the reputed political opposite of that anti-colonial stance. Marilyn Lake and Henry Reynolds, with supporting argument by Carl Nightingale, have traced the ways that the mobilisation of foreign notions and legislation enabled the maintenance or strengthening of the colour line in different white men's countries and cities across the English-speaking world.[31] The goal of the scholars, activists, politicians, administrators and labour leaders who praised and installed the legal infrastructures of racial segregation and immigration restriction was to strengthen whiteness as a durable feature in their cities, provinces and countries. In the state of Victoria and other states of Australia, in California and British Columbia on the other side of the Pacific, in the South African province of Natal, they constantly introduced elements of foreign situations into the domestic debates they created. This took place during extraordinary conjunctures that were common to these different regions, such as the gold rushes in Victoria and California in the mid nineteenth century, but also during ordinary discussions about urban reform and property markets in Baltimore, where comparison of the USA with Africa was always lurking. Between the mid-nineteenth and the early decades of the twentieth century, race activists read, corresponded and visited one another; they packed their reports, press articles and books with foreign examples; they reviewed and commented on foreign parliamentary reports and publications; they suggested adoption of foreign legislations or devices, and they encouraged their municipal or national co-citizens to emulate the foreign example of 'Sister Republics'. The mobilisation of these foreign references in segregation and immigration activities had several outcomes. First, it provided activists with a general framework to under-stand and reinvigorate racial difference, and with examples of evils faced by other white men's countries. Second, it offered a portfolio of solutions, such as the liter-acy test as a barrier to enfranchisement or immigration. Third, it reassured them that they were marching in the sense of history, and brought a touch of univer-sality to their positions. Taking one another as models, pooling factual evidence and marshalling solutions, the different communities of whiteness activists were comforted in their sense of being right and empowered by a cosmopolitan gram-mar of racial knowledge. With their social and political imagination fuelled by the promise of the foreign, they felt confident that they could install white supremacy at home.

▶ Alignment

A few figures, a handful of characters on magazine pages or computer screens: these meet the eye when reading through the annual *Times Higher Education* or Academic Ranking of World Universities (aka Shanghai Ranking of Universities) reports. The same feeling of innocuousness prevails when browsing Moody's or Standard & Poor's listings of credit ratings. Yet, the first have become the compass for university managers and higher education policy makers in many institutions and countries, and the second are the chosen tool that financial and business actors use to reduce the uncertainty of their money-lending activities – despite their role in the financial crises of 2007 and 2011.[32] Ratings have proliferated in the late twentieth and early twenty-first century, their league lists ranking organisations, institutions, places and individuals. Benchmarking has become a keyword in private and public admin-istration, as well in the conduct of professional careers. The annual 'Quality of Life Survey' carried out by Mercer, a consulting firm, ranks cities worldwide for the use of their corporate clients. The non-governmental organisation Transparency International has a Corruption Perception Index to name and shame national gov-ernments. Even scholars can now look for their names on Thomson Reuters' 'Rising Stars' and other ranking lists, whether they want to bolster their ego or their pay cheque.[33] This rating and ranking work drags our attention to a relation where par-ticipants' behaviour and practices are aligned on some common moorings, which validity is recognised in different polities and societies.

These moorings can be of many different types, and relations of alignment occur under different norms, rules and standards. This applies to intellectual categori-sations (left/right, First/Second/Third World) and tenets of political and social life (international law, the market, the state, human rights); freely agreed standards (International Standardisation Organisation norms) and constraining clauses in contract-style agreements (such as International Monetary Fund conditional lend-ing adjustment policies of the 1980s); cascade effects of legislative innovations in different national legislations (the harmonisation of national legislations on terror-ism after the September 11, 2001 attacks); the supranational construction, diffusion and institutionalisation of norms (as in the European Union); daily life details (clothing and its canons) and massive collective practices (Christian missionary work); short-range relations(Parisian painting as an aesthetic canon for German-speaking artists in the middle decades of the nineteenth century) and long-range ones (the regional or global convergence of prices and wages brought by economic integration); categorisation of objects (the Dewey decimal classification for books) or of non-human life forms (natural classification, classification of diseases).

In all these instances and many others, transnational historians can study both the production and outcome of relations of alignment. The result is not always about uniformisation: a common reference does not preclude difference. Projects of alignment have been debated, disputed, contested, accepted and rejected. Such debates have included proposals for other alignments around other canons. Relations of alignment provide an opportunity to study historical processes of uni-versalisation, whereby something is defined and professed to be valid beyond the space and time where it was created or adopted, and its implementation under-taken in the name of this purported universality. Universalisation as a project can go as far as arguing and implementing a worldwide standard. Large religious, polit-ical and social systems have secreted universals, such as the political and economic standards of development suggested by socialism, communism or liberalism. One such intellectual framework was 'modernisation theory', which framed the per-ception of economic regional and national trajectories, as well as the operation of development policies by European and North American governments in the 1950s and 1960s – and to some extent that of the Soviet Union as well.[34] But firms, profes-sional groups and scientific communities also developed 'minor universals' meant to align production processes, lifestyles, codes of conduct or intellectual frame-works on common guidelines to be adopted regardless of context.[35] To understand alignment, historians need to consider both minor and major universals. To take a contemporary example, this means that the relation of alignment is as much about current efforts by Monsanto and other biotechnology firms to make their genetically modified seeds the only source for farmers worldwide, arguing about protection by global intellectual property rights, as it is about the reconfiguration of capitalism that has presided over the establishment of economic deregulation as a paradigm of public economic policies since the late 1970s. This section elaborates on two projects of universalisation that lie somewhere in-between such minor and major universals.

Firstly, we will deal with the standardisation of space and time that unfolded during the nineteenth century, through the installation of the metric system and standard time zones. At the beginning of the nineteenth century, the kilogram and the metre were young legal standards for weight and length, still edging their way into acceptance in France and the few European countries where they had been transported by revolutionary and Napoleonic wars. Time was still very much a measure derived from astronomical events observed at a given latitude and longitude: every city kept its own time and there was no equivalence between these different times. Today, the metric system and standard time zones rule the daily life of billions of people, and provide them with a common reference when it comes to travel, trade, communication or war. They have been the instruments of a huge alignment operation, and a quite recent one. Such changes are often traced back to seminal international agreements between national governments, like the Metre Convention in 1875 and the International Meridian Conference of 1884. These agreements were important, but they did not design or implement the standards of time and measurement in a snap. They took place after decades of debates and pressure, especially from scientific bodies (geographers, astronomers), business and trade interests, and intense campaigns by supporters who advocated standardisation as a tool of civilisation, bound to strengthen peace and harmony throughout the world. They were also resisted, in the same spheres, by anti-standards activists. By and large, there was no clear fault line between supporters and opponents: railway companies, mariners, scientists and free traders could be found on both sides, and national pride as well as vested interests were involved when it came, for instance, to decide on the meridian for timekeeping and calculating longitude,[36] or to accept that a measurement unit made in France would upset the daily habits and fundamental categories in another country. An important aspect of the agreements was that they established agencies to administer and distribute the standard to countries who would decide to opt in, such as the International Bureau of Weights and Measures, although these agencies never received any power to implement the standard. Adoption remained a matter of domestic policy. Moreover, measurement units themselves were designed after a contentious and non-linear process where uniformity was resisted and negotiated.[37] All the more so in that there were alternative systems in both cases: national and regional measures; rival uniform systems like the imperial measures of the British Empire; counter-proposals to adopt decimal time or to take the anti-Greenwich meridian, in the other hemisphere, as the initial meridian.[38]

It took decades to define, implement and complete standard time and standard units, and as much of the process took place within countries as in the international conferences that were regularly called to adjust, develop or refine the standards. Moreover, the seemingly irresistible uniformity of standards never stopped being tweaked at the margins, at the same pace as their adoption. Time zone boundaries are far from rectilinear and have changed over time, while the introduction of daylight saving time (which began during the First World War) has made it possible for specific communities to alter their 'universal time' coordinates.[39] Other weights and measures are still used in countries that have officially gone metric, as in Canada. Yet the metric system is now the official norm in every country of the world except Liberia, Myanmar, the USA, the Independent State of Samoa, the Federated States of Micronesia, Palau, and the Marshall Islands. The standard time zones system, based on the Greenwich meridian, is simply the uniform way to tell and predict time on our planet. A tonne is a tonne wherever the metric system is in operation, and a simple table of time zones makes it possible to calculate time in distinct and distant places. Standard measurement units seem to epitomise the hypothesis of the German historian Jürgen Osterhammel that the nineteenth century is characterised by 'the compression of the reference grid' in political, religious and cultural matters. Standardisation did not lead to uniformity, but to discussions and variations around a smaller set of common references.[40]

One specialist in metrology epitomised the process when he wrote that 'the creation of universality happened through the circulation of particulars', and that this circulation required much energy from its participants.[41] It can be added, in contrast, that particularisation also takes place though the vernacularisation of universals. However, there is not much we know about the circulations that made alignment possible in the case of the metric system and standard time zones, about the teaching and learning process that was involved, about the social and technical adjustments that had to be found. The historical thickness implied by the 'metrication of the world' is still a story being told.[42] But there are other cases where we can document the circulation of particulars that generated alignment around some purported universal, and the way in which different particulars contended to be defined as universal.

Here, we can rely on the growing body of scholarship on 'Muslim transnationalism' that has developed since the late 1980s, and more specifically on studies of the activities of some renewal and revival groups in South Asia in the twentieth century. All these groups exercise da'wa (the call, the activity of spreading the faith) with a concern for returning Muslim religious rituals and beliefs to a state of original purity, which they feel has been lost because of accommodation to mixed spiritual contexts (Hindu, Buddhist or Christian presence, secularism, materialism). The Deobandis, the Wahhabis, the Ahl-I Hadith, the Tablighi Jama'at are distinct intellectual articulations of faith, especially in their relation to the different textual sources of Islam or in the degree of their rejection of other currents of Islam (chiefly sh'ia Islam and Sufism), but all have frequently shared personnel and religious references. They all support a revival of the original practices of Islam, but also contend with one another over their capacity to speak in the name of this 'genuine' Islam. They carry on preaching activities and welfare work, run clinics, mosques and networks of affiliated religious schools.

Some of these groups were already involved in long-distance relations within the worldwide Muslim community (*umma*) in the 1920s, for instance, the India-based Ahl-I Hadith expressly supported the Saud dynasty when it seized power over the holy city of Mecca. The Daru'l-ulum school of higher religious education in Deobandi, India, was already working between and through polities and communities in the early twentieth century. Yet, it was mostly after the Second World War (for the Tablighi Jama'at created in 1927), or in the 1970s and 1980s (for Wahabbism) that they systematised their outreach beyond their region of origin (respectively India and Saudi Arabia). As a whole, their activity has boomed in the last 40 years, although more difficult times have come after the 9/11 attacks in 2001. In their attempts to align Muslim beliefs, rituals and behaviours in Thailand, India, Indonesia, Malaysia (and beyond), each of them has created specific relations across polities and societies that affect both the people who preach the 'true voice of Islam' and those who are preached it.

The Deobandi school has chosen education to reform Islam, and the principles it established for its eight-year course have been transcribed in a number of affiliated schools throughout the Muslim *umma*, together with the texts it published and the legal decrees (*fatwas*) of its scholars.[43] Here, alignment is pursued through the development of a unified intellectual framework. Wahhabism, especially between the 1970s and the 1990s, was the chosen instrument of Saudi Arabian geopolitical strategy, aiming first at resisting Arab secular socialism and later contesting the claims of the Islamic Republic of Iran to be the only genuine Islamic state. Through governmental channels, religious foundations and international non-governmental organisations, oil money was generously distributed to *salafi* (the followers of the pious ancestors) groups in Indonesia, or to Ahl-I Hadith communities in India or Pakistan. These groups used the money to publish books, audio and video tapes celebrating the tenets of Wahhabism; to build mosques; to create madrasas, and to send the most talented students to Imam Muhammad ibn Sa'ud Islamic University in Riyad or to the Medina Islamic University.[44] Here, the alignment strategy relied on building institutions to take charge of the revival and renewal of faith. Tablighi Jama'at, the last of our groups, began its *da'wa* work in 1927, with an emphasis on the communication of the message through inter-individual contact. Now as then, this happens in preaching tours by teams of two to three persons who criss-cross a specific district. They pay regular visits to every house inhabited by Muslims, open discussion about their practice of Islam, and invite them to come to the mosque to listen to recommendations about the appropriate conduct for true believers. When the Tablighi Jama'at decided to expand its activities into the Indian subcontinent after 1947 and the partition of India and Pakistan, and later among the South Asian diaspora in the countries of the Gulf and in the UK, it did not change its modus operandi. It is through inter-individual interaction that the message of alignment was delivered.[45]

There is a second dimension to the relation of alignment that these groups strive to create, which applies to their own members. Here again, different alignment processes play out. For the Deobandi school, it is the relation between guide and disciple (*shaykh/khalifa*), typical of Sufism, that vouches for the dedication of former graduates to implement the curriculum and spirit of the mother school in their own educational activities abroad. The public statements of Ahl-i 'Hadith groups in Pakistan and India, who were among the major beneficiaries of Saudi largesse, converge in the defence of Saudi Arabia as the one and only true Islamic state and model of an Islamic state. Allegiance is key here, and loyalty towards their Saudi patrons has eclipsed the theological differences that Al-I Hadith scholars used to formulate against Wahhabism.[46] As for Tabligh Jama'at, not only do local chapters work in accordance with instructions from their Indian leadership, but they also engineer a sense of belonging to one and only community of souls and bodies among its missionaries: teams are purposely assembled from a mix of nationalities, and the organisation of Tablighi centres looks remarkably similar across different countries. Here, daily practices transform the self, away from worldly concerns and local roots, and create common norms and values for the true believers.[47]

▶ Conclusion

Even the most distracted of readers may have noted that historical relations between and through polities and communities most often combined the different tropes that have been used to organise this chapter. The mobilisation of foreign resources by anti-colonial or whiteness activists included the dedication to a common cause, and eventually an alignment of sorts when they conceived their activities under common notions and keywords. Likewise, the alignment behind standards may result from the capacity of one partner to affect others: this partner will be able to circulate its particular, and make it a universal, thanks to its domination over other participants. Thus the metric system was introduced under colonial rule in regions controlled by France, Portugal, Spain and the Netherlands, and retained after independence. There are few situations where a single type of relation would adequately capture the way participants affect one another. This is why this chapter was built around tropes instead of types: bits and instances with overlapping manifestations rather than neatly bounded categories with their exclusive examples. Further, many other tropes are used by transnational historians to analyse and narrate the relation they are studying: competition, combination or rejection, which is a key notion of Cemil Aydin's *Politics of Anti-Westernism*, are other possible characterisations that have been encountered in previous chapters. None is more worthy of attention than others, and it is up to historians to place the emphasis on one or the other according to the aspects they privilege within the history of entanglements during the last 200–250 years. If we choose to insist on limits to integration, we would certainly be keen to identify relations of rejection or indifference. If we want to indict the steamroller ability of some large economic and political systems to shape the world in their own image, we should most likely focus on relations of dominance. Our vision of a possible global community would be supported effectively if we marshal evidence of relations of alignment and dedication. In any case, the goal is to establish what connections and circulations do to places, people, institutions, polities and societies that they include or leave out. Transnational historians have many other relations to describe, name, scrutinise and criticise before settling on a limited number of archetypes. Our current focus on binaries such as hybridity/hegemony or competition/cooperation may not be the most appropriate conceptual framework to order relations between and across polities and communities. There is still much to imagine and explore, beginning with the durable or transient formations that are created by these relations. That is where the next chapter takes us.

5 Formations

What are the outcomes of these circulations, connections and the relations they result from or install? What do they generate that historians can study to make sense of the past and the present? Where do combinations of links, flows and relations take place and create entities that historians can examine? What are the observation platforms from which historians can follow the blurred line between the domestic and the foreign, tell the story of historical actors and processes that wax and wane through and between the territorial units that frame our professional common sense? How can we reconstruct the making and unmaking of interdependencies between these units? A few years ago, political scientists Thomas Callaghy, Robert Latham and Ronald Kassimir provided an answer to these different questions. Proclaiming their desire to go beyond binary oppositions that came to frame research on **'globalisation'** in the 1990s (global/local, space of flows/space of places, external/internal), they stated their interest in 'what lies silently between' these binaries: 'the rich kernels of specific junctures joining diverse structures, actors, ideas, practices, and institutions with varying ranges in a common and social political frame'.[1] It is in these kernels and their resulting frames that social power, political outcomes, forms of authority, order and meaning are created and implemented. As instances of such kernels, which later in the book they call 'transboundary formations', they mention the civil war in Uganda, the slave trade system of yesteryear, the traffic of arms and diamonds in African civil wars, the mechanics of African debt or the economics of oil in the Niger Delta.

This chapter retains their definition of 'kernels' and 'formations' as a result of the combination of structures, actors and practices with varying range. It also chimes with their identification of moments, places and activities as the backbone of kernels and formations. In doing so, it follows the concern of several social scientists who study circulations, connections and relations, and try to assess their capacity to generate durable frameworks for human life and action in addition or opposition to national frameworks. They also choose the word 'formation' to designate these frameworks.

Scholars of migration conclude that the in-between activities of migrants took place in and created 'transnational social formations'.[2] Drawing on French sociologist Pierre Bourdieu's vocabulary, others propose that research on transnational phenomena needs to define its own unit of study when the national container is irrelevant. They offer the idea of 'transnational social field' as 'a set of multiple interlocking networks of social relationships through which ideas, practices and resources are unequally exchanged, organized, and transformed'.[3] Historians also look for the units and containers where they would be able to both observe and appraise the entanglements they were studying. Mrinalini Sinah, one of the contributors to the 'new imperial history', uses the term 'imperial social formation' as the analytic tool that allows her to hold together disjointed places (India and Britain) and themes (politics, ideology, economy).[4] Ann Laura Stoler and Carole McGranahan, building on the notion of social formations elaborated by Marxist scholars in the 1970s, as complex wholes encompassing political, ideological and economic practices, speak of 'imperial formations' to hold together disjointed elements, tendencies and changing configurations within the history of empires.[5] This chapter partakes in that spirit of holding together elements that are often disjointed, in order to observe and analyse the origin, operation and effects of circulations, connections and relations in the last 200 years or so.

In the earlier chapters, we have walked into many formations and types of formation, from tiny objects like the Berne key to planetary envelopes such as the system of atmospheric winds. Again, no list or typology would do justice to this diversity and it seems wiser in this chapter to present a range of options that can trigger reflection. I have chosen five instances of formations, some of which are familiar frames that historians use to navigate the past and tell their stories. We will first deal with possibly the smallest human formation that can be imagined, the self. As a counterweight to this emphasis on the individual, we will then move to the organisation as a collective entity. Our third sort will be similar to many of those proposed by Callaghy and his colleagues: a 'topical region'. We will end with the staple fodder of historians: the event and the territory. In each instance, we will linger on one selected work after a general presentation.

▶ The self

Single objects and individuals have shown up several times in previous chapters, through their roles in creating connections, launching and severing circulations, generating relations, or as embodiments of these different processes. Here, it is the inner aspect of the individual human being, the self, that will be treated as a 'kernel of junctures'. How is the self affected when personal trajectories straddle different social, political and cultural communities? How do such situations spawn opportunities or constraints for continuity or reinvention of the self? Are there typical 'transnational selves' produced by the lives of those who worked as connectors, were carried away by circulations or performed relations? We can begin with an observation: the question of the self, as a person's essential and unique identity, has itself been the subject of usage, conversations and disputes across borders. The history of the disciplines devoted to the exploration and remediation of the self testifies to this. For a long time, most supporters and practitioners of psychoanalysis considered that their discipline and its concepts were universal. This curative knowledge of the self has been projected and appropriated across polities and societies since the days of Sigmund Freud.[6] More recently, voices have emerged to contest that view: some ethnopsychiatrists have been defending the view that migrants' mental health problems, partly a result of the tension between identity and displacement, were to be addressed through the words and knowledge of the culture of origin.[7] These discussions point to a key issue that has been relentlessly explored by many scholars and intellectuals who have studied the consequences of entanglements upon self-perception. Drawing on W.E.B. Du Bois' notion of 'double consciousness' for US black Americans, on sociologist Abdelmalek Sayad's analysis of the migrant condition as characterised by 'double absence', or on Ashis Nandy and Frantz Fanon's understanding of alienation and the 'enemy within' both the colonised and former-colonised, they chiefly tried to understand or conceptualise the effects of these entanglements on perception and construction of the self in terms of conflicting, split social and psychic identities.[8] Many scholars of migrations, slavery and colonialism thus depicted the 'twoness' of the self, and this can be one of the starting points for transnational historians.

'I only wish I had a home on this globe', once wrote the American Mary Eddy (1864–1923).[9] The citation is from a letter she wrote in 1916, when she lost her eyesight and was confined to a home for incurables in Washington, DC. That was a dreadful moment for Eddy, not only because of the resulting isolation from the outside world, but because she had spent most of her life as a medical doctor in Syria. She was born there of missionary parents, and was one of those second-generation missionaries who were brought up in the local language and tailored their activities to context in order to propagate the Christian faith. Mary Eddy's first and foremost commitment was clearly to spread the Bible and distribute the religious tracts of the Presbyterian Board of Foreign Missions. She chose to be a medical doctor to do so, and for some ten years she provided eye treatment and surgery to women in remote villages and camps of the Ottoman province of Syria (now Syria, Palestine, Lebanon, Israel and Jordan). The different aspects of her activities required her to operate between and across the limits of Syria and the United States, Beirut and Boston. The education of a missionary's child, the life of a missionary and the training of a doctor involved many stints in the USA: study periods in high school or university, furloughs which involved a lot of liaison work with donors, medical treatments for her own failing health. On the other hand, being a medical doctor in the Ottoman Empire was not possible without interaction with the Ottoman authorities and colleagues. Miss Eddy had to get her degree acknowledged by a special committee, and later she would create a sanatorium in partnership with a Syrian medicine professor. Eventually, her work in Syria was only possible with the financial backup of American supporters, and Syria and its Muslim inhabitants were the foundation of the sense of Christian mission that imbued her life. Eddy's distress during her confinement in Washington showed how much her sense of identity and her affects were shaped by this life experience. A friend wrote in 1920 that 'her thoughts were entangled with Syria', and we know she wondered where was the place she could call home. Miss Eddy was eventually taken back to Beirut by her sister, and died there. The tensions of her existence were captured by an obituary written in Arabic for a Beirut-based women's magazine by a Syrian woman who received her education in a Protestant missionary college in Syria. She praised Eddy as a 'patriotic Syrian'. In her own conscience as well as in the perceptions of those who celebrated her (the erection of a statue was even suggested), Miss Eddy was an American missionary whose home on this globe was, eventually, Syria.

Just as anthropologists and ethnologists of migrations are making increasing use of the biographical approach to retrace trajectories of migrants,[10] historians have chosen the prism of the individual to talk about entanglements in the last 200 or so years. This has led some of them to take their distance from twoness, and to underline the multiplicity of strands and layers that contribute to the formation of selves and to the uniqueness of the individuals whose story they are telling. Collectively, the contributors to a recent volume on *Transnational Lives* suggest that participating in circulations, connections and relations can give rise to distinct configurations of the self: some itinerants eventually felt their identity to be that of cosmopolitan dwellers, others maintained a sense of themselves as coming from one very specific place and following a very peculiar trajectory; some rejected a previous version of their selves by exploiting the opportunities of displacement, and others were deprived of their self-esteem and perception by the same displacement.[11] For the historian, it is one of the appeals of the self as a formation that it can help us to capture all these different possibilities and constraints generated by entanglements.

This also underlines the promise of the biography as a narrative framework, because it retraces how individuals come to terms with these opportunities and constraints to make sense of the entanglements that challenge their imagination and beliefs. It does not mean, though, that writing about the self as a formation across and between societies is an easy task: this takes historians out of their comfort zone, upsets publishers as to which national market the book is addressed, and forces scholars and students to read outside their national box and field of interest.[12] Eventually, it may lead historians to write 'heterographies' where what is at stake is not so much to approach the authenticity and agency of the self, as perceived by the subjects of biographies, but their capacity or incapacity to assemble, inhabit and use different selves according to interactions.[13] The results are nonetheless worth the effort as shown by Roger Levine's book on Jan Tzatzoe, whom we encountered in Chapter 2.[14] Thanks to his attention to how Tzatzoe defined him-self and how others defined his identity (his Xhosa brethren, missionaries, British defenders of aboriginals), Levine can balance his capacity to perform his self as an intermediary living in-between and through polities and societies, and the con-straints that, later in time, compel him to don the identity of a faithful subject of the empire in order to survive.

▶ The organisation

Over the course of the last 200 or so years, many structures have been cre-ated to define and perform the tasks involved by connections, circulations and interactions. In the North Atlantic world, some even saw the organisation as an indispensable tool of modern life. It was a leitmotiv for the French social theorist Henri de Saint-Simon when he mused on the future of human society in the early nineteenth century, and journalist William H. Whyte considered organisations and their corporate collectivist ethos as the backbone of mid-twentieth-century USA.[15] Firms, churches, associations and clubs, official intergovernmental organ-isations and journals were established with enthusiasm to prevent, create and maintain activities across and between political and imagined territories. Some of these organisations lived for decades, reinventing themselves under new avatars on different occasions, other disappeared very quickly having succeeded or failed to serve their goals; most remained sketches and dreams. When historians and social scientists paid attention to the study of organisations that served faith, power, revolution, science or the market, they have understandably focused on their programmes, statements and achievements at the expense of their performance as formations. This becomes quite clear in the scholarship about international intergovernmental and non-governmental organisations.

We are far from having a clear idea of the functioning of organisations which were explicitly created to work between and across polities in the last 200 years: the societies and movements that began to organise in the first half of the nine-teenth century, the international unions and bureaux that flourished in the last decades of the nineteenth century, the intergovernmental organisations established by the Treaty of Versailles. The historiography of the League of Nations, the key-stone of the Versailles system, has long been limited to a discussion of the League's capacity to preserve peace and prevent war. Only recently have historians begun to scrutinise systematically its role in defining and implementing rules and stan-dards in different fields, the composition of its personnel, the working process of its apparatus.[16] From that point of view, historians have much to gain from integrating the questions and findings of political scientists and international relations scholars who returned earlier to the study of international intergovernmental organisations, armed with new questions that went beyond might, war and peace.[17] Transnational historians, to answer their own big issues, need to consider these organisations' ability to work between and through different countries, continents or cultures, and their attempts to create common projects, behaviour or norms that weaved distinct and distant societies together.

The history of the Rockefeller Foundation is of special interest from this point of view. It was established in 1913 and became the flagship of the different 'philanthropic' boards created by John D. Rockefeller Senior, his son John D. Rockefeller Jr, and their advisors. For its founder, the creator of Standard Oil, the foundation and his other charities were seen as reciprocation for his God-given money-making gift as well as a magical instrument enabling him to be to be both immensely rich and immensely virtuous by giving away part of the largest fortune of his time. The establishment of the biggest-ever charitable trust was also his most cunning attempt to redeem the public reputation of 'tainted money' attached to the name of Rockefeller as a ruthless promoter of industrial monopoly. The foundation's mission statement was to 'promote the well-being of mankind throughout the world'. Under the supervision of hand-picked trustees, a staff of officers designed and administered this trust in 'scientific giving' with an initial focus on health and social welfare. This scope expanded, and there have been few fields, topics or countries that the foundation has left untouched by its grants to institutions and individuals between 1913 and the present day.[18] The foundation developed its programmes in particular in matters of higher education and scientific research. It supported, created and oriented flows of scholars, monies, scientific literature, concepts and organisation schemes, with a distinct primacy until the 1950s when the Ford Foundation created an even larger international programme.

Despite a radical divergence of interpretation between, on the one hand, scholars who see the Rockefeller Foundation as a cog in a machine designed to make the world safe for a capitalist society, and, on the other, those who celebrate its disinterested goals,[19] the existing literature provides a rich if indirect account of how the foundation has worked. It shows the foundation itself as a formation, a common frame where actors, ideas, structures and levels with varying range came together. This is manifest in the foundation's activities in the first place. The Rockefeller Foundation financed the creation of development research and higher education institutions in many places throughout the world, from the London School of Economics (UK) to the University of Ibadan (Nigeria), and encouraged these institutions to operate as research and training platforms for students and scholars from different national or regional origins. It supported or fostered communities of scholars who shared instruments, methods and visions across national borders in new disciplines or interdisciplinary arrangements (like **area studies**). It organised the alignment of research programmes and education curricula in many different universities belonging to different national systems (for instance with the introduction of laboratory work and a full-time professorship in medical education in the early 20th century). It circulated people and ideas through fellowship programmes that sent, all disciplines included, more than 10,000 individuals from dozens of countries for advanced training and research abroad. On most of these occasions, the foundation cooperated with universities, with national and international professional and scientific associations, with national governments and local authorities. In some regions, especially in Latin America, its action was connected to that of the American federal government and with the interests of Rockefeller business, but it did not merely conflate both: depending on conditions, the foundation operated as a freelance, a pilot fish, a spur, a logistical platform or a follow-up squad in relation to the policies of these two entities. It was a regime maker on its own.

Whereas study of the Rockefeller Foundation and its activities have long been based on its reports, statements and designs, recent studies of the programmes of the foundation have increasingly used the 'grassroots' documents generated by the programme officers who contributed to its daily work, and incorporated the material from the 'receiving end', individuals and institutions who sought, received or refused its help. Latin American scholars have been especially important in the study of the nitty-gritty of the foundation's activities.[20] They have shown that its action was not merely about the imposition of the 'American way'. The projects it supported were largely co-produced by their beneficiaries in conjunction with the local advisors and the permanent or travelling foundation officers installed in South America, Europe and Asia. Moreover, and especially during its first decades of activity, many aspects of the foundation's tenets, such as support for research universities or for preventive medicine, had been elaborated from preliminary observation of conditions abroad (notably in Germany). The geographical range of the foundation's foreign work should not obscure the fact that an important part of its activities took place within the USA itself, and relied on an appropriation of foreign methods, notions and personnel which culminated in the assistance into exile of European intellectuals and artists between the two world wars.[21] In its international activities, the foundation often promoted a composite product which, although stamped with a 'Made in America' label, was ready to be understood, appreciated and appropriated elsewhere. The foundation has been a formation in its own right in its organisational aspects as well. Research on these aspects is growing slowly, as witnessed by attention to the social and professional trajectories of the officers of the foundation and their work. It was not uncommon for these officers, who sometimes spent a long time on location, to end up being as much the informers and accomplices of their local partners as the voice of the New York headquarters.[22] Anne-Emmanuelle Birn, who studied the Mexican activities of the foundation, captured it as a formation when she wrote: 'perhaps uniquely in the first half of the twentieth century the Rockefeller Foundation was at once a national, bilateral, multilateral, international and transnational agency'.[23]

The foundation indeed worked across what we usually see as distinct and nested levels, and appears as a formation where interactions, connections and circulations were generated and where they can be studied.

▶ The topical region

Consider a book that includes many tables about such exciting topics as the number of pigs in the Western world from 1913 to 1938; global meat output between 1955 and 1999; the tonnes of beef, mutton and lamb exported from Argentina; or the trading results of cattle companies and *frigorificos* (slaughtering and refrigeration firms) between the late 1920s and the late 1930s. Few non-economic historians are likely to be entranced by the prospect of going through these tables. But those who are keen to write history in a transnational perspective should. They are included in Richard Perren's volume, which works on the three fronts of transnational history. Perren shows that the meat industry created very strong interdependencies between urban US and British meat markets and the producing regions of Argentina, Uruguay, New Zealand and Australia, with food chains well in place at the end of the nineteenth century. He identifies robust and durable actors who operated across continents in the form of meat firms capable of controlling the whole process from production to consumption. He puts in plain sight how difficult it is to identify what was foreign and domestic in the fate of Latin American cattle born from a Shorthorn or Hereford line imported from England via the United States or Canada, raised in Argentina, processed in a Uruguayan factory operating under German patents and British capital, and shipped to Europe or North America for consumption.[24] Perren is just one among many business and economic historians who retrace trajectories of products, sectors or markets that have thrived in-between and through national economic domains during the last 200 years.

It is not only economic historians who have explored topical regions in order to see what entanglements they created and resulted from. Pascale Casanova thus offers an interpretation of the modern 'republic of letters' that was ruled by a nexus of critics, publishers and literary institutions mostly based in Paris, France, from the late nineteenth to the middle of the twentieth century. They established themselves as gatekeepers of the domain of literature, and played a huge role in defining and implementing the canons in these matters (canons that applied to the evaluation of works and of writers themselves).[25] She suggests that this Parisian nexus, which worked as a 'Greenwich meridian' to appraise literary creations from the world, did much to create a literary field between and through countries, considered as a space where literary rivalries and struggles would play out to establish a hierarchy of genres, authors and national literatures. This had a direct impact on what books were read, translated and sold. Matthew Connelly, in his study of population control policies, their protagonists and their impact, likewise shows this topic to be a formation where actors and institutions of different ranges operated in conjunction and disjunction.[26] In the early twentieth century, it was cooperation and emulation that promoted the success of eugenics in the North Atlantic region, based on the agreement that the white race could and should be improved. From the 1950s onwards, huge flows of foreign aid, technical advisors and world views were funnelled to Asia through massive campaigns. The purpose was to defuse the 'population bomb' and promote the reduction of fertility rates, under the leadership of international governmental and non-governmental organisations – including the Rockefeller Foundation – later backed up by national governments in North America and Europe. However, the national governments that accepted this influx of ideas, people and funds also tweaked the endeavour to their own ends, in order to shape the fate of their newly independent countries. The 'population establishment' and the formation it had brought to life disintegrated in the 1970s, a reminder that there is no irreversible and irresistible trend towards a global level of policies. Connelly and Casanova offer two instances of how a topical formation can be approached and scrutinised based on first-hand research. In so doing, they add another facet to the distinction between transnational history and **world history**.[27] With the latter, the topical region is there from the beginning. Religion, disease, empire, war: world history picks up a 'universal' topic to compare it across time and space through synthesis of an impressive amount of existing research. Transnational history 's topical regions take their cue from the disputes and agreements of historical protagonists, and relies on clues from archives, printed material, interviews and other primary sources.

This does not mean, though, that synthesis cannot be written in a transnational perspective. Taking us back to business history, the selected work of this section shows how to blend original research and second-hand synthesis to write about a topical formation. *Global Electrification. Multinational Enterprise and International Finance in the History of Light and Power, 1878–2007* is not a juxtaposition of histories of electric utility firms in different countries, although it includes a lot of material comparing local or national situations.[28] Rather, it follows enterprises (manufacturers of electric equipment, electricity suppliers, banks, engineering firms) everywhere they contributed to spreading electrification, in distant and distinct cities and countries in most regions of the world. The book is quite an achievement for two other reasons. Firstly, for its authorship. It is penned by three authors who are familiar with original historical material, being specialists in the history of foreign investment, of multinational enterprises and of the electric industries. But, the different chapters also include large contributions of a core group of 11 researchers completed by advice and information provided by some dozens of other historians, all seasoned archive and print material combers. The result offers an interesting way of handling original material and research literature through many different countries and languages without falling into a series of case studies.[29] Secondly, the volume is a systematic attempt to retrace the history of electrification as a formation through the identification of the actors, direction and dynamics that oriented circulating capital and technologies. It reconstructs the conduits 'through which capital, technology and knowledge are moved over borders',[30] and insists on the patterns of interaction across time. Regarding the former, it shows how the capital-intensive dimension of the utilities sector initially created propitious conditions for multinational corporations, and lists the big players that oriented the sector through competition or cooperation, from electric utilities firms to business and financial intermediaries. The initiative and role of freelance engineers, lawyers and municipalities are not downplayed, and they are identified as an important cross-section of the clusters that steered electrification. Regarding patterns of interaction, *Global Electrification* establishes the role of multinational enterprises in the generation and supply of electricity from the 1870s to the 1940s, through foreign direct investment, free-standing companies or financial participation in domestic firms, followed by a period where interdependencies and interconnections were unmade as national capital and national governments outplayed foreign investment, ownership and control. From the late 1980s, international direct investment resumed following the frequent national deregulation of the utilities sector. The volume also refines the identification of the actors. Thus multinational enterprises that conducted electrification between 1878 and 1945 mostly consisted of public utility holding companies, which controlled capital and patents, whereas the return of multinational enterprises into that sector since the late 1980s has taken place under the guise of operating companies.

The book clearly explains that electrification has been a sector where domestic and foreign factors are hard to distinguish: despite many attempts by public authorities to tame foreign ownership and control of the utilities, the free-standing companies shattered that distinction in a number of ways. Societies created by Britons and registered in Canada would operate in Latin American cities, hiring US engineers and installing US equipment, to be taken over by German capital without any alteration of this set-up. Last but not least, the authors dig deep into the mechanisms of the internationalisation of the electricity sector: it was not brought about as much by firms that started business at home and then extended business abroad, as by firms that were created in order to work abroad without any domestic operations. Although the authors do not use the term 'transnational', they do bring answers to all the big issues of transnational history, and their study is an example of the way a topical formation can be scrutinised.

▶ The event

In order to fix the excitement of a day at the Pan-African Festival in Algiers, filmmaker William Klein chose to reconstruct 22 July 1969 in his documentary film.

This former US soldier, who settled in France after the end of the Second World War, captured the festival's atmosphere from many angles relevant to transnational history.[31] The festival was a major public demonstration of the role the Algerian government wanted to play as a vanguard of African anti-colonial activism since independence in 1962 (although a military coup had begun to turn the tables in 1965). In its capital city of Algiers, a sanctuary for African and Third World guerrilla groups and other organisations, it demonstrated the cultural vitality of a continent during a 12-day event that included art performances, debates, lectures and conferences. Mobilising the national repertory of flags, costumes, drama and dance, a number of delegations of Africa's newly independent countries – and of guerrilla movements – rubbed shoulders, celebrated their emancipation and protested against imperialism. The festival also advocated the existence of a pan-African common culture, epitomised in the spoken and musical discourse of US saxophonist Archie Shepp and his quintet when they played on stage with Algerian/Tuareg musicians. But the festival was not only a celebration, it was also a political event that staged multiple confrontations and debates across lines of difference: was pan-Africanism a project for people of black descent or for all those who experienced European colonialism? Was *negritude*, the cultural and political attitude advocated by Aimé Césaire and the then President of Senegal Léopold Sedar Senghor, just a reactionary stance to be overwhelmed by a Marxist and revolutionary conception of the African political future? Were topless sub-Saharan dancers compatible with veiled Algerian women who watched their performance in the streets of Algiers? Was the US Black Panther Party, whose representatives were in attendance, to shift its position from Black Afro-North American nationalism to pan-African revolutionary solidarity? Be that as it may, in the years that followed, memories of Algiers provided many individuals and groups with a vision of what pan-African solidarity meant.

On the eve of the day, another event had embodied a different set of entangled designs, hopes and dreams. There was no actual cheering crowd, but many people remember (or think they remember) sitting in front of their radio or television for live transmission of US astronaut Neil Armstrong's landing on the Moon, on 20 July 1969. Up there, three men concentrated millions of eyes and ears for a brief moment, and marked a turning point in the race to space that had mobilised US and Soviet scientists. Down here in Algiers, a buoyant swirl of performances and declarations carried away those in attendance, and for some it also marked the advent of a new world. In both cases, a moment in time functioned as a site, cause and consequence of circulations, connections and relations. Many other chunks of time have had such a role, and the Algiers festival points us to a number of thematic events in the domain of culture, such as music, cinema and theatre festivals, as well as arts or book fairs, which so far have received none of the attention that historical research has given to world fairs.[32] When one thinks about events as formations in the sense of this chapter, it is probably political upheavals and the years sub-suming their happening that come to mind, and which have received most of the historian's consideration. The Haitian revolution of 1804, the 1848 European revolutionary wave, the Tai Ping Rebellion of 1851, the 1968 protests from Mexico to Belfast, the Eastern European popular movements of 1989 have all been the object of recent works that scrutinise these events as causes and consequences of joint or convergent political mobilisation across distinct and distant places, and recognise them as sites that generated appropriation of foreign elements, projection abroad and some intervention by alien countries, organisations and individuals into the domestic. The 'Age of Revolutions' that extended from the late eighteenth to the mid-nineteenth century is now, again, also read in that perspective,[33] just like the 'Arab Spring' of 2011 will probably attract the attention of transnational historians in the years to come. In order to underline the way in which events may result from arrangements of a number of ideas, actors and stakes that come from between and across nations, continents or regions, this section will emphasise a kind of event known primarily for its capacity to break ties, hinder flows and limit interactions. War.

War, which transforms borders into front lines, blocks trade and migration, anni-hilates cultural exchanges and tears asunder cross-border communities. At least at first sight. Economic historians have thus had few doubts: the wars of the first half of the twentieth century brought **globalisation** to a halt when considered from the point of view of trade or income and wage convergence.[34] War then, would be the nations' last laugh, the great severer. Yet, wars between and within polities have also been creative moments when it comes to connections, circulations and rela-tions. In terms of trade and production, wars not only destroyed but also reoriented or reallocated. Cacao became a rare commodity in Europe in the aftermath of the rebellions against Spanish authority in the early nineteenth century: war stopped the flow and consumption fell.[35] But the American Civil War, far from shattering the international political economy of cotton, reconfigured its growing trade and manufacturing geography by a cascade of new constraints and possibilities.[36] The economic argument can be expanded to other spheres. The West African jihads, which started in the last decades of the sixteenth century but gained new impetus with the Fulani jihads of the early nineteenth century, entailed a multiplication of Islamic education centres within the new Fulani empire, favoured the circulation of the mystical and jurisprudential production of Sufi orders, and created new incen-tives for the Mecca pilgrimage that triggered direct contact with Sufi intellectuals in North Africa and Arabia.[37]

What we see as major milestones of twentieth-century history, the two world wars, generated their 'own' flows of special migrants across nations and continents: exiled groups and individuals, colonial and foreign contract workers, forced work-ers, prisoners of war, displaced persons, troops of occupation, refugee children and war brides. Warfare itself created clusters of ties and flows in different sectors than those in peacetime, as allied countries coordinated logistics, strategic command and weaponry in patterns that involved knowledge, human and capital flows. This was notwithstanding the deployment of huge amounts of cross-border espionage and counter- intelligence to learn about war plans and weapons.[38]

Following wars, the human losses created enduring common commemorations, sites and rituals of mourning and outrage, as well as touchstones for political mobilisations of former veterans. As with the massive reconstruction programmes supported by foreign aid, from post-1918 Belgium to Afghanistan in the 2000s, the destruction of war entailed many connections, circulations and relations. Even the end of actual wars did not mean that all these displacements and relations came to a halt. Remember that one of the earliest academic applications of the term 'transnational' was when the German jurist Max Gutzwiller used it to designate the kind of law that was created and used by the 40 or so permanent mixed arbitration tribunals created after the First World War. These tribunals handled claims of individuals against the Central Powers, mostly investment disputes. Of these bilateral tribunals, the only German–American tribunal examined 13,000 cases. Post-war alliances install durable relations: the history of the North Atlantic Treaty Organisation (NATO) and of the Warsaw Pact is about war plans and strategic coordination within the alliances, and about cross-observation between them,[39] but the expected 'interoperability' of armed forces also gave rise to more trivial details. Since 1951, the Military Standardisation Agency – now the NATO Standardisation Agency – has established more than 2000 standardisation agreements, from combat protocols and map markings to ammunition and air-to-air refuelling procedures. In many aspects, wars are a highly relevant event for transnational historians.

Our chosen case is a very special war, one that did not speak its name for a long time. From 1954 to 1962, and many years after the final settlement, the Algerian War of Independence was called the 'war without a name' in France. Successive French governments defined it as a security enforcement operation, and strove to keep it a strictly internal affair. In contrast, Matthew Connelly unravelled in detail how much the Algerian War of Independence was a result and source of multiple entanglements between countries, regions and political sides.[40] This applies to its causes, with challenges to colonial subordination that came from the mobilisation of overseas energy during the war and the accompanying (unkept) promises of emancipation. It also covers the abundance of different parties who participated directly or indirectly in the war itself: it involved many other protagonists than the French army and the Algerian fighters through economic, military and propaganda assistance or pressure (notably governments from Tunisia, Morocco, Egypt, the USA and communist China, but also the Arab League and the International Red Cross and Red Crescent). Above all, Connelly insists on the very early decision (1948) by the Algerian Liberation Front to internationalise the fight for national independence. The aim was to consolidate their cause with that of North African unity on the one hand, and with the general fight against colonialism on the other. In international arenas like the United Nations, UNESCO, the Bandung conference of non-aligned countries or youth organisation congresses, and with the help of press conferences, radio programmes and film documentaries, the Algerian insurrection was placed before the eyes of the world. In spite of their attempts to keep the Algerian question a national affair, the French authorities eventually contributed to this internationalisation as they launched counter-propaganda in the same arenas and with the same tools, including their attempt to sell the Algerian conflict as a clash of civilisations between Europe and the Muslim world.

After independence in 1962, the Algerian War did not cease to be a focal point for activities across national lines. In international law, it became an important element in the evaluation of situations of autodetermination. In international relations, the Algerian government built on the war's prestige to establish and maintain its clout, as it supported and nurtured national liberation movements in Africa and beyond.[41] This role of vanguard of the Third World was given additional appeal when Frantz Fanon's *Wretched of the Earth* became a standard of anti-colonial literature. Fanon (1925–61), who had been a spokesperson for the Algerian Provisional Government with a special mission to sub-Saharan Africa, contributed to establishing the Algerian War as a major common reference for imperialism's foes. It became one of those wars that captured the imagination of anti-colonial nationalists in many different places in Asia or Africa, after the Aceh wars of the late nineteenth century and the 1905 victory of Japan over Russia.[42] On that front, too, war triggered links, flows and relations well after the battle stopped.

▶ The territory

Another aspect of war is that it often changes the national affiliation of spaces. Tracts of lands, entire cities, whole regions are transferred from one country to another following a defeat or a victory. Some effects of this translation are highly relevant for transnational historians. Reaffiliations have deep effects on the different territories involved, because they revamp ties, flows and relations. Post-war territorial reallocations have generated enduring irredentism in the country whose territory is diminished by the treaty; exile or return for the inhabitants of the said cities or regions; and a burden of social, political and legal problems in the country which gains new territory. These effects were all the more important as the wars of the last 200 years involved countries that defined themselves as national states, that strived to tighten the rights and duties of their citizens, and to increase the national uniformity of norms and rules. Historians have unpacked such formations in different instances.[43] The case of Alsace-Lorraine, a region that moved between

France and Germany on four occasions between 1871 and 1945, exemplifies the ways in which such territories could become places in-between different countries. This was most conspicuous between 1918 and 1939, when Alsace-Lorraine enjoyed a special status within the French republic in terms of labour, religious, welfare and education public policies and legislation. This status was a mix of pre-1871 French legislation that had been maintained by the German authorities, and of rules introduced in the framework of the German Reich between 1871 and 1918. Not only has the region kept this specific body of legislation until the present day, down to minor domains such as hunting regulations, but this peculiar regional legislation acted as a spur and challenge to public policies in France during the inter-war period.

Some territories have emerged as sites and outcomes of entanglements in less exceptional circumstances. It has been mentioned several times in this volume that countries themselves were formations of that type, and the argument has been made forcefully in the recent historiography of Germany or the USA. Cities are another type of territory that historians have read as a formation. Cities are formations in the sense that they have operated as stations of transport, trade emporiums, commanding places of the economy, gateways and destinations for migrants, cultural capitals or centres of revolutionary activities. Historians have paid attention to these different aspects separately, and we have met with several of these in earlier chapters. Beware that not only large cities, big ports and border towns deserve to be read as formations, though. Neighbourhoods, small towns, even villages can be formations in their own right. The small villages of the Swiss Jura, because they were the chosen retreat of the anarchist Bakounin and his followers in the 1860s, functioned as hubs of political activity.[44] The oil and ceresin boom towns of Austrian Galicia attracted European-wide labour and capital in the 1860s.[45] The industrial towns created by the outsourcing of industrial production from Europe and the United States since the middle of the nineteenth century, were formations whose importance did not match their size. Such were the many *saladeros* (salteries) along the Uruguay River, especially that of Fray Bentos with its giant slaughterhouse, processing factory and refrigeration installations. Between the late 1860s and the early 1970s, it was through Fray Bentos that foreign technologies, workforces and urban lifestyles made their way to that part of Uruguay in order to produce Liebig meat extract, more familiar to British consumers as Oxo.[46] The British meat chains had their origins in Fray Bentos and similar beef towns.

The interest in cities, and especially cities of transit and trade, has led to the attempt to replace them in the context of maritime regions. In his *Nouvelle Géographie Universelle*, published between1875 and 1894, the anarchist and geographer Elisée Reclus placed a special emphasis on the port cities of the Mediterranean: his list of *cosmopolites* (cosmopolitan) cities included Tangiers, Alexandria, Smyrna, Odessa, Malta, Salonica and many others. In his eyes, their social complexity and their links to the world epitomised the characterisation of the Mediterranean as a 'space in movement'.[47] Although Reclus was not mentioned by Fernand Braudel, who is the most common 'forerunner' mentioned by historians who have recently advocated a sea-based history, Reclus' characterisation does match what the 'new thalassology' has been doing.[48] The chronological scope of this attempt to make seas and oceans a renewed framework of **area studies** far exceeds our tiny 200–250-year time chunk, of course. But this scholarship is very much in line with the expectations of transnational historians. It deals with sea bodies, or some of their specific routes, subregions and hinterlands, as formations where structures, actors, ideas and practices combined through the channels of trade, migrations, religious or political mobilisations. Although other sea bodies have received substantial attention, the Indian Ocean has been the rising topic for historians who study oceans as formations over the last 200 years. It has benefited from the development of the 'new imperial history' of the British world, from the interest in the history of Muslim connections, circulations and relations, and from the investigation of the historical avatars of globalisation (the Indian Ocean being called by some the 'cradle of globalisation' or the 'first global economy').[49] As a result, trade, cultural, religious and intellectual flows that existed between the East African coast, the Persian Gulf, the seaboards of India and the Malaysian peninsula have been studied afresh. This has led to more than the usual suspects, as shown by the interest of one historian of political, religious and intellectual currents in the region, Mark Frost. It is not surprising that Frost does pay attention to the circle around Rabindranath Tagore and its outreach to the literati of the Indian Ocean, but he also unveils the far less familiar activities of Buddhist religious revival 'agitators and publicists' in Sri Lanka, their attempts to define a multicultural nationalism and their capacity to liaise with the wider Theravada Buddhist community on both sides of the Bay of Bengal.[50]

However, the formidable efforts by historians to study regional territories emerging from connections, circulations and relations does not end with the study of sea-based regions. Regions that we take for granted in our daily lives are thus questioned on their delimitation, including Europe.[51] Regions that historians tend to see as empty, i.e the Sahara desert, are being rediscovered as thick arrangements of study of flows, ties and interactions.[52] Moreover, some regional definitions emerge from the study of interactions, circulations and connections. A recent example is that of Zomia, a region you will not find in your world atlas. Zomia has received attention because of the reactions to the book by Yale University American anthropologist James Scott, who identified the region as one of the last enclaves where peoples have not yet been fully controlled by national states.[53] Indeed, when he coined the word 'Zomia' in 2002, the historian Willem van Schendel wanted it to be a wedge into the canonical geography of area studies. He sees regional definitions of the latter as closed containers whose inception mostly followed the geopolitical concerns of the Cold War, and whose maintenance has been more a matter of academic reproduction than of intellectual relevance.[54] Instead, van Schendel pushes to the fore a region of highlands which straddles several canonical 'areas' (South East Asia, South Asia, Central Asia and East Asia) and different countries (from India to Vietnam and Thailand through China). This region, he argues, shares many features: 'language affinities (...), religious commonalities (...), cultural traits (...), ancient trade networks, and ecological conditions (...)'.[55] To name that region, van Schendel coins the alluring name of Zomia, which he derives from the word *zomi*, i.e. 'highlander' in some languages of the South East Asian massif. If Scott is chiefly concerned by the 'anarchic' features of the region, other researchers read this region as a formation in the sense of this chapter. A special issue of the *Journal of Global History* has recently gathered geographers, anthropologists and historians on these lines.[56]

Its contributors do picture Zomia as a formation that is produced by and has produced connections, circulations and relations. As far as our time span of about 200-250 years is concerned, trade routes criss-crossed these highlands carrying wool, musk, tea and many other products, and Yunnan caravan trade firms gradually evolved into far-flung systems that reached out to the world. This trade was not exclusively licit, with the growing importance of the opium culture and trade from the mid-nineteenth century and later the processing of heroin. Throughout Zomia, ethnic groups that were divided by the delineation of imperial and national borders, like the Thangmi, the Wa and the Hmong, used national and imperial borders to gain shelter from respective governmental authorities, or to generate income by way of seasonal migration, legal and illegal trade. Migrations have taken these peoples to the surrounding lowlands as well as into many distant places in Asia and elsewhere, creating a web of cultural and economic remittances converging on Zomia. And, if surrounding states, colonial authorities or private actors were anxious to penetrate some of these highlands for their resources in raw materials (teak, silver, gold), bringing in foreign capital and workforces, the autonomous mining undertakings of the Wa people also included slave raids into China as late as the 1930s. Many attempts were made from the outside to integrate the people of these regions within national constructions, religious domains, tourist itineraries or geopolitical blocs. Thus Hmong of Laos were hired by the US Central Intelligence Agency during the peripheral conflicts linked to the Vietnam War, and later by the Thai government in its conflict with the Laotian government. For all these entanglements, scholars who study Zomia do not purport that this is a coherent region. There are fiery discussions about its limits and definition. But its heuristic capacity is nonetheless clear: thinking about Zomia brings salience to elements that were invisible in the framework of area studies or national history. It demonstrates that we can shape our territorial units of research according to the issues we want to study, instead of forcing these issues onto existing territories.

▶ Conclusion

'Dig where you are'. Historians who want to adopt a transnational perspective do not need large financial resources, nor ought they to work on faraway lands, or to manage large teams of collaborators to conduct their investigation. For transnational history can also be about one person, one neighbourhood, one event, one object in our close environment. The real challenge is to find ways to replace these elements in the larger formations they are part of. This is where original social and intellectual research arrangements are needed, in order to mobilise a community of scholars between and through national historiographies. As we have seen for anarchism or electrification, these scholars can build a common language including agreements and disagreements, argue about problematised frames, pool information and sources and provide mutual language assistance, although they each retain some specific research interests. The major difficulty, here, is to organise this conversation so that it never boils down to a juxtaposition of territorial monographs. This chapter raises other issues that have to do with the way we do research, and points to some specific methodological issues. This aspect will be examined more closely in the final chapter.

6 On Methodology

'It remains the case that world historians largely rely on secondary sources rather than on their own primary research', writes Patrick Manning in the 'Methods and Materials' chapter of his overview of **world history**.[1] 'Largely' rightly reminds us that some world historians do proceed from primary sources, but the view of the research process as a second-degree one is widely shared in world history and other 'large-scale' attempts to write history, like **big history** or **global history**.[2] Such endorsements have fuelled fears that the adoption of a wide horizon implies a growing estrangement from original material. Thus Bartolomé Yun Casalilla noted that 'Global history involves a clear movement of the historian's laboratory, from the archive to the library.'[3] The recent success of a synthetic essay like that of Chris Bayly seems to support this view.[4] Here, I argue that transnational historians cannot move their laboratory away from original material, whether archival or not. It is when they inch their way through the original material that they see circulations, connections, relations and formations taking shape, and it is when they are in the position to reorganise data, reassemble documentary evidence and gather new material that they can reconstruct their operation and impact. It will not do merely to collate data and evidence that others have dug out and organised from a perspective that did not aim at answering the 'big issues' mentioned in the introduction to this book.

Transnational history is not a collage of several different local, national or regional histories about some topic or other. It is a research-intensive track, and resolutely participates in the 'modest' approach that Frederick Cooper offers as an alternative to the meta-narratives of **globalisation** literature that have hardly any relation to original research and materials. 'My argument', writes Cooper, 'is for precision in specifying how such commodity circuits are constituted, how connections across space are extended and bounded, and how large scale long term processes, such as capitalist development, can be analyzed with due attention to their power, their limitations, and the mechanisms that shape them.'[5] A precise reconstruction of specific ties and flows that have straddled countries, regions, continents and empires, and of their operation and effects, requires primary sources. This makes the appraisal of methodological options an important factor. This chapter examines the posture, methods and material that can help transnational historians in their empirical undertaking.

▶ Stretching our spatial imagination

We historians tend to work within a territorial framework: one city, one country, etc. This is where we gather our data, it is from there that we assemble our argument, and about it that we develop our narrative. Such territories exist prior to our research. We tend to take them for granted because they are embodied in institutions, in archival resources and in the very organisation of our discipline: we are historians of Africa, of Bristol, of Chile, of the Indian Ocean. Beyond the peculiarities of each topic, beyond the specific notions and methods used by historians working in a transnational perspective, lies a common concern. They all make an effort to relocate ties and flows and to assess the orders that presided over and resulted from their development. As a result, transnational history requires us to track objects, capital, norms, organisations, ideas, patterns and people across, between and through the usual territorial categories of our historical understanding. If we stick to our canonical units of understanding – most notably countries but also continents, oceans or cultural areas – we cannot take note of what lives between and through these units. The said objects, capital, organisations and the like slip under the radar and escape our attention merely because they overstep the limits of our territorial specialisation. If we want to identify, follow and capture them, we need to tone up our spatial imagination with a few exercises.

The first of these exercises consists in a gentle horizontal and vertical stretch. Although even the horizontal move, which seems most elementary, is not that easy. Not only is the division of intellectual labour in the discipline of history organised by countries, but it also privileges 'big countries'. How many chairs of Belgian or Laotian history are there outside of Belgium and Laos? If this number is close to zero, is it really because the history of Laos or Belgium has nothing to teach us? Historians tend to specialise in the history of big countries, even when they are comparing countries or writing regional histories. A history of contemporary Europe is most often a history of big countries whose role and attitude are supposed to shape the history of the region: France, Germany, Great Britain. A touch of Italy, and more recently of Eastern Europe, has long been what the most daring historians had to offer in terms of coverage. Entire regions like Scandinavia, small countries like the Netherlands or Switzerland, zones of 'dubious modernity' like southern Europe, are erased from what goes as European history. They count as peripheral, and historians who invest time and energy in research and publication on these places run the risk of being counted as peripheral as well. Yet if our brief is to track people, imagination or things, if we want to understand the order that presides over the direction, orientation and impact of circulating items, if we seek to assess the importance of a specific connection in relation to others, we cannot be confined to working only with 'big countries'. If a historian studies the reach of the American Declaration of Independence, he needs to follow it where it goes, be it

Ghana or Venezuela, and not only to post-war Japan.[6] The history of how US legal culture was used in foreign contexts is equally captivating if studied in 1960s Kenya or in Europe after the Second World War.[7] Likewise, if one seeks to establish the capacity of merchants from the Sind province (India) to find a place in far-flung trading systems from the 1870s, one cannot just look for branches of Hyderabadi firms in a limited number of large trading cities in major countries. Together with Claude Markovits, we must track the 'Sindworkies' in Meknes (Morocco), Tenerife (Canary Islands), Panama, Kingston (Jamaica), Malleija (Malta) or Freetown (Sierra Leone).[8]

Still, if a lateral move in the direction of 'small countries' is a requisite, it is hardly a warm-up. We also need to adjust our vertical gauge. In his take on **world history**, Arif Dirlik suggests that 'the radical challenge of transnational history itself lies in its conjoining of the supranational and the sub-national (or intra-national)'.[9] Some historians have gone further than this conjoining stage, because they think that the grip of the nation, as a concept that originated in the North Atlantic world, does not allow historians to recover the thickness and depth of circulations, connections and relations in regions where the national state was imposed by colonisation (Asia and Africa). In order to rescue history from the nation, they employ the term 'translocality' to qualify their approach.[10] The previous chapters also tried to work with and through the nation, but also above and under it. It was not a difficult task, because many transnational historians are on that wavelength. In *Drawing the Global Colour Line*, the authors contextualise the entanglements in the racial politics of Transvaal, Natal, British Columbia, Victoria and California, without subsuming these regional contexts into national containers. On the same topic, Carl Nightingale has shown that the interchange and implementation of the spatial versions of these worldviews, namely racial residential segregation, also takes place at the level of city politics.[11] The significant units of observation for transnational history can be a neighbourhood, or a few villages, as much as a large oceanic rim.

Now let us move to a set of more demanding exercises. We work within a conception of human societies, polities, activities and non-human factors organised into levels from the local to the global through the national, each fitting on top of the next in a pyramidal structure. This is what geographers have called a 'scalar logic', where spatial scales are given fixed social and cultural attributes and capacities, from neighbourhood to city, city to region, region to nation, nation to continent, continent to planet Earth. In this view, actors and processes operate on one level after another, and the change of scale corresponds to a change in intensity, quality and quantity of their activity. Conversely, transnational history evinces simultaneous operations and presence on different levels and scales, as happens when one follows migrants and their characteristic activities and features in trade, investment, politics or identity.[12] It underlines that actors make scales and play with them, as much as they are constrained by their existence. It also contradicts the nested view of systematic incremental development 'from' one level 'to' another. Studying the organisation of scientific communities belies the systematic notion that the 'national' shapes the 'international' or vice versa: some disciplines began their existence through international congresses without having any national visibility, others coalesced from national components but were redefined as a result of conversations between and through national versions of the disciplines.[13] Large 'philanthropic' organisations like the Rockefeller Foundation did not 'broaden' their horizons from the local to the welfare of humankind: Rockefeller started its programmes simultaneously abroad and in the USA. By and large, the detailed study of a specific territorial formation shows how much its 'local' characteristics are soaked in inputs and outputs that draw from other 'scales': what is qualified as 'local' can have an impact far beyond a specific place, or result from the combination of elements that have transited through many different other places before being 'localised' in one. Vernacularisation and universalisation processes most often combine with one another. By and large, the findings that emerge from the adoption of a transnational perspective force us to cut through what we are used to thinking of as embedded scales. They push the idea of relation over the idea of hierarchy as the key characteristic of links between these levels.

Finally, transnational historians gain from considering space not only as a well-defined and bounded expanse, but as multidimensional, discontinuous and transient. This might be demanding, but it is worth the effort because it allows us to capture actors, projects and patterns that would otherwise fly under the historical radar. Transnational history implies adjusting the space of our research to the questions we tackle, instead of squeezing our questions into national containers.[14] The French historian Marc Bloch pushed this a little further when he urged historians to define the most appropriate research space by starting from the phenomena they observe, instead of relying on 'old, obsolete and falsely convenient pigeonholes that ought to be smashed' [my translation].[15] It has been suggested above that the old pigeonholes, and especially national ones, should not be disposed of too swiftly, because they have shaped too much of modern history to be jettisoned. However, those of us who want to retrace flows and establish ties need to be alert to other types of spatiality than the kind of continuous, territorial and lasting spatiality we are used to. Had the Turkish historian Selçuk Esenbel stuck to nations, civilisations or the typical regions of **area studies**, or to the usual Western/Japan binary that presided over views of post-1858 Japanese relations with the outside world, she would not have been drawn to the study of Japanese connections to pan-Islamist actors located in Tatar Russia, Turkey, Egypt, India and China.[16] The contribution such connections made to the definition of Japanese nationalism and imperial policies would have remained invisible to her. If Benedict Anderson had decided to cast his research into well-rounded and bounded spatial units like South Asia or the Spanish Empire, he would not have been able to reconstruct the intellectual and material resources that Mariano Ponce, José Rizal and Isabelo de Los Reyes were able to harness in their attempt to challenge the Spanish domination in the Philippines.[17] Had he confined himself to examining 'pigeonholes', old or new, his understanding of their activities would have been deprived of 'Italians in Argentina, New Jersey, France and the Basque homeland; Puerto Ricans and Cubans in Haïti, the United States and France; Spaniards in Cuba, France, Brazil and the Philippines; Russians in Paris; Chinese in the Philippines and Japan, (…) and so on'.[18]

Following their lead, transnational historians can take on board the idea to situate their research within different types of space, which do not always match demarcated political, geographical or cultural territories. These 'ad hoc' spaces that we build from our research can show clear demarcations, like the dots, lines and areas we can draw when we retrace the movement of things or people: there is indeed a geography of oil production, processing and consumption, there are definite and scattered locations of migrants from a given village, region or country. But then again other ad hoc spaces are definitely fuzzy, overlapping and not reducible to a specific expanse, for instance the 'thought zones' defined by conversations around a cause or a notion, such as the anti-colonial print culture of the Indian Ocean or the idea of cosmopolitanism.[19] Besides being discontinuous, such spaces may, more often than not, be transient. The rage for cross-border exchange of products and information that dominates transactions at World Fairs, art fairs or film festivals only lasts for a few days or a couple of months. The centre of gravity of the anarchist formation was located in southern and central Europe in the mid-nineteenth century, whereas Latin American cities were a major hub at the outbreak of the First World War. Here again, we should be ready to shift spatial allegiance and attention when necessary.

▶ **Methodological inspirations**

Depending on their intellectual trajectory, political world views, geographical location or subdisciplinary affiliation, historians can turn to various sources of inspiration to work out their sense of spatiality. Historians of empires found inspiration in the work of anthropologists.[20] Many scholars of the history of Mexican migration into the USA thrived on Gloria Anzualda's notion of borderlands as an autonomous space that extended far beyond the strict geographical border regions.[21] 'Zomianists' such as Willem van Schendel or Jean Michaud build from French sociologist Henri Lefebvre's reflections on the production of space.[22] Many also found inspiration in the notion of rhizome, a term that comes from the vegetal world: the rhizome is a horizontal and multiple stem with quite different characteristics to a linear and vertical root as far as the propagation, resilience and filiation of a plant are concerned. The rhizome is a central motif in Gilles Deleuze and Félix Guattari's *Thousand Plateaus,* where it is used as a metaphor for understanding multiplicity.[23] Thinking of ties, flows and interactions in terms of a rhizome makes room for discontinuity, ruptures, new departures and multiple origins, whereas the paradigm of the root is conducive to the search for origin, filiation and genesis. Authors who have shared from this rhizomic outlook can make things easier to grasp, especially when they write fiction or poetry like Edouard Glissant, who has reconnected to the rhizome metaphor some of his developments about creolisation, transversality and conflictual cross-fertilisation in his novels or essays.[24] Social scientist Bruno Latour also built from the idea of the rhizome to juggle the binary distinction between the local and the global. Latour pays attention to what he calls 'non-human' objects and technologies, which have the capacity to be simultaneously here and there because of their essence or the fact they are replicated (the railway, the machine). With these non-human objects and technologies, Latour suggests that we are accessing a new topography where distinct places are always linked to one another by connections. As a result, argues Latour, there is no neat line between the local and the global, between the particular and the general, the specific and the universal. And, he adds, we should not be obsessed by allocating people, facts and processes to one side of this line: what is more important may be what lies in the middle.[25]

However, one does not need to delve into French theory or the complexities of Latour's **actor network theory** to work out our sense of spatiality. My own idiosyncrasies, as a historian trained in France under the double aegis of history and geography, connect me with two sorts of heuristic inspiration and practical suggestions. On the one hand, American geographer John Agnew invites us to reimagine geopolitics. Agnew points to the 'territorial trap', a mode of thought that induces us to speak of the modern national state as inevitably a neatly bounded space; to conceive of domestic and foreign affairs as wholly different realms; and to consider that the territory of a country equates to the boundaries of a society.[26] Agnew also insists that scales and territories were produced in and by history, and that the state-centred view of sovereignty and social organisation is one singular and recent conception of territoriality.[27] On the other hand, we can also draw on British geographers who tried to shake off the view of hierarchised scales that presides over our perception of the world as scholars and citizens. We tend to see the local, the regional, the national and the global as nested into one another like Russian dolls.[28] This 'scalar reasoning', they say, assigns pre-given roles and qualities to each of these levels, and a hierarchy between them. This prevents us from seeing how individuals and collectives exist and operate simultaneously across these levels, and how they activate the existence of these levels through their practice (instead of just being subjected to them). The same British geographers have also insisted on the need to complete our topographical sense of spatiality with a topological dimension, where propinquity is created by discourse and imagination as much as by situation according to strictly spatial coordinates.[29] When writing about connections, circulations, relations and formations, topography needs to be supplemented by topology. The work of the French sociologist Henri Lefebvre, who exhorted social scientists to consider the 'production of space', is a major foundation in both instances.[30]

Sociologists and anthropologists who have been writing and researching globalisation over the last 20 years adopted some of these insights because they helped to explore dimensions made invisible by the joint spell of nested scales and the territorial trap. The sociologist Saskia Sassen offers a illustration of such a shift in spatial imagination: she started from the idea of studying the interaction of 'the global' and 'the local' as discrete entities, and later moved to a position where she questioned the idea of nested scales and concentrated instead on the way that scales are made and unmade, stressing that what we call the 'local' is replete with elements of 'global' origins and vice versa.[31] Historians who work on what lies between and through polities and communities have not been foreign to these ideas. Richard White, as early as 1999, alerted transnational historians to these questions of spatiality. Yet, only recently have these issues been put to the fore by historians.[32] And, as remarked earlier, transnational historians have a specific challenge to uphold: they cannot jettison the usual territorial categories of understanding, if only because regions, continents, cities or countries are **actors' categories**. They have been made and used not only by historians but by the actors and agents of history, and this use has generated situations, roles, values, institutions and behaviours that are part and parcel of the historical processes we study. As a result, the adoption of a brave new spatial imagination is not enough: we also have to devise methods to simultaneously escape the territorial trap and to account for the existence and performance of territories.

▶ Methodological ecumenism and methodological positions

Historians use their honed skills when doing transnational history. Most of them work to combine a wealth of printed and archival material.[33] Others rely on oral histories to work on more recent decades.[34] Teams assemble large databases in order to identify patterns and waves over large chunks of time and space.[35] Images are used as the major sources in the innovative 'visual narratives' and essays conceived by participants to the *Visualizing Cultures* World Wide Web project, in order to deal with the perception and graphic representation of the encounters between Japanese people and the growing Western presence in the nineteenth and twentieth centuries.[36] Narrative strategies also cover a wide range. Some start from a few individuals, like Benedict Anderson in *Under Three Flags*, and reconstruct their worlds. Some choose a few important topics in a national sphere and see how they were infused with foreign experiments and references, as Daniel Rodgers and his *Atlantic Crossings*. As we have seen, transnational historians can organise their plot around a text, an idea, a commodity. It can also be centred on a tract of land,[37] or a social movement.[38] And it is the biographical device that makes it possible for Kris Manjapra to show the significance of the 'interstitial thinker' and Indian Marxist intellectual M. N. Roy, whose activity and thought developed through India, Mexico, Germany, China and the USSR, and on a range of commitments from **Swadeshi** anti-colonial nationalism to world revolution, German social science and 'reconciliation humanism'.[39] Beyond this variety, there are some striking resemblances. The constant emphasis on the content, thickness and depth of circulations, connections, relations and formations amounts to a statement. It also reconnects transnational history to methodological debates that are shared by the social sciences when they try to observe and explain the convergence or divergence of patterns in different units (countries, cultures, social groups).

The debate between function and diffusion is one of these important issues. One of its first occurrences was in London in 1889, when the Royal Anthropological Institute discussed marriage laws and descent patterns. In his comments about a paper that explained convergences between these two traits among some 300 peoples by arguing that their functional relationship was similar in all these societies, Francis Galton suggested that the similitude may instead have resulted from observation, imitation and adaptation between the different societies.[40] This has been called 'Galton's problem' by anthropologists, and they have come up with a number of statistical techniques to try to separate function from diffusion ever since.

The other debate is between system and relation, and is familiar to world historical sociology. For masterminds of world historical sociology like Charles Tilly, Immanuel Wallerstein or John Meyer, there are systematic processes which have driven social change in the last two centuries (chiefly the joint formation of the nation-state system and the worldwide capitalist system). In their eyes, it is the whole, the system, that governs the parts, local societies, countries or empires. In order to support that demonstration, world historical sociologists use 'encompassing comparison', and consider the similarities and differences between units – mostly countries, but also empires – to be the result of their inclusion in the system. Philip McMichael, instead, advocates 'incorporated comparison' where the relations between the parts (countries, empires) are what reveal and realise the whole.[41] He places relation and interaction as key factors, where Tilly or Wallerstein see systemic constraint as the major driver of historical change.

Transnational historians work on the fault lines of these two debates. We can start from circulations and connections to see what relations they create and whether they generate formations of some kind. In so doing, we do not postulate a general framework/system that would script the content, role and place of each flow, every tie and their protagonists. We look for order in the space of flows, but do not proceed from a purported order to read flows. This is the heart of Frederick Cooper's approach: specify the spatial and chronological extent, content, impact of circulations and connections instead of starting from some general system ('globalisation' for Cooper) as unprecedented, irresistible and ubiquitous. This 'modest approach', because of its empirical emphasis, has methodological consequences.

On the one hand, transnational historians need to adopt what sociologist John Urry calls **mobile methods**, in order to follow circulating people, things or imagination.[42] On the other hand, they are well aware of the importance of relocating these mobile items in each of these specific contexts, lest they lose the ability to assess the capacity of these moving persons, ideas or capital to affect existing social or economic arrangements. Anthropologists have faced similar issues. During the 1990s, their attempt to grasp 'global issues' fuelled a very strong critique of the 'field tradition', which was blamed for enclosing research in the straitjacket of a limited territory, thus imprisoning cultures as in a cell. These were the years when James Clifford stressed that 'travel' was as much needed as 'settlement' as a strategy for urban ethnographical research, echoed by George Marcus's urge to 'follow the people' and 'follow the thing'.[43] 'Multi-sited ethnography' became a rallying cry, and was praised for its capacity to capture and record a world on the move. The swing went wild somehow, as noted by Anna Tsing, and there has been a tendency to forget about what was not on the move, and to adopt a view of historical change that contrasted a past and static world bounded in local horizons with a recent and future dynamic world of global flows.[44] Because transnational history is about what circulations do to demarcated territorial units and what the latter do to circulations, historians have a lot to gain from adopting a multi-sited research strategy. This opens the possibility of working with materials that document the specific contribution and position of the different participants to connections, circulations, relations and formations. But we also ought to do justice to the different sites of our multi-sided strategy and to respect their particularity. The workouts in spatiality suggested above offer some solution in that view, because they should prevent us from opposing the local and the global as discrete scales: each site and level is relevant and it is the relation between them that constitutes the whole. The other antidote is relocation: a continuous and pressing concern to contextualise our study of connections and circulations into specific places, moments, events and projects.[45] We need to track and move, but we also need to capture and dig. Three tools of a different nature that can help us to track, to dig, to decide where to dig in what we track, and to tell the others about it. Whence their special place in our toolbox.

▶ In the toolbox of transnational history

First of all, maps. Sociologist John Urry and his 'mobility' colleagues put mapping at the forefront of the mobile methods they urge us to adopt if we want to understand the world of flows, and that seems a worthy piece of advice when we try to capture their topographical dimension.[46] Although there are obvious exceptions, maps are not a common sight in history books, even in countries where the discipline of history has long been associated with geography in terms of training and teaching. When maps appear, it is chiefly as ancillary instruments assigned with the minor mission of locating or illustrating the argument. This is not belied by the books that are cited frequently in this volume. Benedict Anderson only provides two maps, neither of which add to his argument, while Isabel Hofmeyr does not use mapping at all in analysing the trajectories of *The Pilgrim's Progress*. Still, we can draw upon the work of another historian of literature, Franco Moretti, to see how mapping can be an interpretative tool. 'Placing a literary phenomenon in its specific space – mapping it – is not the conclusion of geographical work. It's the beginning (...) One looks at the map and thinks.'[47] And Moretti does think from the maps he draws, as they allow him to track fictional characters, famous books and whole genres. Maps help him to figure out the role of space in literature, as in Jane Austen's novels where loved ones are stranded in some corner of the British Empire, this peripheral location symbolising both ultimate distance and the centrality of England in Austen's plots (Chapter 1). Or, maps give Moretti the opportunity to consider literature in space, and to identify the order that shapes the nineteenth-century flows of translation: maps unravel the intra-national process of centralisation for the publication of foreign novels, the development of a European landscape of readers where different foreign literature genres are only present in specific geographic areas, and the supremacy of the English and French novels which translation waves install as European canons that authors and publishers will emulate for decades (Chapter 3). Of course, Moretti's maps are supported by tables, matrices and charts. All these by-products of quantitative history participate in his explanatory apparatus.

Transnational historians would also benefit from using the visual power of maps to frame the analytical and narrative process, instead of just supporting it. It is quite difficult, and sometimes confusing for the reader, to tell a story that follows a commodity, an individual, a cohort of individuals or an idea across places, continents and languages. The narration of such a trajectory by way of a linear argument, organised in paragraphs and pages, is highly demanding. Maps can help us produce and comprehend the narrative. And, they have long been a chosen instrument for whoever wanted to represent the interdependencies and entanglements between countries and regions: Otto Neurath and Paul Otlet used that form in the 1930s in their atlases,[48] and since Michael Kidron and Ronald Segal published their *State of the World Atlas* in 1981, the atlas has once more been a privileged conduit for interpretations of globalisation.[49] Historians have been reminded that maps can be an effective means of understanding and narration, as suggested by recent publications of atlases that place maps at the centre of the argument instead of at its periphery.[50] Moreover, mapping is now much easier than it used to be. On the one hand, the difficult question of the 'flow map', which is meant to visualise flows as trajectories between origin and destination, is now addressed by dedicated software like Tableau, Flowmap or Flowstrates.[51] And for those who do not want to open the black box of such software, there are many 'ready to use' online packages that make it possible to write by, with and for the map, to insert multimedia content into the map, and to unleash its interpretative and narrative power. That seems to be a boon when it comes to coping with connections, circulations, formations and interactions, the bread and butter of transnational history. Google Maps and Google Earth can be used by historians as building blocks for geolocalisation of historical data, to be fed into open access platforms like GeoTWAIN or Hypercities.[52] Both of these have been developed by historians and social scientists, and are freely available on the web. The latter makes it possible to adopt a 'geo-temporal' analysis and argumentation, and combines mapping with layers of written analysis and original material (archival material, statistics, audio and video excerpts). Another digital platform freely available for academic and non-profit use is VisualEyes, where maps can be weaved together with images, charts, video and data, and where movements, trajectories and locations can be organised along a timeline.[53] Until now, these resources have mostly been used by students in class projects, or to provide a digital avatar to print publications.[54] A recent achievement shows the way for a wider use. In 2012, Simon Burrows and colleagues made available a massive database about the book trade in late eighteenth-century Europe. The database is a treasure trove in itself, making it possible to identify, count and map a specific author or book that was published or traded by the Société Typographique de Neuchatel. But their use of the database is even more suggestive, and it is their combination of maps, data and archival research that gives them the capacity to propose new understanding 'of the French book trade and, dare [they] dream, of the enlightenment'.[55] It is time that transnational historians, in their search for the best instruments to analyse and transmit the history of entanglements, took possession of these tools of the digital humanities.

If 'digging' is accepted as shorthand for the need to embed transnational history into specific contexts, moments and places, then what better methodological suggestion than **historical archaeology**? Although he spoke for early modern situations, Martin Hall argues that historical archaeology, in its concern for 'small things forgotten' (James Deetz), is especially capable of accounting for the way these small things circulated in the networks of colonialism.[56] This capacity to document material culture and to relocate circulating objects in specific contexts is too often overlooked by historians, who still tend to see historical archaeology as a distant and destitute sibling of the queen discipline of history. But historical archaeologists are agile at harnessing documentary and oral sources to the interpretation of their excavations, and we cannot afford not to learn from their achievements. They tell us about the life of specific immigrant communities in cities, or within larger diasporic settings, and provide solid ground for considering hybridisation or creolisation in material culture.[57] Historical archaeology has the power to excavate the ties between a given site and the wider world: in Denver, investigations of the Tremont House Hotel provide clues about the penetration of goods from abroad on the American frontier,[58] while in San Francisco the remains of ocean-going vessels turned into moored, floating warehouses document the role of the city within the oceanic maritime system of trade.[59] Archaeologists have also engaged with important moments, events and sites of entanglements. Archaeological digs help scholars of the African diaspora to discuss the composite nature of the religion and material culture of enslaved Africans in North America,[60] and a recent volume in the *Studies in Contemporary and Historical Archaeology* series includes the launch of Sputnik, the invention of television or Marconi's first transatlantic wireless message.[61] Whenever the historians' sources go 'beyond words', and this is the case when you adopt a transnational perspective, archaeology is a card to be counted on.

However, one needs to have an idea of where to dig in order to increase the chance of a fruitful return. Are there any clues beyond intuition, flair and insight from existing scholarship that can help historians decide where to concentrate their investigations when they try to find order in the space of flows? Social network analysis can deliver that. We can use this robust method to study the ties between a set of actors (such as individuals, organisations, places and polities). These ties can consist in correspondence, trade and business transactions, kinship, textual citation or affiliation to an organisation of some kind. Topology substitutes for topography, as it is social or immaterial relations and not merely spatial paths that are made visible by that method. Network analysis is a quantitative tool, and presents a mathematical expression of the organisation of these ties, which are called 'linkages', and of the resulting 'network' that is formed by the linkages between the elements, which are called 'nodes'. In order to establish linkages, reconstruct the network and analyse its organisation, one needs data. These data will be, for instance, lists of members of corporation boards, if the aim is to estimate the degree of board interlocks between different firms.[62] If a person has directorates of several firms, this does establish a linkage between these firms. It is such data that are fed into software that now runs on personal computers (UCINET and PAJEK are among the most frequently used). This software analyses the general architecture of linkages and presents them in the form of tables, matrices and graphs, the latter being the most visual kind of result. A graph combines a set of points with a set of lines connecting pairs of points. Drawings of networks are used both to discover insights into network structures and to communicate those insights to others.[63] Social network analysis makes it possible to identify hubs within a network, it draws the contours of ties woven by a given individual, it shows how frequently different communities are connected according to different variables, it helps to locate clusters of elements that are more frequently linked to one another than with other elements, and it highlights brokers and intermediaries between different clusters. It is possible to measure structure within a personal network, but most analyses of personal network data 'summarize the composition of the network as a set of variables' or social attributes.[64]

Sociologists have used social network analysis to study linkages between social movements,[65] and historians to study social milieux and ethnic groups, ego-networks (the linkages of individual persons), kinship or migration,[66] mostly within the limits of a country or a city. The number of historians who have used network analysis to support their work on connections, circulations, relations and formations between and through polities and societies is still small.[67] Economic historians have been among the few who have done so with profit, to understand order and movement in flows of goods or capital.[68] As with any method, the advantages and limits of social network analysis are discussed among its practitioners: there are debates on the capacity of the method to qualify the intensity of linkages beyond their mere existence or number, or on the correctness of using chronological precedence of one linkage over others to derive conclusions about their relative importance. The fundamental assumption of social network analysis, that structural differences shown by network analysis are correlated to substantive differences in actual relations between units, is not taken for granted.

Still, the use of social network analysis to study intellectual and literary connections across borders signals two major reasons why transnational historians need to care about it. Historians of translation use it to spot links across lines of national difference, and find it especially useful when it comes to persons or journals that did not belong to the most visible circles of literary life. In Anthony Pym's work on links between 'small journals' in France and Germany,[69] social network analysis shows that cities are the relevant sites for understanding literary linkages, rather than countries, and highlights the role of Belgian, Swiss and Dutch journals and translators as protagonists of an 'intercultural space' that made Franco-German interaction possible and durable. It also called attention to the cross-citations between journals, to the role played by mutual translation (among authors, among journals), to the relations of exchange and opposition between two journals, and to the importance of international linkages for avant garde publications that could not rely on mainstream national authorship and readership. The study of literary circles also points to the heuristic capacity of network analysis. Apropos his work on literary careers in late nineteenth-century Belgium, Christophe Verbruggen insists that social network analysis clears the way for further work.[70] It helps him to capture the structure of Belgian literary journals and authors in their relation with French journals: clusters of authors and journals that are connected by mutual ties ('cohesive subgroups' within networks), journals with a large number of links to others ('centrality'), blocks of journals that have similar linkages with third parties (what network analysis calls 'block modelling'). Social network analysis thus identifies, in relation to their role within the network, 'significant' authors whose career should be reconstructed, or 'important' journals or groups of journals that call for additional investigation. Verbruggen, together with other historians who use social network analysis, concludes that it does not provide an explanation, but raises our awareness of what ought to be explained. 'Profound empirical research based on personal documents such as memoirs, letters and diaries', he says, 'is imperative for a more profound insight into the genesis of network structures.'[71] This is appealing to transnational historians who thrive on empirical research, but who are looking for clues about where exactly to apply their empirical energies in the wide array of possibilities and source material that they work with.

▶ Sources: invention, creative destruction, recycling

Whatever the narrative strategy, whatever the method, historians ultimately depend on material and sources to build their interpretation. Where is the original material that transnational historians need to answer their questions and stimulate their curiosity and imagination? There are no obvious or specific sources for historians who adopt a transnational perspective: even archives that have attracted a huge amount of data and documents about world entanglements result from specific choices or bias, and no single collection suffices to tell well-rounded histories. Existing scholarship suggests some patterns of source creation that recur in recent research, and three such patterns will be presented here.

The first consists in bringing new material or a new type of material into the picture. Oral material clearly fits that bill, such as the dozens of interviews that Ghislaine Lydon has conducted with former caravanners and other protagonists of trans-Saharan trade,[72] or those gathered by Martin Klimke for his study of links between rebel students in Germany and the United States.[73] Orality, just as when

it was used to listen to the 'voice of the weak' in specific national or regional contexts, is certainly a major resource for capturing the activity of those who worked
in-between and through the national units and concerns that have framed the
fabrication and conservation of written records. The production of new source
material also consists in giving new importance to previously neglected material.
This is what the same Lydon has done with a number of family archives and commercial records scattered along the stations of the West African trade roads. This
also goes for the small booklets, newspapers and magazines around the Indian
Ocean which printed excerpts from one another in the early twentieth century.[74]
They contributed to create an Indian Ocean public opinion, but they lived under
the historians' radar for a long time. In fact, some source material that is seen
as trivial, dull or inconsequential from a national angle can turn into a first-class
source when placed under a different light. *Lloyd's List*, published daily from 1837
to document the situation of ships in the different harbours of the world, is now
used by historians of communication to infer the time it took for information to
reach the headquarters of the English insurance firm in London.[75] When they tried
to chart and map the monetary geography of the late nineteenth century, in order
to understand the asymmetrical links of external adjustment that impinged on
trade balance, debt, price levels and interest rates, Marc Flandreau and Clemens
Jobst looked for a way to establish groupings of countries and national currencies
as a basis for qualifying financial interdependence and interconnection.[76] It was
not possible to compute aggregate holdings from banks and financial players, for
lack of data. Accordingly, they chose to use 'course of exchange' bulletins, on the
hypothesis that the quote of one financial market in course of exchange bulletins of
another financial market was a solid clue that there was a sufficiently large demand
and supply to warrant the posting of prices. These quotes are, as they say, a 'proxy
for liquidity'.[77] The course of exchange bulletins, those trite lists used by financial actors of the time, thus became the founding resource of the two economic
historians' network analysis.

In the latter case, the invention of sources almost led to another process, 'creative destruction'. Flandreau and Jobst did ponder the case of countries with several
foreign exchange centres. As they say:

> 'One possibility would have been to identify centres rather than countries. How-
> ever, this was not feasible since a number of listings aggregated foreign regional
> markets: instead of quoting, say, "Antwerp" and/or "Brussels" they reported
> "Belgian centres" (most probably because of nationwide clearing arrangements that
> made regional centres close substitutes of one another for foreign dealers)'.[78]

The reaggregation of data, which would have allowed them to study specific
regional centres instead of countries, was finally not possible because of previous

national aggregation of data. By 'creative destruction', I point to a similar process of dismantling and reassembling existing source material. The case of quantitative data is especially relevant here. Although they have not only or always been collated by national governments, statistical data and categories eventually coalesced to national units when it came to quantifying production, wealth or population. When these quantities are moved across national borders, they are generally quantified as movements between national units taken as monolithic wholes. Economic historians find this a nuisance when they try to understand regional economic aspects, or establish cross-regional comparisons. Kenneth Pomeranz, as he revises the content and factors of the economic divergence between Europe and Asia, echoes his Californian colleague Roy Bin Wong's suggestion that the appropriate units of comparison are not so much countries or continental regions such as 'Europe' and 'Asia' or 'Great Britain' and 'China', but regional entities like the southern Netherlands, northern England, parts of Jiangsu province or of Gujarat.[79] However, economic historians have not yet attempted to dismantle national economic data and reconstruct them differently. Reliance on nationally aggregated data is one of the foundations of **methodological nationalism**.[80]

Likewise, the difficulty of circumventing such nationally organised data has been a roadblock for historians of migrations who wanted to track migrants throughout their trajectory and not only between two countries. But they have tried to work around it. Walt Kamphöfner and Donna Gabaccia create a 'transatlantic record linkage' between the US manuscript census and comparable population lists maintained in European countries, in order to relocate migrants in subnational contexts.[81] Others started from villages rather than countries to show the texture and durability of chain migrations, or from departure ports and passenger lists rather than from national data. Thus it becomes possible to capture patterns such as return migrations, which are invisible when one handles national data, or to compare Asian migrations with transatlantic European migrations.[82] When they look for material other than statistics produced when 'seeing like a state', historians also gain access to the cunning ways devised by participants in the migration system in order to escape the gaze of state power, and consequently its statistics. In his current research about Tamil migration to Malaya at the turn of the nineteenth and twentieth centuries, Sunil Amrith shows how migrant and labour recruitment agents had a creative capacity to play with 'distinctions between immigrants and indigenes, settlers and sojourners', and how they used the propinquity of the Straits settlements and of the French port of Karikal to circumvent British control.[83] Be it for enhancing our capacity to track items that go from one country to another, to identify formations that straddle different countries, or to locate individuals who knew how to slip through the interstices between national or imperial domains, there is much more historians with a transnational perspective can do to tweak nationally aggregated data to their own ends.

A third pattern of source creation is more familiar to historians. Every reorientation of historical research has inspired new investigations of familiar source material in the light of the new approach. This is the case with the transnational perspective. One telling example is the revival of interest in the archives of international organisations. The US historian Matthew Connelly, and other assiduous visitors to such places, remember lonely days spent in the archival repositories of inter- and non-governmental organisations.[84] Indeed, some 15 years ago, it was quite unusual to find many readers in the reading rooms of the League of Nations archives in Geneva, Switzerland – to the point one could even organise workshops in the rooms. Today, the place is buzzing with doctoral students and senior scholars and it can be difficult to get a seat at short notice. While the study of international organisations triggered a 'big yawn' among historians in the 1970s and 1980s, things are quite different now. These organisations are no longer the exclusive province of historians of international relations.

The League of Nations, whose historiographic role was to be the scapegoat for the incapacity of liberal democracies to prevent the Second World War, is now attracting historians who are interested in the fact that the League was an arena, a protagonist, a prime mover in questions of transportation, health, standardisation, migration or energy.[85] A similar interest is noticeable for many of the agencies of the Versailles and San Francisco generation, and it even begins to spill over to the various international unions and bureaux created during the last third of the nineteenth century. The history of the International Labour Organisation, which had been languishing for a long time, has been studied afresh beyond the history of trade unionism or of labour legislation that had attracted attention in previous times. Empirical work based on archives at the ILO and elsewhere demonstrates that the existence and operation of intergovernmental organisations have provided opportunities for communities of reformers to get together (women's groups, moderate anti-colonial groups), that it created spaces for planning and forecasting initiatives and served as a platform for aspiring nationalities and claims by indigenous peoples.[86] Similarly, the history of international non-governmental organisations has entered a research-intensive phase.

Because they acted as connectors, because they carried projects for creating or impeding relations across borders, because they put in motion people, values, ideas and notions, because they created a sphere of action and communities of actors that straddled countries, international organisations and their archives now attract the attention of historians in unprecedented ways. Whether one studies cross-national governance, migrations, health issues, environmental problems, communication infrastructures, social movements or political mobilisation in a transnational perspective, the archives of international organisations can supply elements of an answer. If only because they often acted as black holes, attracting information and interest from or about an incredible range of actors and topics, their archives and libraries are rich seams for transnational historians.

▶ Conclusion

The toolkit required is certainly a lavish one: transnational historians have to find order but account for mobility; they need to integrate a different conception of spatiality but situate their quest for movements within specific contexts; they can use a range of different quantitative or qualitative methods; they may invent new sources as well as revisit or rearrange existing ones. But this makes the transnational agenda rich and varied, one that places a premium on curiosity, imagination and investigation.

These will be much needed as transnational historians often, though not always, have to deal with an issue that is crucial when one is obliged to work across and between lines of difference. To describe a circulation, one must capture it in the different locales that it connects together. To study a relation, one needs to take into account the point of view of the different parties that participate in the interaction. An obvious consequence of these needs is the adoption of multi-sited research, as documentary evidence is often fragmented. But there is more to it, and transnational history is an incentive to develop practices based on the search for symmetrical sourcing. Although it might be fair to deal with the sources applying to only one party in a relation if one's focus is exclusively on this party, the whole story might take a different direction if material shaped by the tools, attitudes and worldviews of the different parties involved is incorporated. This is not just a matter of giving everyone their due share, or giving voice to the dominated and the vanquished. Nor is it a question of getting facts right by comparing different views. What is at stake is the capacity to estimate the expectations of the protagonists, their behaviour, and the results of what happens across lines of difference. We will come nearer to that goal if our research material comes from the different sides of such lines. Sanjay Subrahmanyam, in one attempt to develop this kind of symmetrical sourcing, noted that most historians would agree on that in principle, but would assert that implementation was a totally different matter.[87] This is one of the frontiers of transnational history, but not the only one.

Conclusion

'This book proposes to mark the end of American history as we have known it.'[1] This is the daring assumption Thomas Bender uses as the opening sentence of his *Nations among Nations*. Bender's book is about the making and unmaking of interconnections and interdependencies between America and the rest of the world on the one hand, and on the other it pinpoints the presence of the foreign within domestic American history, and the projection of domestic America into the world out there. As such, Bender does work on two of the three fronts we have mentioned as the 'big issues' to be handled by historians who adopt a transnational perspective. He is adamant that adopting this perspective will make a huge difference to the way American history is written and imagined. British historian Patricia Clavin upholds similar standards in a recent article where she examines the potential of global, transnational and international history to reshape European history. Clavin writes: 'Unearthing connections and networks – however defined – within and across Europe's borders, determining where they break or peter out, will recast our understanding not just of European history, but our understanding of the modern world.'[2]

Is the sky the limit, then? Is transnational history destined to revamp the way historians imagine, research, write, teach and sell history? Should it be openly proposed as the new best way to do history? A more timid position has been adopted throughout this book, which argues that writing history in a transnational perspective is no more and no less than an additional lens for the historian's spectacles. It makes visible some aspects that other lenses do not reveal, but it does not replace the other lenses. It works well for some observations, but is ineffective or even deceptive for others. In line with such a position, this conclusion will begin by reviewing ways in which transnational history can bring added value to specific dimensions of historical knowledge. In the aforementioned article, Patricia Clavin identifies three dimensions where transnational history and its siblings are in a position to bring added value to our understanding of European history, mostly in the twentieth century: time, manner and place. Although I do not address just the field of European twentieth-century history, I will follow these three essential dimensions to elaborate on her statements. But what lies ahead are not just great and exciting prospects, but also limits and difficulties. Some of these will be discussed in a second stage.

▶ Time, manner and place

On the first plane, Patricia Clavin wonders whether transnational history can put pressure on the chronological arrangements of history (periodisation, significant events, watersheds, turning points). She concludes that 'at best, (historians) have put a few dents in historical containers like the First and Second World Wars'. However, the scholarship we have skimmed through is gradually elaborating its own chronological moorings. These have to do with the establishment and disruption of circulations, the longevity of connections, the changing effectiveness of relations, the durability of a formation. And these may or may not match our usual bearings. Take for instance the Cold War. Erez Manela shows that the smallpox eradication programme, a joint venture between US and Soviet governmental agencies, started and thrived at a moment of growing tension between the superpowers. His conclusion, that writing the history of disease control into Cold War history requires some adjustments in the narrative of the latter, directly affects the periodisation of the Cold War.[3] Per Hogselius's dent into Cold War history derives from his study of the transport and trade of natural gas from the USSR to Western Europe. Not only did Austria, Italy, parts of West Germany (Bavaria) and Greece rely heavily or even exclusively on Soviet natural gas, with agreements signed while the Iron Curtain and the North Atlantic Treaty Alliance seemed to rule international politics, but paroxysmal episodes of the Cold War did not necessarily impact on energy provision. It was only two weeks after the invasion of Czechoslovakia by Warsaw Pact forces that Soviet gas began to flow into Austria, following an agreement signed between the Austrian state-owned oil and gas company ÖMV and the Soviet Ministry of Foreign Trade in June 1968.[4] In a recent volume that scrutinises Cold War entanglements from the angle of technology, several authors identify ad hoc temporalities of the Cold War, based on regional stakes or nation-building strategies: from many aspects, they say, the beginning and end of the Cold War do not have the character of the complete ruptures that we assign them.[5] Regarding the world wars mentioned by Clavin, they may lose ground as inevitable limits for books and dissertations. There is, for instance, more and more research being done that straddles the two world wars, and the status of these two periods as thresholds of 'new eras' may change once such studies have nuanced our understanding of how the war affected the longevity of links, redefined circulations and installed new formations. The 'world' dimension of these (and other) wars may also be more finely tuned when we can appraise the extent and importance of circulations and connections that were altered, redirected or created by wars. Most certainly, researchers will not conclude that world wars did not matter, but they will certainly refine the importance of the wars as chronological markers when it comes to understanding certain aspects of history. The study of connections and disconnections, of circulations and changes in their **catchment areas**, of relations and their impact, of specific topical or territorial formations, foretells chronological moorings that will have to be set against the canonical peri-ods and milestones that organise the historical timeline of the last 200 years.[6] The search for ad hoc chronologies may eventually corrode historical containers, but the stakes are far from being recouped here.

Clavin is more confident regarding the variable of 'manner', and she points to the capacity of transnational history to push historians of Europe to 'sharpen the claim to novelty or distinction of any given event or phenomenon'. In this volume, I have argued that historians working in a transnational perspective were working on three fronts: reconstruction and contextualisation of historical interconnections between units of historical understanding, assessment of the blurred line between the foreign and the domestic within these units, and capture and recording of pro-cesses, actors and events that lived through and between these units. On this basis, historians are indeed in a position to **historicise** many events or phenomena. This is what happened when historians of migrations began a conversation with sociol-ogists and anthropologists who felt that the migrants of the late twentieth century were living between two countries in an unprecedented fashion. Historians were spurred on by the social scientists' claim, which allowed them to scrutinise past aspects of present features. It enticed them to shift their research perspective from the study of immigration or emigration to the study of migrations as a chain and a fabric. But they also mobilised their knowledge of nineteenth- or early twentieth-century migrations to show that remittances, political commitment, familial links and entrepreneurial undertakings were familiar to migrants well before the 1980s, and used that knowledge to appraise changes between the nineteenth and the late twentieth centuries. Clavin also notes that transnational history can broaden fields of inquiry, open up new ones and rejuvenate other topics that had been neglected. That is what can be expected from any additional lens adopted by historians, and the preceding chapters have provided different instances of similar gains. But it is not only in terms of 'research results' that the manner of researching and writing history can be affected. Telling the history of entanglements may generate differ-ent ways of organising research, as we have seen, but also different narrative forms and research tools. What the digital sphere has to offer in all these dimensions has yet to be integrated within our methods of researching and teaching transnational history, from text mining to the publication of multimedia historical essays on the World Wide Web and through the production and dissemination of historical research in the form of participatory platforms (wikis, to put it briefly).[7]

As for place, Patricia Clavin states that transnational history is a great incentive to reconsider the writing of national histories and the role of national histories in the writing of European history. On the one hand, transnational history chal-lenges national narratives, by bringing to the fore sub- and supranational units whose importance comes out in the study of connections and circulations. On the other hand, it calls for revisiting national histories, 'notably by focusing on the role of Europe's "smaller nations" and (re)integrating their histories into the study of wider events, trends and institutions'. These two directions have been empha-sised in this book. Certainly, transnational historians do not consider the national unit as the natural container of historical developments in the last 200 years or so, and they frame their problem-solving and problem-setting strategies in ways that do not follow the '*tyrannie du national*'.[8] Still, they also know that nations are valid categories to apprehend historical developments, if only because the national states have generated enough loyalty and institutions to frame historical develop-ments in national terms. Some adjustments to our historical spatial imagination, as suggested in Chapter 6, correspond to Clavin's perception of transnational history's impact on place. They suggest a vertical movement taking on board units larger and smaller than the nation, and a horizontal effort to include countries and regions beyond what historians are used to considering 'good subjects' because they are 'big countries'. But Chapter 6 also hints at other impacts that transnational his-tory may have on our conception of place: the need to work through the different scales that we use to organise our spatial thinking; the consideration of how actors make scale, space and place through circulations, connections and relations; the incorporation of transient and not demarcated space; the emphasis on the reloca-tion of processes and actors in specific contexts. From that point of view, place is not merely the site where transnational historians address their questions about a specific topic: it becomes a crucial dimension of the answers they can provide.

▶ The glass ceilings of transnational history

As suggested by Patricia Clavin's use of the term 'potential', there is still much to be done before it can be said whether and how much the transnational perspective has affected the writing of history. If the sky is the limit, it is also a faraway place, and there might be a glass ceiling between us and the stars. The likelihood of the transnational perspective achieving a lasting place in the historians' armoury does not just depend on the quality of research having been, being or to be done. The proof of the pudding is not only in the eating: it has to do with the atmosphere of the meal, and with the guests' desire to eat it.

At this moment, transnational history is considered with interest and even enthusiasm by many students and scholars. The list of research topics is expanding and scholars show a keen desire to test different narrative forms and analytical methods. This very book, wittingly or unwittingly, nonetheless points to different hurdles that lie across the path of transnational historians. In the first place, it demonstrates that a historian with training in European social history and an inter-est in the North Atlantic world is far from being sufficiently aware of historical connections, circulations and relations in other geographical and topical domains. This is the first layer of our glass ceiling, and we will need a stronger commitment to create and maintain interest between historians of different topics, moments and regions to go through it.[9] But the major challenge may lie beyond the expansion of the intellectual conversation itself. Is it the case that the propitious zeitgeist which propelled the interest in transnational history is changing?

The coming years will certainly be crucial for transnational history, as recent events may mark the wane of factors which had supported its waxing. The changing balance of world power may well favour an emphasis on national history in higher education research and teaching programmes within the up and coming new powerhouses of economic growth like India, China or Brazil. The continuing foreign encroachment in Africa, now augmented by Chinese and Gulf countries' investments, can generate a counter-narrative hostile to ties, flows and relations in that continent. The endemic state of financial, social and economic crisis in Europe and North America may discredit the interest in flows, ties and relations as tokens of the failure of capitalism. Nationalism is on the rise in Hungary and other places. Transnational history, in many aspects, has built its fortune on its promise to contribute to the history of a 'globalised world', despite the appalling pleonastic quality of that cliché. Deglobalisation, initially proposed by the Filipino sociologist Walden Bello as a remedy for the situation of the Global South, is now advocated to solve issues that plague the Global North. Will transnational history keep its appeal if there is a move towards a 'deglobalised world'? Throughout the chapters of this volume, it has been argued that the transnational perspective is also about the capacity of countries and their governements to control entanglements, to protect their citizens from their consequences, and that it is interested in disintegration, the collapse of relations, the interruption and disruption of flows and ties. Therefore I think that a swing back to the *tyrannie du national* should not condemn the attempt to write history in a transnational perspective. A changing context would even push transnational historians to pay more attention to these aspects, still largely under-researched to date. In any case, only the future will give us a better idea of whether the transnational perspective is a historiographical position that can adapt to different weather.

The third layer of the glass ceiling has to do with the reception of transnational history. Michael McGerr, in his 1991 comments on Ian Tyrrell's *American Historical Review* article, mentions that the 'new transnational history' would come at the cost of an estrangement of American historians from their audience, which is still largely nationalistic.[10] Australian historians Ann Curthoys and Marilyn Lake also urge caution: 'Given the intensely local and national relevance of history, then, it seems to us that there are dangers in transnational histories becoming disconnected from local audiences and by extension national political debates.'[11] Both remarks lead us to consider the issue of audience. Who are transnational historians writing for? Who is willing to sit in history classrooms where a transnational perspective of history is adopted? Who are the individuals who want to learn from transnational history? The success of transnational, global, entangled history has had something to do with its capacity to provide a view of the past that matches current and past individuals or family experience of a growing number of people who live between and through nations. Migrants, expatriate professionals, investors, connected nomads would have sort of a vested interest in transnational history. Academic historians themselves may partly fit that description, at a moment when academic training often includes training periods at different universities in foreign countries: the international university job market has expanded well beyond the small circle of luminaries or free riders who were able to seek and find a job abroad only a few decades ago. If transnational history is just meant to provide the kind of narrative that suits the disposition of such social groups, a sort of public history for the mobile classes, its intellectual appeal will not last. Conversely, for some supporters of transnational history, audiences attached to a national paradigm should be exposed to the narrative of connections and circulation in order to transform their outlook. Thomas Bender thus speaks of the capacity of a worldly history of America to 'encourage and sustain a cosmopolitan citizenry, at once proud nationals and humble citizens of the world'.[12] That is indeed a possible answer to Curthoys and Lake (transform local and national political debates into cosmopolitics) and to McGerr (if the audience does not fit, change the audience).

However, it may also turn out that working on the three prongs of transnational history does not lead to an estrangement from nationalistic audiences, nor from local and national political and social stakes. This volume has argued that adopting a transnational perspective does not automatically lead to writing without or against the nation, or to only analysing long-distance connections and long-range circulations. Rather, a transnational perspective shows how deeply the national fabric and the local or national political debate are intertwined with issues, actors and processes that cut through what we are used to conceiving as local or national. To come back to George Orwell's words,[13] more connections and more entanglements do not automatically erode the local or the national, nor do they lead to a brave new world of mutual understanding between different societies and polities. If transnational history wishes to endure, its practitioners will have to relocate the objects of their research, as well as their role as public intellectuals. They cannot live only on a cosmopolitan horizon and audience. Their purchase will also be to explain how and why a transnational perspective can contribute to understanding the historical development of a specific institution, a determined social group, a firm, a community, a neighbourhood, a city, a region or a country.

▶ More later

In any case, the glass ceilings of mood and audience are reminders that the adoption of a transnational perspective is not the 'one ring to rule them all' (Tolkien,

Lord of the Rings). It does not take much insight to realise that not all labour strikes are characterised by the presence of imported strike breakers, by the provision of financial help from abroad, or by participation in an international wave of mobilisation. Or to admit that not every brush stroke by a painter takes its cue from concerns, motifs and colours in distant and distinct places. Or to understand that the conditions of price, production and consumption of a certain product can derive from conditions in a very small and unique place. There are vast domains of historical research that do not require a transnational perspective. Excellent PhD dissertations, great books, suggestive articles and captivating courses will be written and presented without it. That is something we should not forget, in a context of increased competition between universities where 'internationalisation' has become a dogma. From internationalisation of recruitment, exchange agreements and visibility to the forced internationalisation of research and course topics, there is a small step. In many universities, emphasis on 'global' or 'transnational' curricula and research priorities has been the chosen instrument of managers and decision makers, for reasons that do not correspond to the intellectual purchase of such topics.

As a result, there is a tendency to propose transnational history as the new way, or even the new orthodoxy, and it is certainly seen in many quarters as a good way to get funding, find publication outlets and receive attention, credit and interest from colleagues. But the fundamental structures of teaching and research have remained remarkably stable. Curricula are still mostly organised within a national framework, even if there is a growing number of courses that tweak the study of a topic or place to study its ties to the world, and the world presence in it. Likewise, funding programmes that spill over the national container are either dedicated to topics that deal with two countries (and depend on bilateral agreements between two national research agencies), or tailored according to the usual regions and areas. It is relatively easy to find funds for research about 'Europe', it is less so when your research space is transient, uneven and does not match the limits of existing or would-be polities. Transnational historians may want to accept the fact that the conditions of production of historical knowledge are still very much defined at the national level, or the regional one when it comes to the European Union. They may also want to change that. As one who is convinced of the interest in the transnational perspective, and who is aware of its limits, I entertain the hope that transnational historians can participate without being hegemonic. This has been the horizon of this little vade mecum from start to finish.

Notes

▶ Introduction

1 Frederick Jackson Turner, 'The Significance of History', in Ray Allen Billington, ed., *Frontier and Section: Selected Essays of Frederick Jackson Turner* (Englewood Cliffs, NJ, 1961), pp. 20–1.

2 Pascale Rabault-Feuerbahn, ' "Les grandes assises de l'orientalisme." La question interculturelle dans les congrès internationaux des orientalistes (1873–1912)', *Revue Germanique Internationale*, 12 (2010), pp. 47–68.

3 Prasenjit Duara, *Rescuing History from the Nation: Questioning Narratives of Modern China* (Chicago, 1995), p. 4.

4 Andreas Wimmer and Nina Glick-Schiller, 'Methodological Nationalism and Beyond: Nation-State Building, Migration and the Social Sciences', *Global Networks*, 2: 4 (2002), pp. 301–34.

5 Michael Geyer, 'Historical Fictions of Autonomy and the Europeanization of National History', *Central European History*, 22: 3/4 (1989), pp. 316–42.

6 *Journal of Global History* page at http://journals.cambridge.org/action/displayJournal?jid=JGH (accessed 5 March 2013).

7 Michael Geyer, review of Budde, Gunilla; Conrad, Sebastian; Janz, Oliver (ed.): *Transnationale Geschichte. Themen, Tendenzen und Theorien* (Göttingen, 2006), in H-Soz-u-Kult, http://geschichte-transnational.clio-online.net/rezensionen/2006-4-032, published 11 October 2006, accessed 5 March 2013.

8 *The Journal of American History*, 'The Nation and Beyond: Transnational Perspectives on United States History: a Special Issue', 86: 3 (December 1999).

9 William Cunningham, *Growth of English Industry and Commerce during the Early and Middle Ages* (Cambridge, 1890, 2nd edn), vol. 1, p. 8.

10 Marc Bloch, 'Pour une histoire comparée des civilisations européennes', *Revue de Synthèse*, XLVI (1928), pp. 15–50. 'English version: 'A Contribution Towards a Comparative History of European Societies', in Marc Bloch, *Land and Work in Mediaeval Europe. Selected Papers by Marc Bloch* (New York, 1969), pp. 44–81 (translation J.E. Anderson).

11 Marcel Detienne, *Comparing the Incomparable* (Stanford, CA 2008) original edn in French 2000.

12 Michel Espagne, 'Sur les limites du comparatisme en histoire culturelle', *Genèses. Sciences sociales et histoire,* 17: 1 (1994), pp. 112–21.

13 Jürgen Kocka and Heinz-Gerhard Haupt, eds, *Geschichte und Vergleich: Ansätze und Ergebnisse international vergleichender Geschichtsschreibung* (Frankfurt a.M., 1996), p. 10.

14 Johannes Paulmann, 'Internationaler Vergleich und interkultureller Transfer. Zwei Forschungsansätze zur europäischen Geschichte des 18. bis 20. Jahrhunderts', *Historische Zeitschrift,* 267 (1998), pp. 649–85.

15 Christof Mauch and Kiran Klaus Patel, eds, *The United States and Germany During the Twentieth Century. Competition and Convergence* (Cambridge, 2010), original edn in German 2008.

16 Deborah Cohen and Maura O'Connor, eds, *Comparison and History. Europe in Cross-National Perspective* (London, 2004).

17 Nancy L. Green, *Ready-to-Wear and Ready-to-Work: a Century of Industry and Immigrants in Paris and New York* (Durham, NC, 1997).

18 Jerry H. Bentley, *Old World Encounters: Cross-Cultural Contacts and Exchanges in Pre-Modern Times* (New York, 1993); Fernand Braudel, *Civilization and Capitalism, 15th–18th Century* (London, 1981–84),3 vols, original edn in French 1979; Sanjay Subrahmanyam, *Explorations in Connected History* (Delhi, 2005), 2 vols, Victor B.Lieberman, *Strange parallels: Southeast Asia in global context, c. 800–1830* (Cambridge, 2003 and 2012), 2 vols.

19 Martin Krieger, 'Transnationalität in vornationaler Zeit? Ein Plädoyer für eine erweiterte Gesellschaftsgeschichte der frühen Neuzeit', *Geschichte und Gesellschaft,* 30: 1 (2004), pp. 125–36; Angeles Redondo and Bartolomè Yun Casalilla, 'Localism, Global History and Transnational History. A Reflection from the Historian of Early Modern Europe', *Historisk Tidskrift,* 127: 4 (2007), pp. 659–78.

20 Kiran Klaus Patel, 'Überlegungen zu einer transnationalen Geschichte', *Zeitschrift für Geschichtswissenschaft,* 52 (2004), p. 634.

21 Sanjay Subrahmanyam, 'On the Window that was Asia', in *idem, Explorations,* vol. 1, pp. 1–17.

22 Charles S. Maier, 'Consigning the Twentieth Century to History: Alternative Narratives for the Modern Era', *The American Historical Review,* 105: 3 (2000), especially pp. 817–22. Subsequently, Maier indicated that, in his eyes, territoriality was once more on the rise.

23 Saskia Sassen, *Territory, Authority, Rights: From Medieval to Global Assemblages* (Princeton, NJ, 2006).

24 James P. Piscatori, *Islam in a World of Nation-States* (Cambridge, 1986).

25 Sugata Bose, *A Hundred Horizons: The Indian Ocean in an Age of Global Imperialism* (Cambridge, MA, 2006), p. 280.

26 On the national conceptions of the likes of M. N. Roy or Rabindranath Tagore, see Kris Manjapra, *M.N. Roy: Marxism and Colonial Cosmopolitanism* (New Delhi, 2010), chs 1 and 3, and Sugata Bose, *A Hundred Horizons*, ch. 6.

27 James Lorand Matory, *Black Atlantic Religion. Tradition, Transnationalism and Matriarchy in the Rise of the Afro-Brazilian Candomble* (Princeton, NJ, 2005), p. 111.

28 James C. Scott, *Seeing like a State: How Certain Schemes to Improve the Human Condition have Failed* (New Haven, CT, 1998).

29 Patrick Manning, *Navigating World History. Historians Create a Global Past* (New York, 2003).

30 David Christian, *Maps of Time: An Introduction to Big History* (Berkeley, CA, 2004).

31 Despite its open interest in articles dealing with earlier periods, the recently created *Journal of Global History* has mostly attracted articles dealing with the period after the fifteenth century.

32 Simon Schaffer, Lissa Roberts, Kapil Raj and James Delbourgo, eds, *The Brokered World: Go-Betweens and Global Intelligence, 1770–1820* (Sagamore Beach, MA, 2009).

33 Antoinette Burton, 'On the Inadequacy and the Indispensability of the Nation', in *idem*, ed., *After the Imperial Turn: Thinking with and through the Nation* (Durham, NC, 2003), pp. 1–23.

34 Paul H. Kratoska, 'Elites and the Construction of the Nation in Southeast Asia', in Jost Dülffer and Marc Frey, eds, *Elites and Decolonization in the Twentieth Century* (Basingstoke, 2011), pp. 36–55.

35 See John R. Chávez, *Beyond Nations: Evolving Homelands in the North Alantic World, 1400–2000* (New York, 2009) especially chs 4–7; Antoinette Burton, *At the Heart of the Empire: Indians and the Colonial Encounter in Late Victorian Britain* (Berkeley, CA, 1998).

36 C.A. Bayly and Eugenio F. Biagini, eds, *Giuseppe Mazzini and the Globalisation of Democratic Nationalism 1830–1920* (Oxford, 2008).

37 Robin Law, 'Constructing a Real National History: a Comparison of Edward Blyden and Samuel Johnson', in P.F. de Moraes Farias and Karin Barber, eds, *Self-Asssertion and Brokerage: Early Cultural Nationalism in West Africa* (Birmingham, 1990), pp. 78–100.

38 Verkijika G. Fanso, 'The Latent Struggle for Identity and Autonomy in the Southern Cameroons 1916–1946', in Ian Fowler and Verikijika G. Fanso, eds, *Encounter, Transformation and Identity: Peoples of the Western Cameroon Borderlands, 1891–2000* (New York, 2009), pp. 141–50; Roderick D. Bush, *The End of White World Supremacy, Black Internationalism and the Problem of the*

Color Line (Philadelphia, 2009); Michelle Stephens, *Black Empire: the Masculine Global Imaginary of Caribbean Intellectuals in the United States, 1914 to 1962* (Durham, NC, 2005).

39 Mark Frost, 'Wider Opportunities: Religious Revival, Nationalist Awakening and the Global Dimension in Colombo, 1870–1920', *Modern Asian Studies*, 36: 4 (2002), pp. 937–67.

40 Şükrü Hanioğlu, *A Brief History of the Late Ottoman Empire* (Princeton, NJ, 2008), ch. 4; Abbas Amanat, *Pivot of the Universe. Nasir al-Din Shah and the Iranian Monarchy* (Berkeley, CA, 1997), chs 3 and 4; Afaf Lutfi al-Sayyid Marsot, *Egypt in the Reign of Muhammad Ali* (Cambridge, 1984).

41 Arif Dirlik, 'Performing the World: Reality and Representation in the Making of World Histor(ies)', *Journal of World History*, 16: 4 (2005), pp. 406–7.

42 James T. Watson, *Emigration and the Chinese Lineage: the Man in Hong Kong and London* (Berkeley, CA, 1975); Samuel L. Baily, *Immigrants in the Land of Promise: Italians in Buenos Aires and New York City, 1870 to 1914* (Ithaca, NY, 1999); Andrew Hardy, *Red Hills: Migrants and the State in the Highlands of Vietnam* (Copenhagen, 2003).

43 Daniel T. Rodgers, *Atlantic Crossings: Social Politics in a Progressive Age* (Cambridge, MA, 1998).

44 Ulrike Freitag and Achim von Oppen, eds, *Translocality: The Study of Globalising Processes from a Southern Perspective* (Leiden, 2010).

45 Ramón A. Gutiérrez and Elliott Young, 'Transnationalizing Borderlands History', *The Western Historical Quarterly*, 41: 1 (2010), pp. 26–53; Isabel Hofmeyr, 'The Black Atlantic Meets the Indian Ocean: Forging New Paradigms of Transnationalism for the Global South – Literary and Cultural Perspectives', *Social Dynamics*, 33: 2 (2007), pp. 3–32.

46 See respectively Ghislaine Lydon, *On Trans-Saharan Trails. Islamic Law, Trade Networks and Cross-Cultural Exchange in Nineteenth Century Western Africa* (Cambridge, 2009); Alexander Badenoch and Andreas Fickers, eds, *Materializing Europe: Transnational Infrastructures and the Project of Europe* (Basingstoke, 2010); Selçuk Esenbel, *Japan, Turkey and the World of Islam: the Writings of Selcuk Esenbel* (Folkestone, 2009).

47 Benedict Anderson, *Under Three Flags. Anarchism and the Anticolonial Imagination* (London, 2005).

48 Joshua A. Fogel, *Articulating the Sinosphere: Sino-Japanese Relations in Space and Time* (Cambridge, MA, 2009), especially parts 2 and 3, and Shogo Suzuki, 'The Importance of "Othering" in China's National Identity: Sino-Japanese Relations as a Stage of Identity Conflicts', *The Pacific Review*, 20: 1 (2007), pp. 23–47; Michel Espagne and Michael Werner, eds, *Transferts. Les relations intellectuelles dans l'espace franco-allemand* (Paris, 1988); 'Rethinking History and

the Nation-State: Mexico and the United States as a Case Study. A Special Issue', *Journal of American History*, 86: 2 (1999).

49 Gudrun Krämer, *A History of Palestine: From the Ottoman Conquest to the Founding of the State of Israel* (Princeton, NJ, 2008).

50 Alain Tarrius, *La mondialisation par le bas. Les nouveaux nomades de l'économie souterraine* (Paris, 2002); Eric Tagliacozzo, *Secret Trades, Porous Borders: Smuggling and States along a Southeast Asia Frontier, 1865–1915* (Singapore, 2007).

51 Judith Schueler, *Materialising Identity. The Co-Construction of the Gotthard Railway and Swiss National Identity* (Amsterdam, 2008).

52 Donald R. Wright, *The World and a Very Small Place in Africa: A History of Globalization in Niumi, The Gambia* (Armonk, 2004), original edn 1997, chs 4–8.

▶ 1 Meanings and Usages

1 Gustavo Cano, *The Mexico–North Report on Transnationalism* (Washington, DC, 2005), available at http://www.mexnor.org/programs/TRP/MexNor%20Report%20I.pdf (accessed April 2010).

2 Barry Wellman, 'From Little Boxes to Loosely-Bounded Networks: the Privatization and Domestication of Community', and Saskia Sassen, 'Cracked Casings: Notes towards an Analytics for Studying Transnational Processes', both in Janet L Abu-Lughod, ed., *Sociology for the Twenty-First Century: Continuities and Cutting Edges* (Chicago, 1999).

3 Arjun Appadurai, *Modernity at Large. Cultural Dimensions of Globalization* (Minneapolis, 1996), content was published between 1990 and 1995; Paul Gilroy, *The Black Atlantic: Modernity and Double Consciousness* (Cambridge, MA, 1993).

4 Arjun Appadurai, *Modernity*, p. 19.

5 Elsa Chaney, *Supermadre: Women in Politics in Latin America* (Austin, TX, 1979), p. 209.

6 Randolph Bourne, 'Trans-national America', *Atlantic Monthly*, 118 (July 1916), pp. 86–97.

7 Linda Basch *et al.*, *Towards a Transnational Perspective on Migration: Race, Class, Ethnicity, and Nationalism* (New York, 1992); *idem, Nations Unbound: Transnational Projects, Postcolonial Predicaments and De-Territorialized Nation-States* (Amsterdam, 1994).

8 Compare Alejandro Portes and Luis E. Guarnizo, 'Tropical Capitalists: U.S.-Bound Immigration and Small Enterprise Development in the Dominican Republic', in Sergio Díaz-Briquets and Sidney Weintraub, eds, *Migration, Remittances, and Small Business Development: Mexico and Caribbean Basin*

Countries (Boulder, CO, 1991), pp. 101–31 with Alejandro Portes, 'Transnational Communities: their Emergence and Significance in the Contemporary World-System', in Roberto Patricio Korzeniewicz and William C. Smith, eds, *Latin America in the World-Economy* (Westport, CT, 1996), pp. 151–68.

9 Alejandro Portes, 'Introduction: the Debate and Significance of Immigrant Transnationalism', *Global Networks*, 1: 3 (2001), pp. 181–93.

10 Thomas Risse-Kappen, ed., *Bringing Transnational Relations Back In: Non-State Actors, Domestic Structures, and International Institutions* (Cambridge, 1995).

11 Jackie Smith *et al.*, eds, *Transnational Social Movements and Global Politics: Solidarity beyond the State* (Syracuse, NY, 1997); Margaret E. Keck and Kathryn Sikkink, eds, *Activists beyond Borders: Advocacy Networks in International Politics* (Ithaca, NY, 1998).

12 Katherine Verdery, 'Beyond the Nation in Eastern Europe', *Social Text*, 38 (1994), pp. 1–19.

13 Ewa Morawska, 'Disciplinary Agendas and Analytic Strategies of Research on Immigration and Transnationalism: Challenges of Interdisciplinary Knowledge', *International Migration Review*, 37: 3 (2003), pp. 611–40; Roger Waldinger and David Fitzgerald, 'Transnationalism in Question', *American Journal of Sociology*, 109: 5 (2004), pp. 1177–95.

14 Sanjeev Khagram and Peggy Levitt, eds, *The Transnational Studies Reader: Intersections and Innovations* (Oxford, 2008), p. 11.

15 Constantin Pecqueur, *De la paix, de son principe et de sa réalisation* (Paris, 1842), p. 199.

16 Ahmed Zouaoui, *Socialisme et internationalisme. Constantin Pecqueur* (Geneva, 1964).

17 Georg Curtius, *Philologie und Sprachwissenschaft* (Leipzig, 1862), p. 9.

18 I am obliged to Donna Gabaccia for the mention of this quotation in the *Princeton Review*, which put me on to Curtius' trail.

19 For instance, *Atlanta Constitution*, 10 October 1915, 'trans-national highways'.

20 Randolph Bourne, 'Trans-National America', *Atlantic Monthly*, 118 (July 1916), pp. 86–97. This essay has been reprinted in Randolph Bourne, *War and the Intellectuals. Collected Essays*, ed. by Carl Resek (New York, 1964).

21 Max Gutzwiller, 'Das Internationalprivatrecht der durch die Friedensverträge eingesetzten Gemischten Schiedsgerichthöte', *InternationalesJahrbuch für Schiedsgerichtwesen*, 3 (1931), pp. 123–62.

22 Simon Kuznets, 'Foreign Economic Relations of the United States and their Impact upon the Domestic Economy. A Review of Long Term Trends', *Proceedings of the American Philosophical Society*, 92: 4 (1948), pp. 228–43.

23 Peer Zumbansen, 'Transnational Law', in Jan Smits, ed., *Encyclopedia of Comparative Law* (Cheltenham, 2006), pp. 738–54.

24 Karl Kaiser, 'Transnationale Politik ', in Ernst-Otto Czempie, ed., *Die anachro-nistische Souveranität* (Cologne, 1969), pp. 80–109.

25 Robert O. Keohane and Joseph S. Nye Jr, eds, 'Transnational Relations and World Politics', *International Organization*, 25: 3 (1971).

26 *Ibid.*, p. xi.

27 *Ibid.*, p. xii.

28 Thomas Risse-Kappen lists some of the spin-offs in *Bringing Transnational Relations*, especially in note 8.

29 Wimmer and Glick-Schiller, 'Methodological Nationalism'.

30 Stefan Berger, *Writing the Nation. A Global Perspective* (New York, 2007).

31 Immanuel Wallerstein, 'The Unintended Consequences of Cold War Area Stud-ies', in Noam Chomsky, ed., *The Cold War and the University: Toward an Intellectual History of the Postwar Years* (New York, 1997), pp. 195–231.

32 Karl Lamprecht, 'Problems of Universal History', in *idem, What is History? Five Lectures on the Modern Science of History* (New York, 1905), original edn in German 1904, p. 194.

33 Arnold Toynbee, *A Study of History* (New York, 1954), vol. 9.

34 Marshall G.S. Hodgson, 'Hemispheric Interregional History as an Approach to World History', *Journal of World History*, 1: 3 (1954), pp. 715–23.

35 Poul Duedahl, 'Selling Mankind: UNESCO and the Invention of Global History, 1945–76', *Journal of World History*, 22: 1 (2011), pp. 111–33.

36 Gilbert Allardyce, 'Toward World History: American History and the Com-ing of the World History Course', *Journal of World History*, 1: 1 (1990), pp. 23–76.

37 Immanuel Kant, 'Idea for a Universal History with a Cosmopolitan Purpose', in Hans Reiss, ed, *Kant* (Cambridge, 1991), pp. 41–53.

38 Eric J. Hobsbawm, *The Age of Revolution: Europe 1789–1848* (London, 1962), *The Age of Capital: 1848–1875* (London, 1975), *The Age of Empire: 1875–1914* (London, 1987), *The Age of Extremes: the Short Twentieth Century 1914–1991* (London, 1994).

39 See the work of the French historians Jean Aubin and Denys Lombard who have relentlessly explored these issues in South and Southeast Asia since the 1960s, for instance in Jean Aubin and Denys Lombard, *Marchands et hommes d'affaires asiatiques dans l'Océan Indien et la mer de Chine, XIIIe–XXe siècle* (Paris, 1988).

40 Thomas Bender, 'The Revolt against Enclosure: American History Opens Out to the World', in Gary Reichard and Ted Dickson, eds, *America on the World Stage. A Global Approach to U.S. History* (Urbana, IL, 2008), pp. xiii–xxv.

41 Samir Amin, *Unequal Development: an Essay on the Social Formations of Peripheral Capitalism* (New York, 1976), original edn in French 1975.

42 Clark C. Spence, *British Investments and the American Mining Frontier, 1860–1901* (Ithaca, NY, 1958).

43 Sidney Pollard, *Peaceful Conquest. The Industrialisation of Europe 1760–1970* (Oxford, 1981), p. vii; see also Paul Bairoch, *Victoires et déboires: histoire économique et sociale du monde du XVI° siècle à nos jours* (Paris, 1997).

44 Pierre Renouvin and Jean-Baptiste Duroselle, *Introduction à l'histoire des relations internationales* (Paris, 1964), issued a call to study people-to-people relations and *forces profondes* (profound forces) of international relations.

45 Brigitte Schroeder-Gudehus, 'Challenge to Transnational Loyalties: International Scientific Organizations after the First World War', *Science Studies*, 3: 2 (1973), pp. 93–118.

46 Elizabeth Fox Genovese and Eugene D. Genovese, *Fruits of Merchant Capital: Slavery and Bourgeois Property in the Rise and Expansion of Capitalism* (New York, 1983); A.J.H. Latham, *The International Economy and the Undeveloped World 1865–1914* (London, 1978); Alexander Gerschenkron, *Economic Backwardness in Historical Perspective. A Book of Essays* (Cambridge, 1962); Immanuel Wallerstein, *The Modern World-System* (New York, 1974–89).

47 Donald Worster, 'World without Borders: the Internationalizing of Environmental History', *Environmental Review*, 6: 2 (1982), pp. 8–13, and *idem*, ed., *The Ends of the Earth: Perspectives on Modern Environmental History* (Cambridge, 1988).

48 Arthur O. Lovejoy,'The Historiography of Ideas', in *idem, Essays in the History of Ideas* (Baltimore, 1948), pp. 1–13. See also George B. Sanson, *The Western World and Japan: A Study in the Interaction of European and Asiatic Cultures* (New York, 1949).

49 Claude Digeon, *La crise allemande de la pensée française 1870–1914* (Paris, 1959).

50 Marilyn Lake, 'Nationalist Historiography, Feminist Scholarship, and the Promise and Problems of New Transnational Histories: the Australian Case', *Journal of Women's History*, 19: 1 (2007), p. 183.

51 J.W.A. Naber, *Wegbereidsters* (Groningen, 1909). See Karen M. Offen, *European Feminisms 1700–1950: a Political History* (Stanford, CA, 2000), p. 6.

52 For an evaluation of this pattern, see Marcel van der Linden and Frits van Holthoon, eds, *Internationalism in the Labour Movement, 1830–1940* (Leiden,1988), and especially Marcel van der Linden, 'Internationalism in the Labour Movement: Fragments of a Bibliography', vol. II, pp. 624–54.

53 Ernesto Ragioneri, 'Italiani all'estero ed emigrazione di lavoratori italiani: una tema di storia movimento operaio', *Belfagor, Rassegna di varia Umanità*, 17: 6 (1962), pp. 640–69.

54 Robin D.G. Kelley, ' "But a Local Phase of a World Problem": Black History's Global Vision', *The Journal of American History*, 86: 3 (1999), pp. 1015–72.

55 http://legacy.lclark.edu/~tepo/index.html (accessed 5 March 2013).
56 One example is David H. Pinkney, 'American Historians on the European Past', *American Historical Review*, 86: 1 (1981), p. 19, but many others are available in different languages.
57 James A. Fields, Jr, 'Transnationalism and the New Tribe', in Robert O. Keohane and Joseph S. Nye Jr, eds, *Transnational Relations*, pp. 353–72.
58 Prasenjit Duara, the historian of modern China, was one of the few to make a contribution to the group, but describes it as a 'quite brief involvement' (correspondence with the author, November 2007).
59 Khagram and Levitt, eds, *The Transnational Studies Reader*.
60 Ian Tyrrell, 'American Exceptionalism in an Age of International History', *American Historical Review*, 96: 4 (1991), pp. 1031–72. The phrase was suggested to him by a reviewer of his article, the US historian Thomas Bender (correspondence with the author, November 2007).
61 Michael Adas, 'From Settler Colony to Global Hegemon: Integrating the Exceptionalist Narrative of the American Experience into World History', *The American Historical Review*, 106: 5 (2001), pp. 1692–720; Robert Gregg, 'Making the World Safe for American History', in Antoinette Burton, ed., *After the Imperial Turn: Thinking with and through the Nation* (Durham, NC, 2003), pp. 170–85.
62 Thomas Bender, ed., *Rethinking American History in a Global Age* (Berkeley, CA, 2002).
63 Thomas Bender, *A Nation among Nations. America's Place in World History* (New York, 2006); Ian Tyrrell, *Transnational Nation. United States History in Global Perspective since 1789* (New York, 2007).
64 Carmen de la Guardia and Juan Pan-Montojo, 'Reflexiones sobre una Historia Transnacional', special issue 'La historia transnacional', *Studia histórica. Historia Contemporánea*, 16/17 (1998), pp. 9–31. May be the first special issue of a historical journal that used 'transnational history' in its title.
65 *Geschichte und Gesellschaft*, 27: 3 (2001), with introduction by Kocka and contributions by Jürgen Osterhammel, Susanne Sophia Spiliotis and Albert Wirtz. Other contributions in that thread were published in following issues.
66 Kiran Patel, 'Transnations among Transnations? The Debate on Transnational History in the US and Germany', *American Studies*, 53 (2009), pp. 451–72.
67 Espagne and Werner, eds, *Transferts*.
68 Rudolf Muhs *et al.*, eds, *Aneignung und Abwehr: Interkultureller Transfer zwischen Deutschland und Großbritannien im 19. Jahrhundert* (Bodenheim, 1998).
69 Shalini Randeria, 'Geteilte Geschichte, Verwobene Moderne', in Jörn Rüsen *et al.*, eds, *Zukunftsentwürfe- Ideen für eine Kultur der Veränderung* (Frankfurt, 1999), pp. 87–97.

70 Michael Werner and Bénédicte Zimmermann, 'Vergleich, Transfer, Verflechtung. Der Ansatz der *Histoire croisée* und die Herausforderung des Transnationalen', *Geschichte und Gesellschaft* 28 (2002), pp. 607–36.

71 See Sebastian Conrad and Jürgen Osterhammel, eds, *Das Kaiserreich transnational. Deutschland in der Welt, 1871–1914* (Göttingen, 2004); and Philipp Ther, 'Beyond the Nation: the Relational Basis of a Comparative History of Germany and Europe', *Central European History*, 36: 1 (2003), pp. 45–73.

72 Anthony G. Hopkins, 'Globalization. An Agenda for historians', in *idem*, ed., *Globalization in World History* (New York, 2002), p. 2.

73 David Held and Anthony McGrew, *'Globalization'*, in Joel Krieger, ed., The *Oxford Companion to Politics of the World* (New York, 2001), pp. 324–7.

74 Jeffrey G. Williamson, 'Globalization, Convergence, and History', *The Journal of Economic History*, 56: 2 (1996), pp. 277–306.

75 Michael Geyer and Charles Bright, 'For a Unified History of the Twentieth Century', *Radical History Review*, 39 (1987), pp. 69–91 and 'World History in a Global Age', *The American Historical Review*, 100: 4 (1995), pp. 1039–40.

76 Two books that manifest this common interest are Matthew Frye Jacobson, *Barbarian Virtues. The United States Encounters Foreign People at Home and Abroad 1876–1917* (New York, 2000) and Donna R. Gabaccia, *Foreign Relations. American Immigration in Global Perspective* (Princeton, NJ, 2012).

77 Günter Moltmann, ed., *Deutsche Amerikaauswanderung im 19. Jahrhundert. Sozialgeschichtliche Beiträge* (Stuttgart, 1976); Gungwu Wang, *China and the Chinese Overseas* (Singapore, 1991); Donna R. Gabaccia and Fraser M. Ottanelli, eds, *Italian Workers of the World: Labor, Migration, and the Making of Multi-Ethnic Nations* (Urbana, IL, 2001).

78 Jan Lucassen *et al.*, eds, *Migration History in World History. Multidisciplinary Approaches* (Leiden, 2010); Donna R. Gabaccia and Dirk Hoerder, eds, *Connected Seas and Connected Ocean Rims: Indian, Atlantic, and Pacific Oceans and China Seas Migrations from the 1830s to the 1930s* (Leiden, 2011).

79 Frank A. Ninkovich, *The Diplomacy of Ideas: US Foreign Policy and Cultural Relations (1938–1950)* (New York, 1981); Akira Iriye, *The Cold War in Asia* (New York, 1974); and *idem* 'The Internationalization of History. Presidential address to the American Historical Association', *American Historical Review*, 94: 1 (1989), pp. 1–10.

80 See Michael Hogan, 'The "Next Big Thing": the Future of Diplomatic History in a Global Age', *Diplomatic History*, 28: 1 (2004), p. 14.

81 Frederick Cooper and Ann L. Stoler, 'Tensions of Empire: Colonial Control and Visions of Rule', *American Ethnologist*, 16: 4 (1989), pp. 609–21.

82 Antoinette Burton, ed., *After the Imperial Turn: Thinking with and through the Nation* (Durham, NC, 2003).

83 Dale F. Eickelman and James Piscatori, eds, *Muslim Travellers: Pilgrimage, Migration, and the Religious Imagination* (London, 1990).

84 Micol Seigel, 'Beyond Compare: Historical Method after the Transnational Turn', *Radical History Review*, 91 (2005), p. 63.

85 *Idem*, p. 63.

86 May 1949 memorandum, cited by Poul Duedhal, 'Selling Mankind', pp. 111–33.

87 See respectively Akira Iriye, *Global Community: the Role of International Organizations in the Making of the Contemporary World* (Berkeley, 2002) and the 'Nation and Beyond', special issue of the *Journal of American History*.

88 Bender, *A Nation among Nations*, p. 14.

89 Arif Dirlik, 'Performing the World: Reality and Representation in the Making of World Histor(ies)', *Journal of World History*, 16: 4 (2005), pp. 391–410.

90 Akira Iriye, *Global and Transnational History. The Past, Present and Future*, (Basingstoke: 2012) and Patricia Clavin, 'Defining Transnationalism', *Contemporary European History*, 14: 4 (2005), pp. 421–39.

91 Daniel T. Rodgers, *Atlantic Crossings;* Kiran Klaus Patel, *Soldiers of Labor: Labor Service in Nazi Germany and New Deal America, 1933–1945* (Cambridge, 2005).

▶ 2 Connections

1 Cormac Ó Gráda *et al.*, eds, *When the Potato Failed: Causes and Effects of the 'Last' European Subsistence Crisis, 1845–1850* (Turnhout, 2007).

2 D. Graham Burnett, *The Sounding of the Whale. Science and Cetaceans in the Twentieth Century* (Chicago, 2012).

3 For striking exemplifications, see the novel by Carlo Levi, *Christ Stopped at Eboli; the Story of a Year* (New York, 1947) original edn in Italian 1945.

4 Joseph E.Taylor III, 'The Historical Roots of Canadian–American Salmon Wars', in John M. Findlay and Ken Coates, eds, *Parallel Destinies: Canadian–American Relations West of the Rockies* (Seattle, 2002), pp. 155–80.

5 R. J. M. Blackett, *Building an Antislavery Wall: Black Americans in the Atlantic Abolitionist Movement, 1830–1860* (Baton Rouge, 1983).

6 Anthony Reid, 'Nineteenth Century Pan-Islam in Indonesia and Malaya', *Journal of Asian Studies*, 26:2 (1967) pp. 267–83.

7 Stéphane Dudoignon, ed., *Intellectuals in the Modern Islamic World: Transmission, Transformation, Communication* (London, 2006).

8 Patrick Pourchasse and Pierre-Yves Beaurepaire, eds, *Les circulations internationales en Europe: années 1680–années 1780* (Rennes, 2010).

9 Schaffer *et al.*, eds, *The Brokered World*.

10 Abigail Green and Vincent Viaene, eds, *Religious Internationals in the Modern World: Globalization and Faith Communities since 1750* (Basingstoke 2012).

11 Subrahmanyam, *Explorations in Connected History*.

12 Linda Colley, *Captives. Britain, Empire and the World 1600–1850* (London, 2005).

13 Jill Matthews, 'Modern Nomads and National Film History: the Multi-Continental Career of J.D Williams', in Ann Curthoys and Marilyn Lake, eds, *Connected Worlds: History in a Transnational Perspective* (Canberra, 2006), pp. 157–69.

14 Eric Tagliacozzo, *Secret Trades, Porous Borders*; Christophe Bulté, 'Approche économique du secteur de la contrefaçon à Bruxelles (1814–1852)', *Cahiers du Cedic*, 2–4 (2003), pp. 3–78 (http://www.ulb.ac.be/philo/cedic/cahiers/index.html); Wolfgang Eichwede, 'Archipel Samizdat', in *idem*, ed., *Samizdat. Alternative Kultur in Zentral- und Osteuropa: die 60er bis 80er Jahre* (Bremen, 2000), pp. 8–19.

15 Nico Slate, 'A Colored Cosmopolitanism: Cedric Dover's Reading of the Afra-Asian World', in Sugata Bose and Kris Manjapra, eds, *Cosmopolitan Thought Zones. South Asia and the Global Circulation of Ideas* (Basingstoke, 2010), pp. 213–35.

16 Claude Markovits, *The Global World of Indian Merchants, 1750–1947: Traders of Sind from Bukhara to Panama* (Cambridge, 2000); Alain Tarrius, *La remontée des sud: Afghans et Marocains en Europe méridionale* (La Tour d'Aigue, 2007).

17 Edward M. Bruner, *Culture on Tour: Ethnographies of Travel* (Chicago, 2005).

18 Kristin Semens, 'Tourism and Autarky are Conceptually Incompatible. International Tourism Conferences in the Third Reich', in Eric G. E. Zuelow, ed., *Touring beyond the Nation* (Aldershot, 2011), pp. 195–214.

19 Sasha Pack, *Tourism and Dictatorship: Europe's Peaceful Invasion of Franco's Spain* (New York, 2006).

20 Ian R. Tyrrell, *Woman's World/Woman's Empire: the Woman's Christian Temperance Union in International Perspective, 1880–1930* (Chapel Hill, 1991), ch. 5 and *Reforming the World: the Creation of America's Moral Empire* (Princeton, 2010), ch. 2.

21 Sugata Bose, *A Hundred Horizons*, chs 3 and 7.

22 Ghislaine Lydon, *On Trans-Saharan Trails*.

23 Pedro Machado, 'Awash in a Sea of Cloth: South Asia, Cloth and Consumption in the Indian Ocean, 1300–1800', in Prasannan Parthasarathi and Giorgio Riello, eds, *South Asian Textiles in the World* (Oxford, 2008), pp. 53–84.

24 Thomas R. Metcalf, *Imperial Connections. India in the Indian Ocean Arena 1860–1920* (Berkeley, 2007), especially ch. 6.

25 Strickrodt Silke, ' "Afro-Brazilians" of the Western Slave Coast in the Nine-teenth Century', in José C. Curto and Paul E. Lovejoy, eds, *Enslaving Connections, Changing Cultures of Africa and Brazil during the Era of the Slavery* (Amherst, 2004), pp. 213–44.

26 Yong Chen, *Chinese San Francisco 1850–1943: a Transpacific Community* (Stanford, 2000).

27 Madeline Yuan-yin Hsu, *Dreaming of Gold, Dreaming of Home: Transnationalism and Migration between the United States and South China, 1882–1943* (Stanford, 2000).

28 Emmanuelle Loyer, *Paris à New York. Intellectuels et artistes français en exil 1940–1947* (Paris, 2005); Meredith Terretta, 'Cameroonian Nationalists go Global: from Forest Maquis to Pan African Accra', *The Journal of African History*, 51 (2010), pp. 189–212; Ingrid Fey and Karen Racine, eds, *Strange Pilgrimages: Exile, Travel, and National Identity in Latin America, 1800–1990s* (Wilmington, 2000).

29 Benedict Anderson, 'Long Distance Nationalism', in *idem, The Spectre of Comparisons. Nationalism, Southeast Asia and the World* (London, 1998), pp. 58–74.

30 In addition to Metcalf, see also Isabel Hofmeyr, 'Gandhi's Printing Press: Indian Ocean Print Cultures and Cosmopolitanisms', in Sugata Bose and Kris Manjapra, eds, *Cosmopolitan Thought Zones*, pp. 112–30.

31 Richard White, *The Middle Ground: Indians, Empires, and Republics in the Great Lakes Region, 1650–1815* (Cambridge, 1991).

32 John McLeod, 'A Night at "The Cosmopolitan". Axes of Transnational Encounter in the 1930s and 1940s', *Interventions: the International Journal of Postcolonial Studies*, 4: 1 (2002), pp. 53–67.

33 Michael Geyer and Charles Bright, 'World History in a Global Age', *The American Historical Review*, 100: 4 (1995), p. 1040.

34 Mary Louise Pratt, *Imperial Eyes: Travel Writing and Transculturation* (London, 1992); Homi K. Bhabha, *The Location of Culture* (New York, 1994).

35 Serge Gruzinski, *La Pensée Métisse* (Paris, 1999).

36 Eric Tagliacozzo, *Secret Trades, Porous Borders. Smuggling and States along a Southeast Asian Frontier 1865–1915* (New Haven, 2005).

37 Wolfram Siemann, *Deutschlands Ruhe, Sicherheit und Ordnung: die Anfänge der Politischen Polizei 1806–1866* (Tübingen, 1985); Jonathan Gantt, *Irish Terrorism in the Atlantic Community 1865–1922* (Basingstoke, 2010); Cyrille Fijnaut, 'The International Criminal Police Commission and the Fight against Communism, 1923–1945', in Mark Mazower, ed., *The Policing of Politics in the Twentieth Century: Historical Perspectives* (Providence, 1997), pp. 107–28.

38 On daily trespassing, see Edith Sheffer, *Burned Bridge: How East and West Germans made the Iron Curtain* (New York, 2011).

39 Emilia Karaboéva, 'Les visages invisibles de la vie quotidienne: Le cas des camionneurs internationaux de la Bulgarie (1956–1989)', *Divinatio*, 27 (2008), pp. 179–93.

40 James Onley, 'Britain's Native Agents in Arabia and Persia in the Nineteenth Century', *Comparative Studies of South Asia, Africa and the Middle East*, 24: 1 (2004), pp. 129–37.

41 Bernard Heyberger and Chantal Verdeil, eds, *Hommes de l'entre-deux. Parcours individuels et portraits de groupes sur la frontière de la Méditerrannée XVIe–XXe siècle* (Paris, 2009).

42 Mark Ravinder Frost, 'That Great Ocean of Idealism: Calcutta, the Tagore Circle and the Idea of Asia, 1900–1920', Nalanda-Sriwijaya Centre Working Paper 3 (June 2011), http://www.iseas.edu.sg (accessed 15 March 2013).

43 Roger S. Levine, *A Living Man from Africa: Jan Tzatzoe, Xhosa Chief and Missionary, and the Making of Nineteenth-Century South Africa* (New Haven, 2011).

44 Madeline Hsu, 'Trading with Gold Mountain. Jinshanzhuang and Networks of Kinship and Native Place', in Sucheng Chan, ed., *Chinese American Transnationalism: the Flow of People, Resources, and Ideas between China and America during the Exclusion Era* (Philadelphia, 2006), pp. 22–33.

45 Daniel T. Rodgers, *Atlantic Crossings*.

46 *Ibid.*, ch. 4.

47 *Ibid.*, chs 10 and 11.

48 Robert H. Donaldson, ed., *The Soviet Union in the Third World: Successes and Failures* (Boulder, 1981), pp. 336ff.

49 Thomas P. Bernstein and Hua-yu Li, eds, *China Learns from the Soviet Union, 1949–Present* (Lanham, 2010).

50 Mark P. Hampton and Jason P. Abbott, eds, *Offshore Finance Centres and Tax Havens. The Rise of Global Capital* (West Lafayette, 1999); Ronen Palan, *The Offshore World: Sovereign Market, Virtual Places, and Nomad Millionaires* (Ithaca, 2003).

51 Saâdia Elhariri, 'Les Marocaines au cœur d'un nouveau circuit d'échanges marchands: entre ici et là-bas', *Revue Européenne des Migrations Internationales*, 19: 1 (2003), pp. 223–32.

52 Bonnie S. Anderson, *Joyous Greetings: the First International Women's Movement, 1830–1860* (Oxford, 2000).

53 Haiming Liu, *The Transnational History of a Chinese Family: Immigrant Letters, Family Business, and Reverse Migration* (New Brunswick, 2005).

54 JoAnne Yates and Craig N. Murphy, 'Charles Le Maistre: Entrepreneur in International Standardization', *Entreprises et Histoire*, 5 (2008), pp. 10–27.

55 John Braithwaite and Peter Drahos, *Global Business Regulation* (Cambridge, 2000), pp. 588–90.

56 Frederick Cooper, 'What is the Concept of Globalization Good For? An African Historian's Perspective', *African Affairs*, 100: 399 (2001), pp. 189–213.

57 Nicholas Thomas, *Entangled Objects. Exchange, Material Culture and Colonialism in the Pacific* (Cambridge, Mass., 1991).

58 Ruth Benedict, *Patterns of Culture* (Boston, 1934); Bronislaw Malinowski, '*Kula: the Circulating Exchange* of Valuables in the Archipelagoes of Eastern New Guinea', *Man* 20 (1920), pp. 97–105; Arjun Appadurai, ed., *The Social Life of Things. Commodities in Cultural Perspective* (London, 1986).

59 Michael Adas, *Dominance by Design. Technological Imperatives and America's Civilizing Mission* (Cambridge, Mass., 2006).

60 Karl Miller, 'Talking Machine World: Selling the Local in the Global Music Industry 1900–1920', in Anthony G. Hopkins, ed., *Global History. Interactions between the Universal and the Local* (New York, 2006), pp. 160–90.

61 Bose, *A Hundred Oceans,* ch. 6, p. 228.

62 Steven Harris, *Surrealist Art and Thought in the 1930's: Art, Politics, and the Psyche* (Cambridge, 2004).

63 George Ribeill, 'Aux origines de l'utopie du réseau ferroviaire européen intégré', *Histoire & Sociétés*, 21 (2007), pp. 44–59.

64 Sue Matthews *et al., South America Invaded: the Growing Danger of Invasive Alien Species* (Cape Town, 2005).

65 David Edgerton, *The Shock of the Old: Technology and Global History since 1900* (London, 2006), p. 93.

66 Joseph O'Connell, 'Metrology: the Creation of Universality by the Circulation of Particulars', *Social Studies of Science,* 23: 1 (1993), p. 164.

67 Henry B. Lovejoy, 'Drums of Sango: Bata Drum and the Symbolic Reestablishment of Oyo in Colonial Cuba, 1817–1867', in Joel E. Tishken *et al.*, eds, *Sàngó in Africa and the African Diaspora* (Bloomington, 2009), pp. 284–310.

68 Jeremy Prestholdt, 'Similitude and Empire: On Comorian Strategies of Englishness', *Journal of World History*, 18: 2 (2007), p. 113.

69 Mikael Hård and Ruth Oldenziel, *Consumers, Tinkerers, Rebels. The People Who Shaped Europe* (Basingstoke, 2013), ch. 1.

70 'Reading recently a batch of rather shallowly optimistic "progressive" books, I was struck by the automatic way in which people go on repeating certain phrases which were fashionable before 1914. Two great favourites are "the abolition of distance" and "the disappearance of frontiers". I do not know how often I have met with the statements that "the aeroplane and the radio have abolished distance" and "all parts of the world are now interdependent". Actually, the effect of modern inventions has been to increase

nationalism, to make travel enormously more difficult, to cut down the means of communication between one country and another, and to make the various parts of the world less, not more dependent on one another for food and manufactured goods.' George Orwell, *Tribune*, 12 May 1944.

71 Armand Mattelart, *Histoire de l'utopie planétaire. De la cité prophétique à la société globale* (Paris, 1999), p. 124.

72 Deep Kanta Lahiri Choudhury, *Telegraphic Imperialism: Crisis and Panic in the Indian Empire, c.1830–1920* (Basingstoke, 2010), chs 4 and 5.

73 This section draws on the different by-products of the research network Transnational Infrastructures of Europe (TIE), created in 2002. See http://www. tie-project.nl/, accessed 15 March 2013.

74 Vincent Lagendijk, *Electrifying Europe: the Power of Europe in the Construction of Electricity Networks* (Amsterdam, 2008).

75 Per Högselius *et al.*, 'Natural Gas in Cold War Europe: the Making of a Critical Infrastructure', in Anique Hommels *et al.*, eds, *The Making of Europe's Critical Infrastructure: Common Connections and Shared Vulnerabilities* (Basingstoke, 2013).

76 Franck Schipper, *Driving Europe. Building Europe on Roads in the 20th Century* (Amsterdam, 2008); Monika Burri *et al.*, eds, *Die Internationalität der Eisenbahn 1850–1970* (Zurich, 2003).

77 Thomas J. Misa and Johan Schot, 'Inventing Europe: Technology and the Hidden Integration of Europe', *History & Technology*, 21: 2 (2005), pp. 1–19.

78 Per Högselius, 'Fuelling Europe', in *idem et al.*, eds, *From Nature to Networks: the Infrastructural Transformation of Europe* (Basingstoke, forthcoming).

79 Misa and Schot, 'Inventing', p. 9.

80 Michael Nelson, *War of the Black Heavens: the Battle of Western Broadcasting in the Cold War* (Syracuse, 1997).

81 Jamie Frederic Metzl, 'Rwandan Genocide and the International Law of Radio Jamming', *The American Journal of International Law*, 91: 4 (1997), pp. 628–51.

82 Hommels *et al.*, eds, *The Making of Europe's Critical Infrastructure*.

83 Johannes Schweitzer, 'The Birth of Modern Seismology in the Nineteenth and Twentieth Centuries', *Earth Sciences History*, 26: 2 (2007), pp. 263–79.

84 J. R. McNeill, *Something New under the Sun: an Environmental History of the Twentieth-Century World* (New York, 2000).

85 Ulrich Beck, *World Risk Society* (Cambridge, Mass., 1999).

86 Anne-Marie Moulin, 'The Pasteur Institutes between the Two World Wars. The Transformation of the International Sanitary Order', in Paul Weindling, ed., *International Health Organizations and Movements 1918–1939* (Cambridge, 1985), pp. 244–65; Iris Borowy, *Coming to Terms with World Health. The League of Nations Health Organisation 1921–1946* (Frankfurt, 2009).

87 Brett Bennett, 'The El Dorado of Forestry: The Eucalyptus in India, South Africa, and Thailand, 1850–2000', *International Review of Social History*, 55 (2010), supplement, pp. 27–50; Ravi Rajan, *Modernizing Nature: Forestry and Imperial Eco-development 1800–1950* (Oxford, 2006).

88 Kurk Dorsey, *The Dawn of Conservation Diplomacy: U.S.–Canadian Wildlife Protection Treaties in the Progressive Era* (Seattle, 1998).

89 Ulrike Lindner, 'Transnational Movements between Colonial Empires: Migrant Workers from the British Cape Colony in the German Diamond Town of Lüderitzbucht', *European Review of History: Revue Européenne d'Histoire*, 16: 5 (2009), pp. 679–95.

90 Charles F. Feinstein, *An Economic History of South Africa: Conquest, Discrimination and Development* (Cambridge, 2005), ch. 5; Alan H. Jeeves, *Migrant Labour and South Africa's Mining Economy: the Struggle for the Gold Mines' Labour Supply* (Montreal, 1985).

91 Jean-Jacques Van Helten, 'Empire and High Finance: South Africa and the International Gold Standard 1890–1914', *The Journal of African History*, 23: 4 (1982), pp. 529–48.

92 Christopher Lever, *They Dined on Eland. The Story of the Acclimatisation Societies* (London, 1992).

93 Jane Carruthers and Libby Robin, 'Taxonomic Imperialism in the Battles for Acacia: Identity and Science in South Africa and Australia', *Transactions of the Royal Society of South Africa*, 65: 1 (2010), p. 48.

94 Stephen B. Jones, *Boundary-Making; a Handbook for Statesmen, Treaty Editors, and Boundary Commissioners* (Washington, 1945).

95 'AHR Forum: Oceans of History', *The American Historical Review*, 111: 3 (2006).

96 Peter Gleick, 'Water and Conflict', *International Security* 18: 1 (1993), pp. 79–112.

97 Mark Cioc, *The Rhine: an Eco-Biography, 1815–2000* (Seattle, 2002).

98 Joseph E. Taylor III, 'Boundary Terminology', *Environmental History*, 13: 3 (2008), p. 5.

99 See Roger Blench, 'Pastoralists and National Borders in Nigeria', in Paul Nugent and A. I. Asiwaju, eds, *African Boundaries: Barriers, Conduits, and Opportunities* (London, 1996), pp. 118–28.

100 Taylor, 'Boundary'.

101 Rodgers, *Atlantic Crossings*, p. 5.

▶ 3 Circulations

1 Michael Billig, *Banal Nationalism* (London, 1995).

2 John Hutchinson, *Nations as Zones of Conflict* (London, 2005), ch. 2; Anne Marie Thiesse, 'National Identities: a Transnational Paradigm', in Alain

Dieckhoff and Christophe Jaffrelot, eds, *Revisiting Nationalism: Theories and Processes* (London, 2005), pp. 122–43.

3 Manjapra, *M.N. Roy*, ch. 1.

4 See Jeffrey Byrne, 'Our Own Special Brand of Socialism: Algeria and the Contest of Modernities in the 1960s'. *Diplomatic History*, 33: 3 (2009) pp. 427–47 and his forthcoming *The Pilot Nation: Revolutionary Algeria in the Third World's Vanguard.*

5 Compare David Todd, 'John Bowring and the Global Dissemination of Free Trade', *Historical Journal*, 51 (2008), pp. 373–97 and Mark Metzler, 'The Cosmopolitanism of National Economics: Friedrich List in a Japanese Mirror', in Hopkins, ed., *Global History*, pp. 98–130.

6 Edgerton, *The Shock of the Old.*

7 Marie-Monique Robin, *Escadrons de la mort, l'école française* (Paris, 2004).

8 See above, chapter 2 note 70.

9 Compare Wolfram Kaiser, *Christian Democracy and the Origins of European Union* (Cambridge, 2007) with Andrea Mammone, *Transnational Neofascism. The Extreme Right in France and Italy since 1945* (Cambridge, 2012).

10 The notion of regime is traced through its different elaborations in the expanded online bibliographical companion, which can be obtained by writing to pys.th.2013@gmail.com.

11 John Urry, *Sociology beyond Societies: Mobilities for the Twenty-First Century* (London, 2000).

12 'Historical Memory, Global Movements and Violence: Paul Gilroy and Arjun Appadurai in Conversation', interview with Paul Gilroy and Arjun Appadurai by Vikki Bell, *Theory, Culture & Society*, 16: 2 (1999), pp. 21–40.

13 John Urry, *Global Complexity* (Malden, 2003).

14 Saskia Sassen, 'Introduction: Locating Cities on Global Circuits', in *idem, Global Networks, Linked Cities* (New York, 2002), pp. 1–38.

15 Isabel Hofmeyr, *The Portable Bunyan. A Transnational History of the Pilgrim's Progress* (Princeton, 2004).

16 Marilyn Lake and Henry Reynolds, *Drawing the Global Colour Line: White Men's Countries and the International Challenge of Racial Equality* (Cambridge, 2008), p. 4.

17 Michael Egan, 'Mercury's Web. Some Reflections on Following Nature across Time and Place', *Radical History Review*, 107 (2010), pp. 111–26.

18 Anouche Kunth, 'Le portrait confisqué de Joseph Mantachev. Histoire d'exils et de spoliations', *L'Homme*, 195–196 (2010), pp. 283–306.

19 Marie Percot, 'Indian Nurses in the Gulf: Two Generations of Female Migration', *South Asia Research*, 26: 1 (2006), pp. 41–62 and 'Indian Nurses in the Gulf: from Job Opportunity to Life Strategy', in Anuja Agrawal, ed., *Migrant Women and Work* (New Delhi, 2006), pp. 155–76.

20 Hans Konrad Van Tilburg, 'Vessels of Exchange: the Global Shipwright in the Pacific', in Jerry H. Bentley *et al.*, eds, *Seascapes: Maritime Histories, Littoral Cultures, and Transoceanic Exchanges* (Honolulu, 2007), pp. 38–52.

21 *Modern Intellectual History*, 7: 2 (2010), is devoted to the *Gita*.

22 Erwin Panofsky, *Studies in Iconology: Humanistic Themes in the Art of the Renaissance* (New York: 1939), pp. 70–71.

23 On the circulation of housing reform ideas in the North Atlantic world, see Thomas Adam, *Intercultural Transfers and the Making of the Modern World* (Basingstoke, 2011), ch. 2.

24 Kapil Raj, *Relocating Modern Science. Circulation and the Construction of Knowledge in South Asia and Europe 1650–1900* (Basingstoke, 2007).

25 Guy Attewell, 'Interweaving Substance Trajectories: *Tiryaq*, Circulation and Therapeutic Transformation in the Nineteenth Century', in Anne Digby *et al.*, eds, *Crossing Colonial Historiographies: Histories of Colonial and Indigenous Medicines in Transnational Perspective* (Newcastle, 2010), pp. 1–20.

26 Aleksandra Majstorac-Kobiljski, 'American Missionary Colleges in Beirut and Kyoto 1860–1920', PhD dissertation (The City University of New York, 2010).

27 Martin Dodge and Rob Kitchin, *Atlas of Cyberspace* (Harlow, 2008).

28 Steven Topik *et al.*, *From Silver to Cocaine: Latin American Commodity Chains and the Building of the World Economy, 1500–2000* (Durham, 2006).

29 Virginie Rozée, 'Cross-Border Oocyte Donation in Europe', paper presented at the 27th Annual Meeting of European Society of Human Reproduction and Embryology, Stockholm, Sweden, 2011.

30 Marc Levinson, *The Box: How the Shipping Container made the World Smaller and the World Economy Bigger* (Princeton, 2006).

31 Frank H.H. King *et al.*, *The History of the Hongkong and Shanghai Banking Corporation* (New York, 1987–91).

32 Marc Flandreau and Clemens Jobst, 'The Ties that Divide: a Network Analysis of the International Monetary System, 1890–1910', *The Journal of Economic History*, 65: 4 (2005), pp. 977–1007.

33 France Nerlich, *La peinture française en Allemagne (1815–1870)* (Paris, 2010).

34 See the expanded bibliography for Chapter 4 in the online bibliographical companion, which can be obtained by writing to pys.th.2013@gmail.com.

35 Kirk Shaffer, 'Tropical Libertarians: Anarchist Movements and Networks in the Caribbean, Southern United States, and Mexico, 1890s–1920s', in Steven Hirsch and Lucien van der Walt, eds, *Anarchism and Syndicalism in the Colonial and Postcolonial World, 1870–1940: the Praxis of National Liberation, Internationalism, and Social Revolution* (Leiden, 2010), pp. 273–320.

36 Raj, *Relocating Science*, p. 226.

37 Erik van der Vleuten and Vincent Lagendijk, 'Transnational Infrastructure Vulnerability. The Historical Shaping of the European Blackout', *Energy Policy*, 38: 4 (2010), pp. 2042–52.

38 For an overview of the current situation, see Glenn Morgan *et al.*, eds, *The Multinational Firm. Organizing across Institutional and National Divides* (Oxford, 2001).

39 For combination within a collection of essays, see Michael O. West *et al.*, eds, *From Toussaint to Tupac: the Black International since the Age of Revolution* (Chapel Hill, 2009); for combination in a field of study, compare Haiming Liu, *The Transnational History of a Chinese Family: Immigrant Letters, Family Business, and Reverse Migration* (New Brunswick, 2005) with Look Lai Walton, *Indentured Labor, Caribbean Sugar: Chinese and Indian Migrants to the British West Indies 1838–1928* (Baltimore, 1993).

40 Cemil Aydin, *The Politics of Anti-Westernism in Asia: Visions of World Order in Pan-Islamic and Pan-Asian Thought* (New York, 2007); Caitlin E. Murdock, *Changing Places: Society, Culture, and Territory in the Saxon–Bohemian Borderlands, 1870–1946* (Ann Arbor, 2010).

41 Wimmer and Glick Schiller, 'Methodological Nationalism'.

42 Freitag and von Oppen, eds, *Translocality*.

43 Dudoignon *et al.*, *Intellectuals in the Modern Islamic World*, part 1, pp. 3–159.

44 Steven Topik and William Gervase Clarence-Smith, eds, *The Global Coffee Economy in Africa, Asia, and Latin America, 1500–1989* (Cambridge, 2003); John M. Talbot, *Grounds for Agreement: the Political Economy of the Coffee Commodity Chain* (Lanham, 2004).

45 W. M. Mathew, *The House of Gibbs and the Peruvian Guano Monopoly* (London, 1981).

46 Franco Moretti, *Atlas of the European Novel, 1800–1900* (London, 1998), p. 157.

47 Michel Espagne, *Les transferts culturels franco-allemands* (Paris, 1999), chs 2 and 8.

48 Robert W. Rydell and Rob Kroes, *Buffalo Bill in Bologna: the Americanization of the World, 1869–1922* (Chicago, 2005); Allan Mitchell, *The German Influence in France after 1870: the Formation of the French Republic* (Chapel Hill, 1979).

49 Mira Wilkins, *The History of Foreign Investment in the United States to 1914* (Cambridge, Mass., 1989).

50 Frederick Cooper and Ann Laura Stoler, 'Between Metropole and Colony: Rethinking a Research Agenda', in *idem*, eds, *Tensions of Empire: Colonial Cultures in a Bourgeois World* (Berkeley, 1997), pp. 1–58.

51 Ariane Landuyt, 'Il modello rimosso. Pragmatismo, etica, solidarietà e principio federativo nelle interrelazioni tra socialismo belga e socialismo italiano',

in Maurizio Ridolfi, ed., *Alessandro Schiavi. Indagine sociale, culture politiche e tradizione socialista nel primo '900* (Cesena, 1994), pp. 15–30.

52 Ezekiel B. Gebissa, 'Khat in the Horn of Africa: Historical Perspectives and Current Trends', *Journal of Ethnopharmacology*, 132: 3 (2010), pp. 607–14; Cyrus Schayegh, 'The Many Worlds of Abud Yasin; or, What Narcotics Trafficking in the Interwar Middle East Can Tell Us about Territorialization', *American Historical Review*, 116: 2 (2011), pp. 273–306.

53 R. Michael Feener *et al.*, eds, *Islamic Connections: Muslim Societies in South and Southeast Asia* (Singapore, 2009), and for circulations between Europe and Asia, Christiane Brosius and Roland Wenzlhuemer, eds, *Transcultural Turbulences. Towards a Multi-Sited Reading of Image Flows* (Heidelberg, 2011).

54 Gerd Gemünden, 'Between Karl May and Karl Marx: the DEFA *Indianerfilme* (1965–1983)', *New German Critique*, 82 (2001), pp. 25–38.

55 Sudha Rajagopalan, *Indian Films in Soviet Cinemas. The Culture of Movie-Going after Stalin* (Bloomington, 2009).

56 Brian Larkin, 'Degraded Images, Distorted Sounds: Nigerian Video and the Infrastructure of Piracy', *Public Culture*, 16: 2 (2004), pp. 289–314.

57 Hamid Naficy, *An Accented Cinema: Exilic and Diasporic Filmmaking* (Princeton, 2001).

58 Jeffrey E. Hanes, *The City as Subject: Seki Hajime and the Reinvention of Modern Osaka* (Berkeley, 2002).

59 Frank Grüner and Ines Prodöhl, eds, 'Ethnic Ghettos and Transcultural Processes in a Globalised City: New Research on Harbin', *Itinerario. International Journal on the History of European Expansion and Global Interaction*, 35: 3 (2011); Thomas Lahusen, ed., 'Harbin and Manchuria: Place, Space, and Identity', *South Atlantic Quarterly*, 99: 1 (2000).

60 Carl Levy, 'Social Histories of Anarchism', *Journal for the Study of Radicalism*, 4: 2 (2010), pp. 1–44.

61 Benedict Anderson, *Under Three Flags. Anarchism and the Anticolonial Imagination* (London, 2005); Ilham Khuri-Makdisi, *The Eastern Mediterranean and the Making of Global Radicalism, 1860–1914* (Berkeley, 2010); Michael Silvestri, 'The Bomb, Bhadralok, Bhagavad Gita, and Dan Breem: Terrorism in Bengal and Its Relations to the European Experience', *Terrorism and Political Violence*, 21 (2009), pp. 1–27.

62 Michael Schmidt and Lucien van der Walt, eds, *Black Flame: the Revolutionary Class Politics of Anarchism and Syndicalism* (Edinburgh, 2009); Steven Hirsch and Lucien van der Walt, eds, *Anarchism and Syndicalism in the Colonial and Postcolonial World, 1870–1940: the Praxis of National Liberation, Internationalism, and Social Revolution* (Amsterdam, 2010).

63 Rodman W. Paul, 'The Great California Grain War: the Grangers Challenge the Wheat King', *Pacific Historical Review*, 27 (1958), pp. 333–49.

64 This short can be watched at http://www.archive.org/details/D.w.Griffith-ACornerInWheat1909 (accessed 4 January 2012).

65 Samuel Truett and Elliott Young, eds, *Continental Crossroads: Remapping U.S.– Mexico Borderlands History* (Durham, 2004).

66 *Cent ans de l'Office international de bibliographie: 1895–1995* (Mons, 1995). The most complete view in English is W. Boyd Rayward, *The Universe of Information: the Work of Paul Otlet for Documentation and International Organisation* (Moscow, 1975).

67 Catherine Ann Cline, *E.D. Morel, 1873–1924: the Strategies of Protest* (Belfast, 1980).

68 David Bassens *et al.*, 'Setting Shari'a Standards: on the Role, Power and Spatialities of Interlocking Shari'a boards in Islamic Financial Services', *Geoforum*, 42:1 (2010), pp. 94–103.

69 Quentin Deluermoz, 'La fabrique "d'Empires inversés"?: le judo à la conquête de l'Europe et du monde', in Pierre Singaravélou and Julien Sorez, eds, *L'empire des sports: une histoire de la mondialisation culturelle* (Paris, 2010), pp. 117–37.

70 Christopher Rowland, ed., *The Cambridge Companion to Liberation Theology.*(Cambridge, 2007); Barry Carr, 'Mexican Communism 1968–1981: Eurocommunism in the Americas?' *Journal of Latin American Studies*, 17 (1985), pp. 201–28.

71 Eric Helleiner and Jonathan Kirshner, *The Future of the Dollar* (Ithaca, 2009).

72 Thomas P. Hughes, *Networks of Power. Electrification in Western Society 1880–1930* (Baltimore, 1983). For an application to nineteenth- and twentieth-century Europe, Erik van der Vleuten *et al.*, 'Europe's System Builders', *Contemporary European History*, 16: 3 (2007), pp. 321–47.

73 Werner Abelshauser *et al.*, *German Industry and Global Enterprise. BASF: the History of a Company* (Cambridge, 2004).

74 Diane White Oyler, *The History of the N'ko Alphabet and its Role in Mande Transnational Identity: Words as Weapons* (Cherry Hill, 2005), chs 5 and 7.

75 Francis E. Peters, *The Hajj: the Muslim Pilgrimage to Mecca and the Holy Places* (Princeton, 1994).

76 His trilogy of *The Information Age* was published between 1996 and 1998.

77 From the list of books recently published, see for instance Gary B. Magee and Andrew S. Thompson, *Empire and Globalization. Networks of People, Goods and Capital in the British World c.1850–1914* (Cambridge, 2010) or Berthold Unfried *et al.*, eds, *Transnationale Netzwerke im 20. Jahrhundert. Historische Erkundungen zu Ideen und Praktiken, Individuen und Organisationen* (Leipzig, 2008).

78 Manuel Castells, 'Informationalism, Networks and the Network Society: a Theoretical Blueprint', in *idem*, ed., *The Network Society: a Cross-Cultural Perspective* (Cheltenham, 2004), pp. 3–45.

79 Manuel Castells, *The Rise of the Network Society* (Cambridge, Mass., 1996), ch. 6.

80 'AHR Conversation: On Transnational History', *American Historical Review*, 111: 5 (2006), pp. 1449–50.

▶ 4 Relations

1 David G. Herrmann, *The Arming of Europe and the Making of the First World War* (Princeton, 1996); Michael Howard, 'Men against Fire, Expectations of War in 1914', *International Security*, 9: 1 (1984), pp. 41–57.

2 Abril Trigo, 'Shifting Paradigms: from Transculturation to Hybridity. A Theoretical Critique', in Rita de Grandis and Zilá Bernd, eds, *Unforeseeable Americas: Questioning Cultural Hybridity in the Americas* (Amsterdam, 2000), pp. 85–111.

3 Ariel Dorfman and Armand Mattelart, *How to Read Donald Duck: Imperialist Ideology in the Disney Comic* (New York, 1975), original edn in Spanish 1974.

4 Néstor García Canclini, *Hybrid Cultures: Strategies for Entering and Leaving Modernity* (Minneapolis, 2005), original edn in Spanish 2001.

5 Rob Kroes, '*Americanisation: What are we Talking about?*', in Rob Kroes *et al.*, eds, *Cultural Transmissions and Receptions: American Mass Culture in Europe* (Amsterdam, 1993), pp. 302–18.

6 Compare Michel Espagne and Michael Werner, 'La construction d'une référence culturelle allemande en France, genèse et histoire', *Annales. Économies Sociétés Civilisations*, 42: 4 (1987), pp. 969–92, with Michel Espagne, *Les transferts culturels franco-allemands* (Paris, 1999).

7 Peter Burke, 'Translating Knowledge, Translating Cultures', in Michael North, ed., *Kultureller Austausch in der Frühen Neuzeit* (Cologne, 2009), pp. 69–77.

8 Peter Burke, *Cultural Hybridity* (Cambridge, 2009), ch. 2.

9 Information is derived from the online resource on the history of horticulture in Lyon, *Horti-Lyon*, http://www.horti-lyon.fr/, accessed 19 March 2013.

10 Alfred W. Crosby, Jr, *The Columbian Exchange: Biological and Cultural Consequences of 1492* (Westport, 1972).

11 Margaret O. Meredith, 'Friendship and Knowledge. Correspondence and Communication in Northern Trans-Atlantic Natural History 1780–1815', in James Delburgo *et al.*, eds, *The Brokered World*, pp. 151–91.

12 Stefan-Ludwig Hoffmann, *The Politics of Sociability: Freemasonry and German Civil Society, 1840–1918* (Ann Arbor, 2007), original edn in German 2000, part 3; Jessica L. Harland-Jacobs, *Builders of Empire: Freemasons and British Imperialism, 1717–1927* (Chapel Hill, 2007).

13 Matthew Brown, *Adventuring through Spanish Colonies: Simón Bolívar, Foreign Mercenaries and the Birth of New Nations* (Liverpool, 2006); Clément Thibaud,

Républiques en armes. Les armées de Bolívar dans la guerre d'Indépendance en Colombie et au Venezuela (Rennes, 2006).

14 Eric Pécout, 'The International Armed Volunteers: Pilgrims of a Transnational Risorgimento', *Journal of Modern Italian Studies*, 14: 4 (2009), p. 414.

15 Yuko Takigawa, 'Contrast of Japanese Materials and Knowledge used by Cuvier, Valenciennes and Siebold to Describe Japanese Fish and Aquatic Animals in the 19th Century', paper presented at the conference 'Mobility and Circulation of Knowledge', Université Paris Diderot, Paris, November 2011.

16 Jean-Paul Gaudillère, *Inventer la biomédecine. La France, l'Amérique et la production des savoirs du vivant après 1945* (Paris, 2002), ch. 7.

17 Elisabeth Crawford *et al.*, eds, *Denationalizing Science: the Contexts of International Scientific Practice* (Dordrecht, 1993).

18 Adolphe Quételet, *Sciences mathématiques et physiques au commencement du XIXème siècle* (Brussels, 1867).

19 See respectively Mircea Babes and Marc-Antoine Kaeser, eds, *Archaeologists without Boundaries: towards a History of International Archaeological Congresses (1866–2006)* (Oxford, 2009); Pierre Marage and Grégoire Wallenborn, eds, *The Solvay Councils and the Birth of Modern Physics* (Bern, 1999); Anthony Hallam, *Great Geological Controversies* (Oxford, 1983) and Naomi Oreskes, *The Rejection of Continental Drift: Theory and Method in American Earth Science* (New York, 1999); Anne Rasmussen, 'L'amitié, une valeur scientifique. Les amitiés internationales des savants au tournant du siècle', *Jean Jaurès. Cahier Trimestriels*, 143 (1997), pp. 77–95.

20 Geert J. Somsen, 'A History of Universalism: Conceptions of the Internationality of Science from the Enlightenment to the Cold War', *Minerva*, 46 (2008), pp. 361–79.

21 Pascal Blanchard *et al.*, eds, *Human Zoos: Science and Spectacle in the Age of Colonial Empires* (Liverpool, 2008), original edn in French 2004.

22 The relation between asymmetry and reciprocity is at the heart of Serge Gruzinski's work on Mexico in the sixteenth and seventeenth centuries, beginning with *The Mestizo Mind: the Intellectual Dynamics of Colonization and Globalization* (New York, 2002), original edn in French 1999.

23 Victoria de Grazia, *Irresistible Empire: America's Advance through Twentieth Century Europe* (Cambridge, Mass., 2005); Michael Adas, *Dominance by Design: Technological Imperatives and America's Civilizing Mission* (Cambridge, Mass., 2006).

24 Kristin L. Hoganson, *Consumers' Imperium: the Global Production of American Domesticity, 1865–1920* (Chapel Hill, 2007); Ian Tyrrell, *Reforming the World: the Creation of America's Moral Empire* (Princeton, 2010).

25 Ian Tyrrell, *Woman's World/Woman's Empire*.

26　Michael Baxandall, *Patterns of Intentions: on the Historical Explanation of Pictures* (New Haven, 1985), pp. 59–60.

27　William Rubin, ed., *'Primitivism' in 20th Century Art: Affinity of the Tribal and the Modern* (New York, 1984).

28　Vicente L. Rafael, *The Promise of the Foreign: Nationalism and the Technics of Translation in the Spanish Philippines* (Durham, NC, 2005).

29　Benedict Anderson, *Under Three Flags. Anarchism and the Anticolonial Imagination* (London, 2005).

30　Rebecca E. Karl, *Staging the World: Chinese Nationalism at the Turn of the Twentieth Century* (Durham, 2002).

31　Lake and Reynolds, *Drawing the Global Colour Line*; Carl Nightingale, 'The Transnational Contexts of Early Twentieth-Century American Urban Segregation', *Journal of Social History*, 39: 3 (2006), pp. 667–702 and *Segregation: a Global History of Divided Cities* (Chicago, 2012), chs 5–10.

32　John Hunt, 'Credit Rating Agencies and the "Worldwide Credit Crisis": the Limits of Reputation, the Insufficiency of Reform, and a Proposal for Improvement', *Columbia Business Law Review*, 1 (2009), pp. 109–209.

33　For a glimpse on Thomson Reuters' multiple rankings of individual scientists, go to http://sciencewatch.com/dr/.

34　Nils Gilman, *Mandarins of the Future: Modernization Theory in Cold War America* (Baltimore, 2003).

35　The phrase is tweaked from Jay Winter's 'minor utopias', in *Dreams of Peace and Freedom: Utopian Moments in the Twentieth Century* (New Haven, 2006).

36　Martin H. Geyer, 'Prime Meridians, National Time, and the Symbolic Authority of Capitals in the Nineteenth Century', in Andreas W. Daum and Christof Mauch, eds, *Berlin, Washington, 1800–2000: Capital Cities, Cultural Representation, and National Identities* (Washington, DC, 2005), pp. 79–100.

37　Martin H. Geyer, 'One Language for the World. The Metric System, International Coinage, Gold Standard and the Rise of Internationalism 1850–1900', in Martin H. Geyer and Johannes Paulmann, eds, *The Mechanics of Internationalism: Culture, Society, and Politics from the 1840s to the First World War* (London, 2001), pp. 55–92.

38　Hector Vera, 'Decimal Time: Misadventures of a Revolutionary Idea, 1793–2008', *KronoScope: Journal for the Study of Time*, 9: 1–2 (2009), pp. 29–48.

39　Ian R. Bartky, *One Time Fits All: the Campaigns for Global Uniformity* (Stanford, 2007), chs 10 and 11.

40　Jürgen Osterhammel, *Die Verwandlung der Welt: eine Geschichte des 19. Jahrhunderts* (Munich, 2009), p. 1294.

41　Joseph O'Connell, 'Metrology: the Creation of Universality by the Circulation of Particulars', *Social Studies of Science*, 23: 1 (1993), pp. 129–73.

42 Hector Vera, 'The Social Life of Measures: Metrication in the United States and Mexico, 1789–2004', Ph.D. dissertation (The New School for Social Research, 2011).

43 Dietrich Reetz, 'The Deoband Universe: What Makes a Transcultural and Transnational Educational Movement of Islam?', *Comparative Studies of South Asia, Africa and the Middle East*, 27: 1 (2007), pp. 139–59.

44 Mariam Abou Zahab, 'Salafism in Pakistan. The Ahl-e Hadith Movement', in Roel Meijer, ed., *Global Salafism: Islam's New Religious Movement* (New York, 2009), pp. 126–42; Noorhaidi Hasan, 'The Salafi Movement in Indonesia: Transnational Dynamics and Local Development', *Comparative Studies of South Asia, Africa and the Middle East*, 27: 1 (2007), pp. 83–94.

45 Marc Gaborieau, 'The Transformation of Tablîghî Jamâat into a Transnational Movement', in Muhammad Khalid Masud, ed., *Travellers in Faith. Studies of the Tablîghî Jamâat as a Transnational Islamic Faith Movement for Faith Renewal* (Leiden, 2000), pp. 121–38.

46 Yoginder Sikkand, 'Stoking the Flames: Intra-Muslim Rivalries in India and the Saudi Connection', *Comparative Studies of South Asia, Africa and the Middle East*, 27: 1 (2007), pp. 95–108.

47 Alexander Horstmann, 'The Tablighi Jama'at, Transnational Islam, and the Transformation of the Self between Southern Thailand and South Asia', *Comparative Studies of South Asia, Africa and the Middle East*, 27: 1 (2007), pp. 26–40.

▶ 5 Formations

1 Thomas M. Callaghy *et al.*, eds, *Intervention and Transnationalism in Africa: Global–Local Networks of Power* (Cambridge, 2001), p. 6.

2 Luis Eduardo Guarnizo, 'The Emergence of a Transnational Social Formation and the Mirage of Return Migration among Dominican Transmigrants', *Identities: Global Studies in Culture and Power*, 4: 2 (1997), pp. 281–322.

3 Peggy Levitt and Nina Glick Schiller, 'Conceptualizing Simultaneity: a Transnational Social Field Perspective on Society', *International Migration Review*, 38: 3 (2004), p. 1009.

4 Mrinalini Sinha, *Colonial Masculinity: the 'Manly Englishman' and the 'Effeminate Bengali' in the Late Nineteenth Century* (Manchester, 1995), p. 2.

5 Ann Laura Stoler and Carole McGranahan, 'Introduction', in Ann Laura Stoler *et al.*, eds, *Imperial Formations* (Santa Fe, 2007), pp. 8–9.

6 Joy Damousi and Mariano Ben Plotkin, eds, *The Transnational Unconscious. Essays in the History of Psychoanalysis and Transnationalism* (Basingstoke, 2006).

7 Tobie Nathan, *Nous ne sommes pas seuls au monde* (Paris, 2001).

8 W.E.B. Du Bois, *The Souls of Black Folk* (Chicago, 1903), p. 4; Abdelmalek Sayad, *The Suffering of the Immigrant* (Cambridge, 2004), original edn in French 1999; Ashis Nandy, *The Intimate Enemy: Loss and Recovery of Self under Colonialism* (Delhi, 1983); Frantz Fanon, *Black Skin, White Masks* (New York, 1967), original edn in French 1952.

9 Ellen Fleischmann, ' "I only wish I had a home on this globe": Transnational Biography and Dr. Mary Eddy', *Journal of Women's History*, 21: 3 (2009), pp. 108–30.

10 Minna-Kristiina Ruokonen-Engler, *'Unsichtbare' Migration? Transnationale Positionierungen finnischer Migrantinnen. Eine biographieanalytische Studie* (Bielefeld, 2011).

11 Desley Deacon *et al.*, eds, *Transnational Lives. Biographies of Global Modernity 1700–present* (Basingstoke, 2010).

12 Desley Deacon *et al.*, 'Introduction', in *idem, Transnational Ties. Australian Lives in the World* (Canberra, 2008), pp. xvi–xvii.

13 Clifton Crais and Pamela Scully, *Sara Baartman and the Hottentot Venus: a Ghost Story and a Biography* (Princeton, 2009).

14 Levine, *A Living Man from Africa*.

15 Henri de Saint-Simon, *Selected Writings* (New York, 1952); William H. Whyte, *The Organization Man* (New York, 1956).

16 Compare Zara Steiner, *The Lights that Failed. European International History 1919–33* (Oxford, 2007) with Patricia Clavin and Jens Wilhelm Wessels, 'Transnationalism and the League of Nations: Understanding the Work of its Economic and Financial Organization', *Contemporary European History*, 14: 4 (2005), pp. 465–92.

17 Michael Barnett and Martha Finnemore, *Rules for the World: International Organizations in Global Politics* (Ithaca, 2004).

18 The Foundation's annual reports since 1913 are available at http://www.rockefellerfoundation.org/about-us/annual-reports.

19 Martin Bulmer, 'Philanthropic Foundations and the Development of the Social Sciences in the Early Twentieth Century: a Reply to Donald Fisher', *Sociology*, 18 (1984), pp. 572–9; Donald Fisher, 'Philanthropic Foundations and the Social Sciences: a Response to Martin Bulmer', *Sociology*, 18 (1984), pp. 581–7.

20 Anne-Emanuelle Birn, *Marriage of Convenience: Rockefeller International Health and Revolutionary Mexico* (Rochester, 2006).

21 Giulana Gemelli, ed., *The 'Unacceptables'. American Foundations and Refugee Scholars between the Two Wars and After* (Brussels, 2000).

22 Pierre-Yves Saunier and Ludovic Tournès, '*Philanthropies Croisées*: a Joint Venture in Public Health at Lyon (1917–1940)', *French History*, 23: 2 (2009), pp. 216–40.

23 Anne-Emanuelle Birn, 'Wa(i)ves of Influence: Rockefeller Public Health in Mexico, 1920–50', *Studies in History and Philosophy of Science Part C*, 31: 3 (2000), p. 381.

24 Richard Perren, *Taste, Trade and Technology: the Development of the International Meat Industry since 1840* (Aldershot, 2006).

25 Pascale Casanova, *The World Republic of Letters* (Cambridge, MA, 2004), original edn in French 1999.

26 Matthew Connelly, *Fatal Misconception: the Struggle to Control World Population* (Cambridge, MA, 2008).

27 Around a similar intent to interweave disease and international politics, compare the book by world historian John R. McNeill's *Mosquito Empires: Ecology and War in the Greater Caribbean, 1620–1914* (New York, 2010) with Sunil S. Amrith, *Decolonizing International Health: India and Southeast Asia, 1930–65* (Basingstoke, 2006).

28 William J. Hausman *et al.*, *Global Electrification: Multinational Enterprise and International Finance in the History of Light and Power, 1878–2007* (Cambridge, 2008).

29 For another original attempt at multi-authorship, see Jonathan Bignell and Andreas Fickers, eds, *A European Television History* (Malden, 2008).

30 Hausman *et al.*, *Global Electrification*, p. 41.

31 William Klein, *Le Festival pan-africain d'Alger*, ONCIC (Algerian National Film Board), 1969, 120 mins.

32 Paul Greenhalgh, *Ephemeral Vistas: the Expositions Universelles, Great Exhibitions and World's Fairs, 1851–1939* (Manchester, 1987).

33 David Armitage and Sanjay Subrahmanyam, eds, *The Age of Revolutions in Global Context, c.1760–1840* (Basingstoke, 2010).

34 The year 1914 is a landmark in Kevin O'Rourke and Jeffrey G. Williamson, *Globalization and History: the Evolution of a Nineteenth-Century Atlantic Economy* (Cambridge, MA, 1999) as well as in Stephen Broadberry and Kevin O'Rourke, eds, *The Cambridge Economic History of Modern Europe* (Cambridge, 2010).

35 Sarah Moss and Alec Badenoch, *Chocolate. A Global History* (London, 2009), pp. 54–5.

36 Sven Beckert, 'Emancipation and Empire: Reconstructing the Worldwide Web of Cotton Production in the Age of the American Civil War', *The American Historical Review*, 109: 5 (2004), pp. 1405–38.

37 David Robinson, *The Holy War of Umar Tal: the Western Sudan in the Mid-Nineteenth Century* (Oxford, 1985).

38 Christopher Andrew and Jeremy Noakes, eds, *Intelligence and International Relations, 1900–1945* (Exeter, 1987).

39 Vojtech Mastny, *Learning from the Enemy: NATO as a Model for the Warsaw Pact* (Zurich, 2001).
40 Matthew J. Connelly, *A Diplomatic Revolution: Algeria's Fight for Independence and the Origins of the Post-Cold War Era* (Oxford, 2002).
41 Jeffrey Byrne, 'Our Own Special Brand of Socialism: Algeria and the Contest of Modernities in the 1960s', *Diplomatic History* 33: 3 (2009), pp. 427–47.
42 Aydin, *The Politics of Anti-Westernism in Asia*, esp. ch. 4.
43 Tibor Frank and Frank Hadler, eds, *Disputed Territories and Shared Pasts: Overlapping National Histories in Modern Europe* (Basingstoke, 2011).
44 Marianne Enckell, *La Fédération jurassienne. Les origines de l'anarchisme en Suisse* (Lausanne, 1971); and the special issue 'L'Anarchisme dans les montagnes', *Revue Neuchâteloise*, 55–56 (1971).
45 Alison Fleig Frank, *Oil Empire: Visions of Prosperity in Austrian Galicia* (Cambridge, 2005).
46 René Boretto Ovalle, *Historiografía de la ciudad de Fray Bentos. Los antecedentes. Fundación y desarrollo social, económico y cultural. Periodo 1857–1890* (Fray Bentos, 2000).
47 See Raffaele Cattedra, 'Élisée Reclus et la Méditerranée', in Jean Paul Bord *et al.*, *Élisée Reclus, Paul Vidal de la Blache. Le géographe, la cité et le monde hier et aujourd'hui* (Paris, 2009), pp. 69–112.
48 Forum 'Oceans of History', *American Historical Review*, 111: 3 (2006).
49 For characterisations of the Indian Ocean as a 'cradle of globalisation', see Markus Vink, 'Indian Ocean Studies and the New Thalassology', *Journal of Global History*, 2: 1 (2007), p. 47, note 23.
50 Compare Mark Ravinder Frost, 'Wider Opportunities: Religious Revival, Nationalist Awakening and the Global Dimension in Colombo, 1870–1920', *Modern Asian Studies*, 36: 4 (2002), pp. 937–67, and *idem*, 'That Great Ocean of Idealism: Calcutta, the Tagore Circle and the Idea of Asia,1900–1920', Nalanda-Sriwijaya Centre Working Paper, 3, published June 2011, http://www.iseas.edu.sg (accessed 16 April 2013).
51 Philipp Ther, 'Comparisons, Cultural Transfers and the Study of Networks: Towards a Transnational History of Europe', in Heinz-Gerhard Haupt and Jürgen Kocka, eds, *Comparative and Transnational History. Central European Approaches and New Perspectives* (New York, 2009), pp. 204–25.
52 Lydon, *On Trans-Saharan Trails*; Laurence Marfaing and Steffen Wippel, *Les relations trans-sahariennes a l'epoque contemporaine. Un espace en constante mutation* (Paris, 2004).
53 James C. Scott, *The Art of Not Being Governed: an Anarchist History of Upland Southeast Asia* (New Haven, 2009).

54 Willem van Schendel, 'Geographies of Knowing, Geographies of Ignorance: Jumping Scale in Southeast Asia', *Environment and Planning D: Society and Space*, 20 (2002), pp. 647–68.

55 *Ibid.*, pp. 654–5.

56 *Journal of Global History*, 5: 2 (2010).

▶ 6 On Methodology

1 Patrick Manning, 'Methods and Materials', in Marnie Hugues-Warrington, ed., *Palgrave Advances in World Histories* (Basingstoke, 2005), p. 49.

2 Pamela Kyle Crossley, *What is Global History?* (Cambridge, 2008), pp. 3–4.

3 Bartolomé Yun-Casalilla, 'Localism, Global History and Transnational History. A Reflection from the Historian of Early Modern Europe', *Historisk Tidskrift*, 127: 4 (2007), p. 16.

4 C.A. Bayly, *The Birth of the Modern World, 1780–1914: Global Connections and Comparisons* (Malden, 2004).

5 Frederick Cooper, 'What is the Concept of Globalization Good For? An African Historian's Perspective', *African Affairs*, 100: 399 (2001), p. 211.

6 David Armitage, *The Declaration of Independence: a Global History* (Cambridge, MA, 2007).

7 Mary L. Dudziak, *Exporting American Dreams: Thurgood Marshall's African Journey* (Oxford, 2008); Antonin Cohen, 'Constitutionalism without Constitution: Transnational Elites between Political Mobilization and Legal Expertise in the Making of a Constitution for Europe (1940s-1960s)', *Law & Social Inquiry*, 32: 1 (2007), pp. 109–35.

8 Markovits, *The Global World of Indian Merchants*, especially ch. 3.

9 Arif Dirlik, '"Performing the World": Reality and Representation in the Making of World Histor(ies)', *Journal of World History*, 16: 4 (2005), pp. 391–410.

10 Ulrike Freitag, ed., *Translocality. The Study of Globalizing Processes from a Southern Perspective* (Leiden, 2010).

11 Carl Nightingale, 'The Transnational Contexts of Early Twentieth-Century American Urban Segregation', *Journal of Social History*, 39: 3 (2006), pp. 667–702.

12 Gregor Benton and Edmund Terence Gomez, *The Chinese in Britain 1800–Present. Economy, Transnationalism, Identity* (Basingstoke, 2008).

13 Mircea Babes and Marc-Antoine Kaeser, eds, *Archaeologists without Boundaries: towards a History of International Archaeological Congresses (1866–2006)* (Oxford, 2009); Johan Heilbron et al., 'Towards a Transnational History of the

Social Sciences', *Journal of the History of the Behavioral Sciences*, 44: 2 (2008), pp. 146–60.

14 Carmen de la Guardia and Juan Pan-Montojo, 'Reflexiones sobre una Historia Transnacional', *Studia histórica. Historia Contemporánea*, 16/17 (1998), pp. 28–9.

15 'Fascicule de candidature au Collège de France', in Marc Bloch, *Histoire et Histoires* (Paris, 1965), p.126.

16 Selçuk Esenbel, 'Japan's Global Claim to Asia and the World of Islam: Transnational Nationalism and World Power, 1900–1945', *American Historical Review*, 109: 4 (2004), pp. 1140–70.

17 Anderson, *Under Three Flags.*

18 *Idem*, p. 4.

19 Bose and Manjapra, *Cosmopolitan Thought Zones.*

20 Akhil Gupta and James Ferguson 'Beyond "Culture": Space, Identity, and the Politics of Difference', special issue 'Space, Identity, and the Politics of Difference', *Cultural Anthropology*, 7: 1 (1992), pp. 6–23.

21 Gloria Anzaldúa, *Borderlands/La Frontera: the New Mestiza* (San Francisco, 1987).

22 Henri Lefebvre, *The Production of Space* (Oxford, 1991), original edn in French 1974.

23 Gilles Deleuze and Félix Guattari, *A Thousand Plateaus* (London, 2004), original edn in French 1980.

24 Édouard Glissant, *Poetics of Relation* (Ann Arbor, 1997), original edn in French 1990; *idem., Traité du Tout-Monde* (Paris, 1997).

25 Bruno Latour, *We Have Never Been Modern* (New York, 1993), original edn in French 1991.

26 John Agnew, 'The Territorial Trap: the Geographical Assumptions of International Relations Theory', *Review of International Political Economy*, 1: 1 (1994), pp. 53–80.

27 *Idem, Globalization and Sovereignty* (Lanham, 2009).

28 Ash Amin, 'Spatialities of Globalisation', *Environment and Planning A*, 34 (2002) pp. 385–99.

29 John Allen, *Lost Geographies of Power* (Oxford, 2003).

30 Henri Lefebvre, *The Production of Space.*

31 Compare her *Global City* (Princeton, 1991) with her *Sociology of Globalization* (New York, 2007).

32 Richard White, 'The Nationalization of Nature', *The Journal of American History*, 86:3 (1999), pp. 976–86; Matthias Middell and Katja Naumann, 'Global History and the Spatial Turn: from the Impact of Area Studies to the Study of Critical Junctures of Globalization', *Journal of Global History*, 5: 1 (2010), pp. 149–70; Michael G. Müller and Cornelius Torp, 'Conceptualising Transnational Spaces in History', *European Review of History*, 16: 5 (2009), pp. 609–17.

33 Jonathan Gantt, *Irish Terrorism in the Atlantic Community* (Basingstoke, 2010).

34 A. James Hammerton and Alistair Thomson, *'Ten Pound Poms': Australia's Invisible Migrants* (Manchester, 2005).

35 The World Labour Group Database includes 91,487 mentions of labour unrest in 168 countries between 1870 and 1996 and was used, among others, by historical sociologist Beverly J. Silver in her *Forces of Labor: Workers' Movements and Globalization since 1870* (Cambridge, 2003).

36 http://ocw.mit.edu/ans7870/21f/21f.027/home/vis_menu.html (accessed 21 December 2012).

37 Samuel Truett, *Fugitive Landscapes. The Forgotten History of the U.S.–Mexico Borderlands* (New Haven, 2006).

38 Martin Klimke, *The Other Alliance. Student Protest in West Germany & the United States in the Global Sixties* (Princeton, 2010).

39 Manjapra, *M. N. Roy*.

40 Edward B. Tylor, 'On a Method of Investigating the Development of Institutions; Applied to Laws of Marriage and Descent', *The Journal of the Anthropological Institute of Great Britain and Ireland*, 18 (1889), pp. 245–72.

41 Philip McMichael, 'Incorporating Comparison within a World-Historical Perspective: an Alternative Comparative Method', *American Sociological Review*, 55: 3 (1990), pp. 385–97.

42 Monika Büscher et al., eds, *Mobile Methods* (Oxford, 2011).

43 James Clifford, 'Traveling Cultures', in Lawrence Grossberg et al., eds, *Cultural Studies* (New York, 1992), pp. 96–116; George E. Marcus, 'Ethnography in/of the World-System: the Emergence of Multi-Sited Ethnography', *Annual Review of Anthropology*, 24 (1995), pp. 95–117.

44 Anna Tsing, 'The Global Situation', *Cultural Anthropology*, 15: 3 (2000), pp. 327–60.

45 Raj, *Relocating Modern Science*; Yves Cohen, 'Circulatory Localities. The Example of Stalinism in the 1930s', *Kritika: Explorations in Russian and Eurasian History*, 11: 1 (2010), pp. 11–45.

46 Jonas Larsen et al., *Mobilities, Networks, Geographies* (London, 2006).

47 Franco Moretti, *Atlas of the European Novel 1800–1900* (London, 1998), original edn in Italian 1997, p. 7.

48 Otto Neurath, *Gesellschaft und Wirtschaft* (Leipzig, 1930).

49 Michael Kidron and Ronald Segal, *State of the World Atlas* (London: Heinemann, 1981).

50 Pierre-Yves Beaurepaire and Silvia Marzagalli, *Atlas de la Révolution Française. Circulations des hommes et des idées* (Paris, 2010); Sergio Luzzatto and Gabriele Pedullà, *Atlante della letteratura italiana* (Turin, 2010–11).

51 http://flowmap.geog.uu.nl/, accessed 16 April, 2013; Ilya Boyandin, 'Flowstrates: an Approach for Visual Exploration of Temporal Origin–Destination Data', *Computer Graphics Forum*, 30: 10 (2011), pp. 971–80.

52 GeoTWAIN was created by a team within the 'Asia and Europe in a global context' cluster at the University of Heidelberg, Germany: http://kjc-sv006.kjc. uni-heidelberg.de/geotwain/WebService/.

Hypercities was developed in collaboration by the University of California at Los Angeles and the University of Southern California: http://hypercities.com/ about/.

53 VisualEyes is an undertaking of the Virginia Center for Digital History (University of Virginia, United States of America): http://www.viseyes.org/.

54 *Urban History*, special issue on 'Transnational Urbanism in the Americas', 36: 2 (2009), http://journals.cambridge.org/fulltext_content/supplementary/uhy36_ 2supp001/index.html, accessed 21 December 2011.

55 Simon Burrows, Mark Curran, Vincent Hiribarren, Sarah Kattau, Henry Merivale, eds, *The French Book Trade in Enlightenment Europe, 1769–1794. Mapping the Trade of the Société typographique de Neuchâtel*, Leeds, University of Leeds, 2012, http://chop.leeds.ac.uk/stn/ accessed 24 March 2013; Simon Burrows and Mark Curran 'How Swiss was the Société Typographique de Neuchâtel? A Digital Case Study of French Book Trade Networks', *Journal of Digital Humanities*, 1:3 (2012), http://journalofdigitalhumanities.org, accessed 24 March 2013.

56 Martin Hall, *Archaeology and the Modern World: Colonial Transcripts in South Africa and the Chesapeake* (London, 2000).

57 Roberta S. Greenwood, *Down by the Station: Los Angeles Chinatown, 1880– 1933* (Los Angeles, 1996); Christopher Fennell, ed., *African Diaspora Archaeology* (Columbus, 2008); Timothy Clack, ed., *Archaeology, Syncretism, and Creolisation* (Oxford, forthcoming).

58 Sarah M. Nelson et al., *Denver: an Archaeological History* (Boulder, 2008), esp. ch. 5.

59 James P. Delgado, *Gold Rush Port: the Maritime Archaeology of San Francisco's Waterfront* (Berkeley, 2009).

60 See Theresa A. Singleton, 'African Diaspora Archaelogy in Dialogue', in Kevin A. Yelvington, ed., *Afro-Atlantic Dialogues: Anthropology in the Diaspora* (Santa Fe, 2006), pp. 249–87.

61 John Schofield, ed., *Defining Moments: Dramatic Archaeologies of the Twentieth Century* (Oxford, 2009).

62 Mary Fennema, *International Networks of Banks and Industry* (The Hague, 1982).

63 Linton Freeman, 'Visualising Social Networks', *Journal of Social Structure*, 1:1 (2000), http://www.cmu.edu/joss/content/articles/volume1/Freeman.html, accessed 31 August 2012.

64 C. McCarty et al., 'A Comparison of Social Network Mapping and Personal Network Visualization', *Field Methods*, 19: 2 (2007), 145–62.

65 Naomi Rosenthal et al., 'Social Movements and Network Analysis: a Case Study of Nineteenth-Century Women's Reform in New York State', *American Journal of Sociology*, 90: 5 (1985), pp. 1022–54.

66 Charles Wheterell, 'Historical Social Network Analysis', *International Review of Social History*, 43 (1998), pp. 125–44.

67 See for instance Roland Wenzlhuemer, 'The Dematerialization of Telecommunication: Communication Centres and Peripheries in Europe and the World, 1850–1920', *Journal of Global History*, 2: 3 (2007), pp. 345–72.

68 David A. Smith and Douglas R.White, 'Structure and Dynamics of the Global Economy: Network Analysis of International Trade 1965–1980', *Social Forces*, 70: 4 (1992), pp. 857–93; Marc Flandreau and Clemens Jobst, 'The Ties that Divide: a Network Analysis of the International Monetary System, 1890–1910', *The Journal of Economic History*, 65: 4 (2005), pp. 977–1007.

69 Anthony Pym, 'Cross-Cultural Networking: Translators in the French-German Network of *Petites Revues* at the End of the Nineteenth Century', *Meta*, 52: 4 (2007), pp. 744–62.

70 Christophe Verbruggen, 'Literary Strategy during Flanders's Golden Decades (1880–1914): Combining Social Network Analysis and Prosopography', in Katharine Keats-Rohan and Christian Settipani, eds, *Prosopography: Approaches and Applications. A Handbook* (Oxford, 2007), pp. 579–99.

71 *Ibid.*, p. 599.

72 Lydon, *On Trans-Saharan Trails*.

73 Klimke, *The Other Alliance*.

74 Elizabeth Hofmeyr, 'Gandhi's Printing Press: Indian Ocean Print Cultures and Cosmopolitanisms', in Sugata Bose and Kris Manjapra, eds, *Cosmopolitan Thought Zones*, pp. 112–30.

75 Roland Wenzlhuemer, ed., special issue 'Global Communication. Telecommunication and Global Flows of Information in the Late 19th and Early 20th Century', *Historical Social Research*, 35: 1 (2010).

76 Flandreau and Jobst, 'The Ties that Divide'.

77 *Ibid.*, p. 7.

78 *Ibid.*, p. 11.

79 Kenneth Pomeranz, *The Great Divergence: China, Europe, and the Making of the Modern World Economy* (Princeton, 2000), pp. 7ff.

80 Wimmer and Glick-Schiller, 'Methodological Nationalism', p. 306.

81 Robert P. Swierenga, *Faith and Family: Dutch Immigration and Settlement in the United States, 1820–1920* (New York, 2000).

82 Adam McKeown, 'Chinese Emigration in Global Context, 1850–1940', *Journal of Global History*, 1: 5 (2010), pp. 107ff.

83 Sunil Amrith, 'Indians Overseas? Governing Tamil Migration to Malaya, 1870–1941', *Past and Present*, 208 (2010), pp. 231–61.
84 'AHR Conversation: On Transnational History', p. 1453.
85 Susan Pedersen, 'Back to the League of Nations', *American Historical Review*, 112: 4 (2007), pp. 1091–117.
86 Jasmien van Daele et al., eds, *ILO Histories: Essays on the International Labour Organization and its Impact on the World during the Twentieth Century* (Bern, 2010); Frank Schipper, *Driving Europe. Building Europe on Roads in the Twentieth Century* (Amsterdam, 2008); Luis Rodríguez-Piñero, *Indigenous Peoples, Postcolonialism, and International Law. The ILO Regime (1919–1989)* (Oxford, 2006).
87 Sanjay Subrahmanyam, 'On Indian Views of the Portuguese in Asia, 1500–1700', in *Explorations in Connected History. From the Tagus to the Ganges* (Oxford, 2005), pp. 18–44.

▶ Conclusion

1 Thomas Bender, *A Nation among Nations: America's Place in World History* (New York, 2006), p. 3.
2 Patricia Clavin, 'Time, Manner, Place: Writing Modern European History in Global, Transnational and International Contexts', *European History Quarterly*, 40: 4 (2010), pp. 624–40.
3 Erez Manela, 'A Pox on Your Narrative: Writing Disease Control into Cold War History', *Diplomatic History*, 34: 2 (2010), pp. 299–323.
4 Per Hogselius et al., 'Natural Gas in Cold War Europe: the Making of a Critical Transnational Infrastructure', in Anique Hommels et al., eds, *The Making of Europe's Critical Infrastructure*. Basingstoke.
5 Gabrielle Hecht, ed., *Entangled Geographies: Empire and Technopolitics in the Global Cold War* (Cambridge, MA, 2011).
6 For such attempts in world history, see Jerry H. Bentley, 'Cross-Cultural Interaction and Periodization in World History', *The American Historical Review*, 101: 3 (1996), pp. 749–70; and about globalisation, Chris A. Bayly, 'Archaic and Modern Globalization in the Eurasian and African Arena ca. 1750–1850', in A.G Hopkins, ed., *Globalization in World History* (New York, 2002), pp. 45–72.
7 For a view of current developments in digital humanities, readers should visit or subscribe to the news and choices of *Digital Humanities Now*, serviced by the Roy Rosenzweig Center for History and New Media at George Mason University http://digitalhumanitiesnow.org/.
8 The phrase is Gérard Noiriel's, who used it in a different context, *La tyrannie du national. Le droit d'asile en Europe, 1793–1993* (Paris, 1991).

9 Dominic Sachsenmaier, *Global Perspectives on Global History: Theories and Approaches in a Connected World* (Cambridge, 2011).

10 Michael McGerr, 'The Price of the "New Transnational History" ', *The American Historical Review*, 96: 4 (1991), p. 1066.

11 Ann Curthoys and Marilyn Lake, eds, *Connected Worlds: History in Transnational Perspective* (Canberra, 2005), p. 14.

12 Bender, *Nation among Nations*, p. 14.

13 See above, chapter 2, note 70.

Glossary

actor network theory (ANT):   first developed in science and technology studies, this concept considers humans and non-humans (machines, artefacts) on a par for their role in interactions that create human societies and their environment.

actors' categories: a category that historical actors use to perceive, organise, make sense of and act on their environment.

area studies: interdisciplinary fields of research dedicated to large regions (Middle East, South East Asia). Born in the 1920s, area studies was institutionalised after the Second World War, chiefly as a tool for Cold War policies of the US federal government.

borderland studies: an interdisciplinary field of research devoted to the study of regions and limits that separate and link territories, states and nations.

catchment area/drainage basin: the area of land which is drained by a river.

circuit: an arrangement of linkages that is consciously installed and maintained in order to gain access to resources and possibilities located in different places across national borders.

comparative history: the systematic attempt to compare historical developments in different societies and polities, mostly national ones, in search of causation.

connected history/connected histories: an approach formalised by Sanjay Subrahmanyam to direct attention to conjunctures, circulations and vocabularies that plugged polities and societies into one another in early modern Eurasia.

global history: previously used as a synonym of world history, the phrase gained new meaning in the 1990s when it came to designate the historical study of globalisation understood as a process of integration and differentiation caused by interactions between societies.

globalisation: although it had been around for quite a while, the term gained currency in the 1980s to describe the planetary scope of economic operations and financial transactions.

histoire croisée: in its original formulation by Bénédicte Zimmermann and Michael Werner, more than the history of entanglements between societies and polities. *Histoire croisée* also includes 'the operations by which researchers themselves cross scales, categories, and viewpoints'.

historical archaeology: the form of archaeology that studies societies from the sixteenth century onwards.

historicisation: the operation that consists in restoring ideas, people, patterns and trends to a specific context, mostly a time but also a place and a society.

interfaces: sites of interactions between different entities.

large technological systems: American historian of technology Thomas P. Hugues (1983) defined them as coherent structures comprised of interacting, interconnected technical components placed under some central control (also called large technical systems).

methodological nationalism: according to Herminio Martins, the assumption that the nation is the natural form of polities and societies in the modern world, and the incorporation of that view into humanities and social science work.

mobile methods: under that term, the British sociologist John Urry placed specific methods that can be used to capture mobility and to improve the capacity of researchers to move in order to follow mobile objects of study.

modular production system: an industrial model that developed in the 1990s, based on the abandonment of direct manufacturing by leading US firms in electronics (Apple, IBM, Sun, Dell). Each 'module' of the production chain was increasingly contracted to a third party called a 'contract manufacturer'.

monad: an elementary individual substance which reflects the order of the world and from which the world's properties are derived.

neo-Europes: a term introduced by historian Alfred W. Crosby in 1986 to designate lands of the temperate zones where Europeans migrated en masse with their biological environment (plants, animals) between the 1820s and the 1960s. Australia and New Zealand, the Americas and the southern cone of South America.

realised category: a category of perception, organisation and action on the world that is incorporated in society and in human minds and bodies through the travail of legislation, education and institutions.

Swadeshi: the Bengali word for self-sufficiency, and the motto of the anti-colonial national movement of the early twentieth century that resisted the partition of Bengal by the boycott of British goods.

transculturation: an approach to culture that places the emphasis on hybridity and process. The Cuban anthropologist Fernando Ortiz, who coined the term in 1940, insisted on entanglements between cultures, and how cultures are outcomes of entanglements.

Transfergeschichte: the German term to name the field of historical research that developed around the study of the circulation of cultural products between national spheres.

translocality: a notion elaborated by scholars of Asia, Africa and the Middle East in order to study transfers and connections taking place below the elite level, outside the West and within the regions identified by area studies.

universal history: a genre of history writing that appeared in the third to fourth centuries BCE, and initially attempted to write the history of humankind in the form of annals of every period, place and moment. Now revived, under the name of 'big history', as a synthetic search for large patterns of the history of the universe, earth and humankind in the last 13.7 billion years.

world history: as a discipline, world history came of age in the 1960s in the United States of America in the form of the high school world history course. It insists on general patterns and trends in human history. World history has flourished as a teaching and research undertaking since the 1990s.

zeitgeist: generally attributed to the German philosopher Georg Wilhelm Friedrich Hegel, the notion of zeitgeist designates the purported unifying spirit of an age.

Further reading

The core texts are cited in the notes of the chapters, and this section merely suggests a limited number of additional readings. The choice has been made to range across a number of topics, places, moments and disciplines. A more expansive bibliography, organised along the chapters structure of this volume, can be obtained by writing to pys.th.2013@gmail.com.

▶ Introduction

Readers of German will enjoy the first primer on transnational history to have been published, Margrit Pernau, *Transnationale Geschichte* (Göttingen, 2011). The gateway *Geschichte.Transnational* is the best resource on current work by historians about what lies between and through polities and communities. Since 2004, it has been publishing book reviews, conference reports and projects announcements in English, German and French: http://geschichte-transnational.clio-online. net/transnat.asp. Among the many history journals that carry articles of interest for transnational historians, some need to be browsed very regularly: *Itinerario. International Journal on the History of European Expansion and Global Interaction*, *Journal of Global History*, *Journal of World History*, *Comparativ – Zeitschrift für Globalgeschichte und vergleichende Gesellschaftsforschung*, and *International Review of Social History*. The *Palgrave Dictionary of Transnational History* (Basingstoke, 2009) includes 451 entries on a range of topics. European History Online, a site launched in 2011 by the Leibniz Institute of European History in Mainz (Germany), includes a large and growing number of essays about entanglements within Europe and with the rest of the world: http://www.ieg-ego.eu/.

▶ Chapter 1: Trajectories, Meanings and Usages

The Transnational Studies Reader: Intersections and Innovations, edited by Sanjeev Khagram and Peggy Levitt (Abingdon, 2008) is a first port of call to identify authors and fields who endorsed transnational approaches in the last four decades, across different disciplines of the social sciences. The most complete book-length presentation of 'transnationalism' as a new paradigm to study migrants and migrations is Steven Vertovec, *Transnationalism* (London, 2009). A detailed history of the term 'transnational' and its derivatives is available in Pierre-Yves Saunier 'Transnational', in Akira Iriye and Pierre-Yves Saunier, eds, *The Palgrave Dictionary of Transnational History* (Basingstoke, 2009), pp. 1047–1055. Among the contributions generated by AGORA, the powerhouse of transnational history in Germany, pay special attention to Shalini Randeria and Andreas Eckert, eds, *Jenseits des Eurozentrismus: Postkoloniale Perspektiven in den Geschichts- und Kulturwissenschaften* (Frankfurt, 2002), and to the article by Michael Werner and Bénédicte Zimmermann that was originally published in German in 2002 and translated in many languages thereafter: 'Beyond comparison. *Histoire croisée* and the challenge of reflexivity', *History and Theory*, 45 (2006), pp. 145–66. Big History, conceived as a new formulation of universal history and the search for large patterns, arouses much interest among world historians now. See Fred Spier, *Big History and the Future of Humanity* (Chichester, 2010), to be completed by David Christian 'The return of universal history', *History and Theory*, 49:4 (2010) pp. 6–27. One of the first collective attempts by historians to engage the history of globalization has been the volume coordinated by Anthony Hopkins, *Globalization in World History* (New York, 2002). In 2007, the *History Workshop Journal* published a series of contributions on the same topic in a special section 'Feature global times and spaces: on historicizing the global', 64:1 (2007).

▶ ## Chapter 2: Human Connectors

Wide ranging contributions on migrants as connectors have been gathered by Donna R. Gabaccia and Dirk Hoerder, eds, *Connecting Seas and Connected Ocean Rims. Indian, Atlantic, and Pacific Oceans and China Seas Migrations from the 1830s to the 1930s* (Leiden, 2011). Traders as intermediaries and their mutiple positions are the object of James Onley, *The Arabian Frontier of the British Raj: Merchants, Rulers, and the British in the Nineteenth Century Gulf* (Oxford, 2007), and Anne K. Bang has written about the religious Indian Ocean connections of a prominent Sufi figure in her *Sufis and Scholars of the Sea: Family Networks in East Africa, 1860–1925* (London, 2003). For collective and individual portraits of intermediaries that worked across the colonial line, see Benjamin N. Lawrance *et al.*, *Intermediaries, Interpreters, and Clerks: African Employees in the Making of Colonial Africa* (Madison, 2006). On the role of returnee slaves on the Western Coast of Africa, works in Portuguese deserve special attention, such as Milton Guran, *Agudás. Os Brasileiros do Benin* (Rio de Janeiro, 1999). The history of travel is in full bloom, and one outstanding commercial on line collection of sources ought to be mentioned here: *Travel Writing, Spectacle and World History* (Adam Matthew Digital, 2010) at http://www.amdigital.co.uk/m-collections/collection/travel-writing-spectacle-and-world-history/. Maurizio Isabella brings the travail of Italian political exiles alive in *Risorgimento in Exile: Italian Émigrés and the Liberal International in the post-Napoleonic Era* (Oxford, 2009). Lionel Lambourne, *Japonisme: Cultural Crossings between Japan and the West* (London, 2005) pictures the whole milieu of intermediaries that made the 'crossings' of Japanese art possible. A significant recent development is the integration of history of intermediaries who mediated between the communist world and the developing countries in the history of post-war development policies, as in Jost Dülffer and Marc Frey, eds, *Elites and Decolonization in the Twentieth Century* (Basingstoke, 2011).

▶ Chapter 3: Non-Human Intermediaries

Taken together, four books offer an introduction to the capacity of different types of things to connect societies and communities: Frank Dikotter, *Exotic Commodities: Modern Objects and Everyday life in China* (New York, 2006); Holger Jebens, ed., *Cargo, Cult, and Culture Critique* (Honolulu, 2004); Joel Roeber *The Hidden Market: Corruption in the International Arms Trade* (New York, 2001) and Jeremy Prestholdt, *Domesticating the World: African Consumerism and the Genealogies of Globalization* (Berkeley, 2008). The history of technological infrastructures is best approached through the work of the Transnational Infrastructures of Europe research group, notably Erik van der Vleuten and Arne Kaijser, eds, *Networking Europe. Transnational Infrastructures and the Shaping of Europe 1850–2000* (Sagamore Beach, 2006). For natural connectors, another combination of further readings can be recommended: Ike Okonta and Oronto Douglas, *Where Vultures Feast: Shell, Human Rights, and Oil in the Niger Delta* (San Francisco, 2001); Christopher Lever, *They Dined on Eland. The Story of the Acclimatisation Societies* (London, 1992), Richard Grove and John Chappell, eds, *El Niño, History and Crisis* (Cambridge, 2000). In addition to the Indian and Atlantic Ocean research mentioned in this chapter, readers can sail on other oceans and sea bodies under the guidance of Donald B. Freeman, *The Straits of Malacca: Gateway or Gauntlet?* (Montreal, 2003), Paul D'Arcy *The People of the Sea: Environment, Identity and History in Oceania* (Honolulu, 2006), and Charles King, *The Black Sea: A History* (Oxford, 2004).

▶ Chapter 4: Circulations

To start with, a collection about the circulation of words and notions with Carol Gluck and Anna Lowenhaupt Tsing, eds, *Words in Motion. Toward a Global Lexicon*

(Durham, 2009). People on the move in Europe have been covered in a recent reference volume, Klaus J. Bade et al., eds, *The Encyclopedia of Migration and Minorities in Europe: From the 17th Century to the Present* (Cambridge, 2011). To go beyond the usual Italian, Chinese or Jewish diasporas, try Ulrike Freitag *Indian Ocean Migrants and State Formation in Hadhramaut: Reforming the Homeland* (Leiden, 2003). To move away from the Atlantic history of of cultural circulations, try Katherine E. Zirbel, 'Playing it both ways: local Egyptian performers between regional identity and international markets' in Walter Armbrust, ed., *Mass Mediations: New Approaches to Popular Culture in the Middle East and Beyond* (Berkeley, 2000). For commodities, there is still much to learn from Sidney W. Mintz's *Sweetness and Power: The Place of Sugar in Modern History* (New York, 1985), to be read alongside the anniversary journal issue dedicated to its publication (*Food and Foodways*, 16: 2, 2008). Another vintage book, yet about the peregrinations of a manufactured object, is Robert Bruce Davies, *Peacefully working to Conquer the World: Singer Sewing Machines in Foreign Markets, 1854–1920* (New York, 1976). Religious circulations certainly are not only about pilgrims, but there is currently a number of ongoing projects about the Hajj, including that of Eileen Kane on the neglected Russian Hajj, to be discovered with her 'Odessa as a Hajj hub, 1880s–1910s' in John Randolph and Eugene Avrutin, eds, *Russia in Motion. Cultures of Human Mobility since 1850*, (Urbana, 2012). Capital flows in the form of securities, stocks and bonds market have been minutely reconstructed by Ranald C. Michie, *The Global Securities Market: A History* (Oxford, 2006). For books on circulations generated by cross-observation or spatial propinquity, the following selection will provide a diverse range: Willem van Schendel, *The Bengal Borderland: beyond State and Nation in South Asia*, (London, 2005); Michel Espagne and Matthias Middell, eds, *Von der Elbe bis an die Seine: Kulturtransfer zwischen Sachsen und Frankreich im 18. Und 19. Jahrhundert* (Leipzig, 1993) and Renee Worringer, *Ottoman Imagination and the Rising Sun: The Middle East, Japan, and Non-Western Modernity at the Turn of the 20th Century* (forthcoming, 2014).

▶ Chapter 5: Relations

On occasions where different parties join for a cause across borders, discover an interesting mix of situations with Cemil Aydin, *The Politics of Anti-Westernism in Asia: Visions of World Order in Pan-Islamic and Pan-Asian Thought* (New York, 2007); Volker Heins *Nongovernmental Organizations in International Society: Struggles over Recognition* (New York, 2008); Roger D. Launius et al., eds, *Globalizing Polar Science: Reconsidering the International Polar and Geophysical Years* (New York, 2010) and Michael Jackson, *Fallen Sparrows: The International Brigades in the Spanish Civil War* (Philadelphia,1994). The projects and nuances that characterize the relation of dominance show up clearly in Antoinette Burton, *At the Heart of the Empire: Indians* and the Colonial Encounter in Late Victorian Britain (Berkeley, 1998) and Nicholas J. Cull, *The Cold War and the United States Information Agency: American Propaganda and Public Diplomacy, 1945–1989* (Cambridge, 2008). In order to appraise the manifold aspects of the impact of American culture Europe, browse the Amsterdam Monographs in American Studies, published by Rodopi under the direction of Rob Kroes. Two studies give a clear view of how artists and artistic currents, movements or schools mobilize foreign elements to develop their artistic and social positions: Béatrice Joyeux-Prunel, '*Nul n'est prophète en son pays*'? *L'internationalisation de la peinture avant-gardiste parisienne (1855–1914)* (Paris, 2009), on painting and painters, and Sujatha Fernandes, *Close to the Edge: In Search of the Global Hip Hop Generation* (London, 2011) on current musical trends. For the production of legal norms, see Isabella Löhr, *Die Globalisierung geistiger Eigentumsrechte. Neue Strukturen der internationalen Zusammenarbeit 1886–1952* (Göttingen, 2010) and Yves Dezalay and Bryant G. Garth, *Global Prescriptions: the Production, Exportation, and Importation of a New Legal Orthodoxy* (Ann Arbor, 2002). The latter focuses on the last decades of the twentieth century. A study of nineteenth-century classification efforts in the natural science is Jim Endersby *Imperial Nature: Joseph Hooker and the Practices of Victorian Science* (Chicago, 2008).

▶ Chapter 6: Formations

The contributors to Rosamund Dalziell, ed., *Selves Crossing Cultures: Autobiography and Globalization* (Melbourne, 2002), offer many reflections on the self as a site of intersection. The studies of international organisations conducted by Madeleine Herren and her team in Heidelberg, Germany, are now coming to fruition, and her forthcoming collection, *Networks in Times of Transition. Toward a Transcultural History of International Organisations* (Dordrecht, 2013) is awaited. In the same field, an important book for historians of international organisations is Michael Barnett and Martha Finnemore, *Rules for the World. International Organizations in Global Politics* (Ithaca, 2004). Both Steven Topik *et al.*, eds, *From Silver to Cocaine: Latin American Commodity Chains and the Building of the World Economy, 1500–2000* (Durham, 2006) and Youssef Cassis, *Capitals of Capital: a History of International Financial Centres, 1780–2005* (Cambridge, 2006) are a great help to understand the topical formations created around commodities and capital. Laurent Dubois has depicted the entangled echoes of the Haitian Revolution in *Avengers of the New World: the Story of the Haitian Revolution* (Cambridge, MA, 2004). With the contributors of Gerd-Rainer Horn and Padraic Kenney, eds, *Transnational Moments of Change: Europe 1945, 1968, 1989* (Lanham, 2004), readers will access a set of events at the other end of the space of time covered in this volume. Places are sites of intersection in history and in historiography. The latter is the object of Tibor Frank and Frank Hadler, eds,

Disputed Territories and Shared Pasts: Overlapping National Histories in Modern Europe (Basingstoke, 2011), and the former comes to the fore in Takeshi Hamashita, *Trade and Finance in Late Imperial China Maritime Customs and Open Port Market Zones* (Singapore, 2012) and in Christophe Charle, *Théâtres en capitales. Naissance de la société du spectacle, Paris, Berlin, Londres, Vienne 1860–1914* (Paris, 2008).

▶ Chapter 7: On methodology

A complete introduction to the work of Henri Lefebvre and his reflections on spatiality can be found in *State, Space, World: Selected Essays by Henri Lefebvre*, edited by Neil Brenner and Stuart Elden (Minneapolis, 2009). Richard White, in 'The Nationalization of Nature', *The Journal of American History*, 86: 3 (1999), pp. 976–986, gives a clear account of the spatial implications of transnational history. In addition to the contribution of geographers, the anthropologist Frederik Barth was among the firsts who insisted on the capacity of groups and individuals to 'make scales'. See especially the introduction and conclusion of Frederik Barth, ed., *Scale and Social Organization* (Oslo, 1978). The journal *Historical Archaeology* has published several special issues on the archaeology of migrant communities, diasporas, maritime cities, missions or colonies that include the last 200–250 years. Charles Wheterell gave a good presentation of social network analys in 'Historical social network analysis', *International Review of Social History*, 43 (1998), pp. 125–44. On maps and their importance for narrating circulations, Béatrice Joyeux-Prunel 'Chiffres et cartes. Enjeux d'une 'histoire totale' de l'art', http://www.thes-arts.com/index.php?option=com_content&view=article&id=106, published September 2010 (accessed 22 March 2013).

Index

Page numbers indicating glossary entries are shown in bold. Names that begin 'Mc' are arranged in the index as if 'Mac'.

Printed in China